"In his compelling book *Silence Can Kill*, Arthur Simon's illuminating vision of a moral center reveals in sharp relief the limitations of private charity and the important role of public justice in ending hunger and addressing other deeply rooted inequalities. Simon commendably appeals to our best instincts as citizens in his forceful call to join the public and winnable fight against human suffering."

— WILLIAM JULIUS WILSON, Harvard University

"An inspiration and a call to action. *Silence Can Kill* is a guidebook for changing the world and an urgent invitation to take on the task."

— E. J. DIONNE JR., *Washington Post*

"A thought-provoking read, *Silence Can Kill* should inspire each one of us to do our part—however small—in combating hunger. Art Simon emphasizes the power of citizen advocacy in shaping our nation's hunger policy. He makes a credible case that ending hunger is a surprisingly attainable goal—one that can be achieved through determination and a unified voice. More than just informative, this book is a call to action."

— SENATOR BOB DOLE

"In *Silence Can Kill*, the author challenges Christians to demand that there be no hungry people in our world. Through the window of Bread for the World, Simon sets out what is needed for food justice and why we resist. We have the ability to feed a hungry world, but we lack the will. Readers will come away challenged and (I hope) engaged in the campaign to speak up and save our neighbors and our planet."

— SIMONE CAMPBELL, CEO,
Network Lobby and leader of Nuns on the Bus

"Who among us would choose the brokenness, strife, and ugliness we are witnessing in our nation today? Our country desperately needs the inspiring and healing vision of *Silence Can Kill*."

—SPENCER BACHUS, former congressman
and chair of the House Financial Services Committee

"In the face of the most profound partisan division, we need a cause that can once again unite us. Ending hunger can be that cause. This is a hugely important book, compelling in its argument, morally urgent, the culminating contribution of one of America's most important, practical, Christian moral leaders of the last fifty years. I recommend this book with the highest enthusiasm."

— DAVID P. GUSHEE,
Mercer University, and immediate
past president of the American Academy
of Religion and the Society of Christian Ethics

"In *Silence Can Kill*, Arthur Simon draws upon his extraordinary experience as founder of Bread for the World, a citizen lobby to end national and world hunger. He paints a compelling picture of an America where hunger and injustice are evils of the past once the obstacles of doubt, silence, and the political divide are removed. Simon powerfully advocates a joint effort of private charities, government, communities, and families to end hunger and create a just economy for all Americans. *Silence Can Kill* is a must-read for everyone desiring an America 'we the people' need."

— BARBARA WILLIAMS-SKINNER, president,
Skinner Leadership Institute

"Art Simon is a drum major! *Silence Can Kill* is a towering and compelling moral vision to end hunger! Art Simon combines a deep analysis of the root causes of poverty with an inspirational hope that ending hunger is indeed possible in our generation."

— GABRIEL SALGUERO, president,
National Latino Evangelical Coalition

"Arthur Simon, at age 88, asks us to come together across partisan lines to end hunger and improve opportunity for all Americans. We need this book now."

— DAVID BECKMANN, president,
Bread for the World

"Arthur Simon has spent a lifetime issuing much-needed wake-up calls to force America to confront the horrid realities of domestic and international hunger. He does it again in *Silence Can Kill*, a searing indictment of our failing status quo that allows mass food deprivation at a time of soaring wealth at the top. The book is on target on all the big issues: that hunger saps us morally and economically, that charity alone can't fix the problem, but that the problem of hunger can indeed be solved by building a people's movement to compel governments to enact the proven public policies to end it."

— JOEL BERG, CEO, Hunger Free America

"In this era of increasing national and global wealth disparities, *Silence Can Kill* is a pivotal treatise on the causes, consequences, and remedies to address hunger and poverty. With a twenty-first-century prophetic imagination for justice and food security for all peoples, Simon offers a comprehensive analysis and compelling questions to all those with a heart to hear and a commitment to democratic values."

— IVA CARUTHERS, General Secretary,
Samuel DeWitt Proctor Conference

"*Silence Can Kill* is a timely call to intensified citizen engagement in advocacy to end hunger now. Drawing on decades of experience mobilizing Christians of diverse traditions to work together, Art Simon is both prophetic and pastoral, idealistic and practical. Americans have long been generous with charitable contributions and volunteering to help their vulnerable neighbors. Simon points out that citizens must also press government to fulfill its indispensable role in allocating resources and setting policies that offer help and opportunity to those living with poverty and hunger. At key moments in our history, Americans have risen to the challenge, with transformative results. We can draw strength from past successes even as we redouble our efforts in the face of current needs. If silence can kill, a united Christian witness to God's love and justice can bring life and hope to millions of our struggling neighbors."

— GALEN CAREY, vice president for government relations,
National Association of Evangelicals

Silence Can Kill

Speaking Up to End Hunger and
Make Our Economy Work for Everyone

Arthur Simon

WILLIAM B. EERDMANS PUBLISHING COMPANY
GRAND RAPIDS, MICHIGAN

Wm. B. Eerdmans Publishing Co.
4035 Park East Court SE, Grand Rapids, Michigan 49546
www.eerdmans.com

Published 2019
Printed in the United States of America

25 24 23 22 21 20 19   1 2 3 4 5 6 7

ISBN 978-0-8028-7747-5

Library of Congress Cataloging-in-Publication Data

A catalog record for this book is available from the Library of Congress.

To my wife Shirley
who is a treasured gift of love

Contents

IV. WE CAN ACT ON A COMPELLING VISION

Foreword

Mother Teresa inspired me with her concern for the poor and downtrodden. But it was Art Simon who stirred me to action by asking, "Why?" Why, amid such unprecedented affluence, are there still hungry people in the United States? With his book *Silence Can Kill*, Art explains how we can be active in our citizenship—and how advocacy gives our compassion traction.

Forty years ago, on the streets of Seattle, a stranger handed me a copy of Art Simon's book *Bread for the World*. The incident seemed odd, but for some reason I accepted the book and read it. *Bread for the World* taught me about the economics of hunger and how it can be addressed. It freed me to see the structural basis of poverty. I realized that poverty in a wealthy world is, in part, a matter of structure—and that, in a well-functioning democracy, structural poverty can be remedied by a caring and engaged citizenry. Art taught me, as a Christian who cares about people in poverty, that getting political in order to address the problem of hunger is not only OK—it's the right thing to do.

Art's new book, *Silence Can Kill*, gets us up-to-date on these same themes, with a smart and pragmatic approach that mixes active citizenship with walking the talk as a person of faith. And I am both delighted and honored to share some thoughts about this book and Art's message in this foreword.

Some people strive to love their neighbors. Others just strive to be safe and comfortable. And the case for tackling hunger can be framed either way. A great lesson I've learned through my travels is that, even if you're motivated only by greed, if you know what's good for you, you don't want to be filthy rich in a desperately poor world. It's not a nice place to raise your children.

Since I read Art's earlier book back in the 1970s, I've spent four months each year—a third of my life—on the road, learning about the world . . . and learning about my own country at the same time. When you travel, you can visit lands facing more extreme versions of the same challenges confronting the United States, and you can see what happens if the trajectory of our problems is not changed. By viewing your own country from afar, you also learn about it in ways you never could back home. You see both the consequences of inaction (or wrong action) and the impact of governance—good and bad. You return home with a fire in your belly to make a difference. Art Simon has dedicated his life to tending (and stoking) such fires.

Assuming we want to end hunger, we need to recognize the relative value of charity versus government policy. Charity is important. But reading *Silence Can Kill* makes it clear—in the same way Art introduced me to these concepts in *Bread for the World* forty years ago—that all the charity in America combined has only a small fraction of the impact on our nation's poor and hungry that government policy has. It's great to have a photo on your mantel of a single child you helped feed, but it is much more important to help shape a world in which parents can work hard and provide for their own children.

While the wisdom of *Silence Can Kill* resonates with people of any faith, as a Christian I appreciated the reminder that if you want an effective, Christ-like approach to hunger, it's not only OK to get political—you *must* get political. This book explains how silence is violence. Hunger and poverty are real in our country. And ignoring them is violence in slow motion.

Political discourse in America is a harsh mirror—it reflects what people really care about. And in our democracy today, most politicians figure there's not much interest in talking about hunger. This can change, but not without an awakening.

Capitalism—the free-market system—is like a religion in America. As a business owner, I'm thankful for the freewheeling environment in which I get to run my company. I can employ people well, produce good stuff at a good price, and make plenty of money. But I also know that in an unbridled free market, buying power rules. If my cat has more buying power than your child, my cat gets the tuna. These days in our country, there are a lot of fat cats. There are more homeless people . . . and more people with second homes. There are more people in prison . . . and more people living in gated communities. There are a lot of good people who are afraid . . . and, because of that fear, more Americans are aspiring to build not bridges but walls.

Art Simon teaches us that, for our ship of state, the free market is the engine—and it's a powerful engine. But it's not the steering wheel. Our society's steering wheel is our government (the collective "we"). The engine is morally neutral—it could be selling apples or sex, cars or cocaine. And by tapping into the profit motive to rev that engine, we as a society can be blinded by greed and end up heading, full steam, in a direction not true to our society's values. So regulation is essential if the free market is to contribute to the common good even as it enriches individuals. Our national budget is, therefore, a moral document.

It's clear that Art Simon spends a lot of time thinking about hunger. In this book, we consider dimensions that had never occurred to us. Art notes that Congress can, in a spasm of fear and greed, incited by shrill media voices, cut billions of dollars from food assistance for hungry Americans (for example, ending SNAP, more than $60 billion in groceries). Art demonstrates that the very existence of hunger in the USA costs our society more money than it would take to end hunger. Reading his book gives me—as a reader, as a concerned citizen, and as a person with a Christian compassion for the poor—empathy for the hungry and gets me excited about realistic ways to tackle the problem.

In this book, Art Simon instills hope and seeks to unite us in this challenge to end hunger in the USA. That's setting the bar high. But it can be done. We are all part of "the body politic." We are political whether we realize it or not. When it comes to hunger, silence is a political act. Art reassures us that, if you choose active citizenship and work to end hunger, compassion and truth are an easier sell than greed and deceit, and that a societal spotlight is more efficient and effective than a thousand points of light.

Lobbying our government is, in itself, neither good nor bad. It's a question of what you are lobbying for. If you believe that hunger is bad, then lobbying against it is good. But if you claim to care about the hungry and then—in the privacy of the voting booth—elect leaders who do not support economic justice, that's a disconnect. An enlightened citizen knows that the outcome of an election has a bigger impact on the poor than on the rest of us. And knowing that makes how we vote a moral decision.

This book is both a powerful argument and a manual for making a difference. It offers a wise and insightful foundation for understanding the whys and hows of effectively fighting hunger. *Silence Can Kill* moves us to augment our charity by embracing advocacy.

Now read this book . . . and get to work!

RICK STEVES

Preface: A Lens of Hope

While I was working on the initial draft of this book, public frustration and anger erupted in the 2016 presidential contests, unleashing a flood of protest and producing an outcome that revealed how close we have come to letting our great democratic experiment lose its way.

That outburst serves as a canary in our political mine. To continue on the present course of growing inequalities and partisan division would be folly. As the wiser pundits from across the political spectrum have been urging, we need a vision that instills hope and unites us. *That is exactly what this book proposes.*

The first half (Parts I and II) sees ending hunger in America as a moral imperative—*but not a stand-alone goal.* Hunger thrives on the racial, social, and economic extremes that are eating away at the soul of our nation and pulling us apart. But ending hunger could now become the cause that brings us together across partisan lines to make our economy include everyone and work for everybody. Because the goal of ending hunger is so decent and clearly within reach, the pursuit of it in the United States would enable us to see more clearly the connections between hunger and those deeper problems that underlie our discontent—which is the focus of the book's second half (Parts III and IV). Put simply, in a handful of years we could "repeal" hunger and begin to replace it with a more inclusive economy. That is a promising alternative to our current political dysfunctions.

We also have at our fingertips the ability to exert stronger leadership in helping to end extreme hunger and poverty throughout the world.

Obstacles stand in the way. The first obstacle is doubt that hunger can be nearly eliminated. Chapter 2 makes the case for doing so in the United States, where the price we pay for letting hunger persist far outweighs the cost of erasing it. Chapter 3 contends that ending most extreme hunger and poverty worldwide by the year 2030—as the nations of the world have pledged to do—is a daunting but not an impossible goal.

A second obstacle is our silence. Americans by the millions assist hungry people through charity but remain enablers of hunger through their silence as citizens. Religious congregations, as well as the media, excel in featuring the response of charity to hunger, especially when disasters occur or during seasons of giving. As commendable as such encouragement is, it conveys the impression that charity is the main way or even the only way citizens have of responding. People are led to think that the role of charity is far more consequential than the role of government in addressing hunger, when the opposite is the case by a wide margin. As a result, few of us who support such charities also urge our members of Congress to act so that the nation as a whole does its part in addressing hunger and poverty.

The consequence of our silence is more than regrettable. It impairs and shortens lives on a massive scale. The truth is that you, the reader, and the impact you can have on our government, are of critical importance in getting the United States to take leadership in eliminating hunger here and reducing it abroad. Chapters 4 to 7 explain why charity is much too limited to end hunger and why government must take the lead.

A third obstacle is our political divide, which hobbles our ability to govern. Two sides tend to speak past each other about the causes of hunger and poverty rather than sharing insights and finding common ground. Liberals point to severe inequalities, conservatives to behavioral problems, as though we face an either/or dilemma. Rigid views lock horns and block solutions, feeding the view that government is inept at solving problems.

Suppose instead a handful of Democrat and Republican leaders work across party lines to get Congress to establish, as a dead-serious national goal, ending the shame of hunger in the world's richest nation, while accelerating our efforts toward ending it globally. Setting those goals and starting the process to achieve them would not only save and enhance countless lives; it would also clarify our vision for addressing extreme inequalities that tie us in knots and set us against one another. What this book proposes, however, is not a split-the-difference political compromise, but a bipartisan way forward that reflects the nation's founding ideals of what America was meant to be. Getting Congress to take such leadership would give Americans, especially young Americans who have soured on politics, a cause worth embracing and one that could breathe new life into our troubled democracy.

That brings me to the second half of this book—Parts III and IV. Erasing most hunger in the United States by improving and expanding our current federal food assistance programs would also reduce poverty, but it would still leave many Americans poor or nearly so, swimming against a current of inequalities without a job or working at very low wages. So while reducing hunger in our nation through the quick-fix of food assistance, we should also tackle the more basic and enduring solution of a more inclusive economy so that all who can and should work have a chance to earn an adequate living.

For that reason the second half of the book focuses on making the economy work for everyone. Chapter 8 addresses the social and racial inequalities that plague us; chapter 9, the erosion of family life; chapter 10, the dilemma of taxes and soaring deficits; and chapter 11, the way toward fixing an economy that is strong in aggregate but fails too many of us. An agreement to work together to end hunger would enable us to see more clearly how to make our economy function well for everyone, a challenge that currently leaves us spinning our wheels.

Make America great? Now *there* is a lens of hope for doing it.

In projecting that hope, this book affirms both charity and justice, because both are necessary for ending hunger and making our economy fair and inclusive. Charity is often contrasted with justice. That is a useful but also misleading distinction because it oversimplifies. Charities working to reduce hunger and poverty are offering help that is due recipients by virtue of their need and our common humanity. The worth of those being helped is not dependent upon our judgment of their worthiness. The assistance offered is often a hand up as well as a hand out, a way of helping people so they can help themselves. There is a strong element of justice in that.

In reducing hunger and poverty, charities benefit both recipients and donors. I have been involved in various ways for most of my life in supporting such agencies and have seen firsthand what a difference they can make both here and abroad. The difference is not trivial.

But I have also seen the limitations of charity. As a Lutheran parish pastor, I lived and worked with a racial diversity of people on New York City's Lower East Side, many of them economically poor. Their struggles prompted me and others to launch a national citizens' lobby against hunger, Bread for the World. Why a *citizens'* lobby? Because conveying our views to government leaders is a way in which each of us can help the entire nation deal more effectively with hunger as well as the poverty that lies behind it.

Charity does much good, but not when it diverts attention from our public responsibility. This book dispels the myth that charity is an adequate response to hunger. Of course, free enterprise by itself cannot do so either. Neither can the government nor families nor communities. None of these alone can come close to ending hunger, but in combination we can eliminate most of it, if we determine to do so. However, *only the government of "we the people" can exert the essential leadership of making it a national commitment.*

In referring to hunger and poverty, people occasionally say, "Let charity do it." They rarely mean that literally. They commonly mean, "Let free enterprise create jobs, and let charities take care of people in distress." In other words, reduce or bypass the role of government. That is a terrible mistake. It overlooks the limitations of free enterprise. It lays on charities a burden that lies way beyond their capacity. And it leads citizens to neglect the great privilege that is ours as Americans to help determine the nation's well-being and our being well governed.

Free enterprise, charity, and government, along with families, communities, and good neighbors—all are necessary for ending hunger and reducing inequalities, each with its respective strengths, each respecting its limitations, and each with its distinctive obligations. This book stresses the responsibility that is ours as citizens and explains why it is crucial, at this particular moment in history, that we press our nation's leaders to get solidly behind the goals of eliminating hunger and making our economy fair. Utopian? Those goals are so decent and so clearly within our grasp that we would be fools to dismiss them as unachievable.

I make the case for this as an appeal to all people of good will, religious and secular alike. However, because churches are inclined to promote only charity as a response to hunger and poverty, the final chapter challenges people of faith to see the contradiction between what they profess to believe and their silence at the political level while others suffer and die.

Whether you are religious or not, Democrat, Independent, or Republican, it is time for all of us to end our silence and speak up.

ARTHUR SIMON
January 2019

Disclosure: My views are influenced by the work of Bread for the World, the citizens' lobby that I helped to found and in which I am still actively engaged. However, I freely express my own thinking in this book. Bread for the World is not responsible for opinions of mine that wander beyond its agenda.

PART I

Ending Most Hunger
Is within Reach

1

Silence Can Kill

The most tragic problem is silence.

—Rabbi Joachim Prinz,
March on Washington, August 28, 1963[1]

Silence may be golden, but it can also kill.

When Adolf Hitler rose to power in Germany and began unleashing horror on Jews, the majority of respectable people in Germany, including churchgoing Christians, watched in silence. There were various reasons for their silence, among them the desire to avoid "getting involved in politics," but their silence was deeply political because it gave unwitting consent to the unfolding slaughter of millions of people, including six million Holocaust victims, during World War II.

Today hunger is directly or indirectly responsible for the deaths of at least six million people each year, half of them young children.[2] That's 60 million in a decade. Their untimely deaths are avoidable, as are the suffering and disabilities they endure during their shortened stay on earth. Yet all that it takes to ensure the continuation of hunger is the silence of well-meaning citizens.

Let me explain.

The world has seen dramatic gains against hunger and poverty in recent decades. The share of its population that is *chronically undernourished* has sharply receded. The world is now within reach of putting a near end to that kind of hunger. The Greeks called such a moment a *kairos* to distinguish a transcendent opportunity from *chronos*, ordinary chronological time. Less than a century ago chronic hunger—undernourishment that goes on and on—was a way of life for most of the world's people. But a historic escape from hunger has been occurring, and by 2017 about 11 percent of the human family was chronically undernourished. That marks tremendous progress,

3

though still a calamity for 821 million of us—one out of every nine people—who face extreme hunger.[3]

Today we understand better than ever what it takes to end hunger, and the nations of the world may be more determined than ever to do it. In September 2015 they launched Sustainable Development Goals (SDGs), the most ambitious international effort in history to wipe out extreme hunger and extreme poverty, and to do it by the year 2030.[4] The US commitment—or lack of it—in this effort will weigh heavily in determining the outcome. The nation's political upheaval in 2016 may have delayed such a commitment on our part or even thrown it into reverse. That makes the response of citizens all the more important, as our nation struggles to find its way.

What about hunger in the United States? Our country cut in half the percentage of people living in poverty and hunger during the 1960s and 1970s.[5] Then we slipped and have still not regained momentum. Yet we could end almost all food insecurity and much of the poverty in our country within a handful of years, and in partnership with other nations we could provide key leadership toward bringing extreme hunger and poverty to a near conclusion globally by 2030.

These things we *could* do. But there is nothing easy or inevitable about doing them. Even erasing hunger in America will take personal as well as public commitments on a sizable scale. The question is: Can we muster the necessary will?

From Good Intentions to National Commitment

The will to end hunger must be engraved in national policy. Feeling sorry for hungry people is not enough. Wishing hard for hunger to end won't help much either, unless it inspires action. Private enterprise and private charity play essential roles in preventing hunger, but even in combination they are not enough. The eradication of hunger requires a national commitment; and in our country that must be concretely expressed by congressional action and presidential leadership. Such a national commitment, however, is not likely to happen until enough citizens get sufficiently aroused to speak up, and speak often, to the nation's decision-makers and persuade them to act.

Many of us want hunger to end. Americans in large numbers contribute money or time to private agencies that offer assistance to relieve hunger and poverty; but so far most of us who do this remain silent before "the powers that be." Silence sends a message to the nation's lawmakers that we consider the current level of hunger acceptable; some see it as unavoidable, and others conclude that the problem is best left to charity. But this "acceptable" level of hunger leaves hundreds of millions of children and adults trapped in suffering globally, and tens of millions of Americans in households that cannot always provide adequate nourishment.

Too few of us are speaking this truth to our own members of Congress. To speak out is to save lives and to enhance the lives of others. To remain silent is to cast a vote for misery and death to persist. That is the silence that kills—*our* silence.

Please understand. The killing occurs not by malicious intent. It is a consequence in part of our failure as citizens to demand that our nation's policymakers take action against hunger and the poverty that spawns it. Our silence allows the nation to give a tepid response, when a serious effort could bring hunger to a virtual end in this country and set the pace for ending most remaining hunger worldwide.

As it was during the Nazi era in Germany, silence today is political. Far from avoiding politics, it counts as support for the continuation of hunger and the underlying inequalities that it reflects. The result is poor health, disability, and premature death for many.

In short, our silence takes a lethal toll.

This book has a twofold purpose: to make the case for breaking that silence, and to use the goal of ending hunger as a wedge for making our entire economy more humane. Doing so would not only save lives, it might also save our democracy.

The public tremors that led to the political earthquake of 2016 are symptoms of the nation's weak underbelly of despair and exclusion that divides us and undermines our ability to govern. How do we get our bearings? How can we work together and move forward? This book tries to cut through some of our noisy disagreements by starting with the clear, simple, decent, nonpartisan step of deciding to erase hunger in our richly endowed nation. Taking that step together would not only help us feel better about ourselves and one another, it would also give us a clearer vision of how our economy could serve the common good.

Three Claims

The first half of this book makes two claims: (1) that the prospect of ending most remaining hunger, both in our own country and globally, is within reach; and (2) that the silence of US citizens about it *at the political level* is a big factor in the continuation of hunger. Therefore it is a silence that kills.

Neither claim is self-evident. Each requires plausible evidence. Chapters 2 and 3 address the first claim, and Part II (chapters 4 through 7) addresses the second claim. Snapshots of history help document and explain the case I make. Like a sampling of photos from your family album they highlight a few main points but omit a lot of detail.

The second half of this book (Parts III and IV) builds on a third claim: (3) that a commitment to end hunger could be a corrective lens for our current political crisis and enable us to make our nation more responsive to the social, racial, and economic inequalities that diminish our democracy and threaten its survival.

2

We Could Soon End Most US Hunger

Many social problems seem complex beyond hope.
But dramatic progress against hunger is not.

—Michael Gerson[1]

I spent more than two decades on the Lower East Side of Manhattan, a section of New York City made famous more than a century ago by journalist Jacob Riis in *How the Other Half Lives,* and the place where Michael Harrington said he "first came into contact with the terrible reality of involuntary poverty" through Dorothy Day and the Catholic Worker movement.[2] Shortly after I arrived there in 1961, Harrington's *The Other America* alerted the nation to the depth and extent of US poverty and helped trigger the "war" against it.

Many of the people with whom I lived and worked as a parish pastor were caught in a constellation of problems that afflict poor people. Along the way I wrote about some of them, hoping that would help others understand why those who get caught in poverty often cannot escape it.[3] They included a family of four, whose father's disability kept him moving from job to job, the family moving from one run-down apartment to another, and the two children moving in and out of school. I sketched a mother's hard life of raising a family while coping with racial barriers, and three seniors who battled threadbare years as body and income faded away. These folks exhibited courage—sometimes joy—in the face of adversity.

The contagious laughter of children often carried me through the day. But too often those kids reached a point at which the light in their eyes began to dim, as they came to see themselves traveling down a road on which their dreams were slipping away. Economic poverty accounted for much of this, but so did family and social surroundings. Fading hope was robbing them of determination to invest in the future.

7

Hunger as Food Insecurity

If by random selection you were to become a child growing up in our country today, you would have one chance in five or six of living in poverty, and about the same odds of being in a home that is "food-insecure," the official US designation for living in or on the edge of hunger. Food insecurity is a more moderate form of deprivation than the chronic hunger that is so lethal in much of the world. But it is no picnic for the 40 million Americans (one in every eight, including 13 million children) in households that have to skimp on food or miss meals when money runs out, many of them just one unexpected setback from a major crisis.

- Food insecurity claimed 11.8 percent of US households in 2017, and almost one-third of food-insecure households faced *very low* food security with periodic episodes of not having money to buy enough food.[4]
- Poverty also claimed one out of every eight Americans (12.3 percent).[5]

You may think hunger and poverty in the United States can't be terrible, and compared to extremes in many countries, that is usually the case. A poor American family may have television, beds with mattresses, central heat, air conditioning (almost half do), indoor plumbing, a refrigerator, and maybe an old car. That level of poverty would strike a poor family in a developing country as lavish. Until recent times kings and emperors lacked such things, but that did not make them hungry; nor do modern appliances make poor Americans well fed. Would selling its TV allow a family to eat better for a month or two? Perhaps, but what about the next month? Sell a bed? Doing without such things is no solution to hunger or poverty in twenty-first-century America, when having a computer or a smartphone is often a way for people to learn of opportunities and work their way ahead. For children, access to a computer is part of growing up in a world where even unskilled jobs increasingly require basic tech savvy.

Angela Brill and two children live on her meager earnings of $1,300 a month. With the cost of rent, utilities, food, clothing, out-of-pocket medical care, transportation, school expenses and more, getting by is a daily struggle. The federal "food stamp" program, now called SNAP (Supplemental Nutrition Assistance Program), allows deductions for some of their expenses, which enables her family to qualify for a net income of $640 a month and gives them food benefits of $312 on their SNAP debit card, reloaded each month for buying groceries.[6] "Without that," Angela says, "we couldn't begin to manage." SNAP's benefit for her family averages $1.16 a person for each meal, and at their income level they are expected to pay out-of-pocket for any additional food. They usually get a monthly bag of groceries from a food pantry, though getting there and back by bus or lining up a ride takes time and energy that are in painfully short supply. The family still has to skimp on food near the end of the month when their SNAP benefits are used up. Despite Angela's care in shopping, their diet is strong on calories and weak on fruits, vegetables, and proteins. Her quest for food is a daily concern, but even worse for 19 million Americans with monthly incomes less than half of the official poverty line of $1,702 for a family of three,[7] and worse yet for people at the bottom who survive on $2 a day or less.[8]

On a sliding scale, SNAP benefits taper off and end for those with incomes at 130 percent of the poverty line. Because it enables many people to have an adequate or near-adequate diet, SNAP cushions the level of food insecurity for both poor and near-poor Americans, yet leaves many of them still struggling for food and coming up short on nutrition.

In 2017 the nation spent $99 billion on federal food and nutrition programs to help alleviate hunger in America—a lot of money, but less than three cents of every dollar spent by the government or about a half-a-penny of each dollar from the nation's total income. Of the $99 billion, $68 billion paid for the SNAP program.[9] Other federal programs offer school lunches and sometimes breakfast to children; supplemental nutrition for women, infants, and children (WIC); and food through a handful of smaller programs. SNAP, however, is the backbone of the nation's food assistance, providing far more of it than all other food assistance programs—government as well as private charities—combined.

Two striking numbers in the box on page 10: (1) only 55 percent of Feeding America network recipients said they were SNAP recipients, and (2) 50 percent of its client households lived above the poverty line.[10] This tells us that many food-insecure Americans are middle-class workers who have fallen on hard times—often sickness, job loss, or separation. The figures indicate a sizable overlap between what is needed to overcome hunger and what is needed to make the economy work for everyone.

SNAP Under Attack

Those who qualify for SNAP benefits are legally entitled to them, so when the Great Recession of 2007-2009 began to peak, the number of SNAP recipients increased sharply. SNAP fulfilled its purpose as a safety-net for millions of newly desperate Americans, which pushed its cost to record levels. That triggered renewed efforts in Congress to reduce its funding. SNAP, the argument goes, is a handout that creates dependence on government and discourages people from seeking work, so hunger or the threat of hunger will prod them to find jobs. Most able-bodied, unemployed adults without children are limited to three months of benefits unless they are

Feeding America

Though small compared to federal food assistance, charity plays a sizable role, mainly as part of a network related to Feeding America, the umbrella agency for most of the nation's food banks, which serve 46,000 local agencies that operate 60,000 food programs such as food pantries and soup kitchens. In 2016-17 the Feeding America network of 200 regional food banks and local outlets provided $8.5 billion worth of food and grocery items to more than 46 million Americans.[1] The Feeding America network serves as an emergency backup to SNAP and other federal nutrition programs. SNAP was designed from the start to help people through difficult times by offering them a diet meant "for temporary or emergency use."[2] So when assistance falls short, people often turn to private charities for help—but 79 percent of those who do, report that their most common coping strategy is buying cheap food.[3] That 46 million of us received food from these charities, yet 41 million of us still live in food-insecure households, is striking evidence that our government's food safety-net fails to meet the nutritional needs of a large number of Americans, even with the help of charities.

Feeding America periodically publishes an extensive study of its hunger network, which gives us one of the best available descriptions of what food insecurity is like in America, including the 55 percent of its recipients who reported currently receiving SNAP for food assistance and those who did not.[4] In 2014 Feeding America's data showed the choices that recipients of food charity have had to make:

- 69 percent between food and utilities;
- 67 percent between food and transportation;
- 66 percent between food and medical care;
- 57 percent between food and housing;
- 31 percent between food and education.[5]

In 58 percent of households served, someone in the household had high blood pressure, 33 percent included someone with diabetes, 55 percent reported medical debts, 29 percent had no health insurance, 50 percent fell below the poverty line (including 62 percent in households with one or more child), and 84 percent were food-insecure.[6]

participating in a workfare or job-training program.[11] In 2016 almost two-thirds of SNAP recipients came from households with children, elderly, or disabled persons who need care; and one-third (32 percent) of SNAP households had at least one working adult. The average SNAP household income was only 61 percent of the poverty line.[12] Should we withhold food from such people, among them military personnel and veterans? Seeing food assistance and sloth, rather than poverty, as the problem conveniently shifts the responsibility for hunger from us to poverty's victims. Hunger is *their* fault.

SNAP often reflects in-and-out participation and sometimes long-term dependency. During a recent four-year stretch, more than a third of the nation's population had at least one spell of poverty lasting two months or more.[13] SNAP offers one way to make it through those tough periods. It gives people a hand up. It serves as a ladder as well as a safety-net.

A study examining the eventual outcome for early food-stamp recipients found that on average they contributed more to the economy than did non-recipients who also qualified for but were not on food stamps.[14] In his autobiography, *Gifted Hands*, neurosurgeon and now US Secretary of Housing and Urban Development Ben Carson reports that he grew up in a single-parent family and received government aid in the form of eyeglasses, a jobs program, and food stamps (SNAP), though he opposes reliance on public assistance.[15]

Michael Gerson, syndicated *Washington Post* columnist, frequent guest on PBS News, and a compassionate conservative, sees SNAP as a moral issue. He notes that this now-automated program is both efficient and effective and could be expanded with little increase in its administration. We know when recipients run out of food each month, he writes, "so how is it then possible to justify funding three weeks of food instead of four? What additional dependence, what added moral hazard could a full month of eating possibly create?"

His answer: "There are no good excuses."[16]

Occasionally a few members of Congress have a "food stamp experience" by grocery shopping on a SNAP allowance. I have never heard of a congressperson who has lived on that for a week and then voted for a cut in SNAP. "Moderate" hunger may not seem so bad if, like me, you are comfortable and well fed; but to a child who has to go to school without breakfast and can't concentrate, it's bad. To a mother or father who has to choose between food and rent or medicine, it's bad. To a family like Angela's, whose monthly SNAP benefits run out before the end of the month, it's bad.

Hunger was no picnic for Wisconsin's David Obey, who served forty years in Congress, eight of these as chairman of the powerful House Appropriations Committee. Obey had a difficult childhood. His parents divorced and his mother worked but "couldn't make enough money to keep afloat." They had to start selling things to a secondhand store and pawnshop to get through the last week of the month. "It was a terrible feeling, and I will never forget it until the day I die," says Obey. He recalls a week before Christmas when the family was facing a particularly hard time and the Lemke family came to the front door with a bag of groceries. His mother was so grateful she began crying. David was so embarrassed and ashamed that he ran upstairs and refused to come down to thank the Lemkes. "Today, I still feel that frustration and anger when I run into people who are in that same circumstance and especially when I see homeless people. . . . How little it takes—bad luck, sickness—to be pushed back to that awful edge."[17]

Could We End Hunger in America?

The United States is the richest nation on earth, the world's largest food exporter,[18] and the self-proclaimed champion of liberty and justice for all. In 1964 we launched a much-heralded "War on Poverty." Yet in 2017, 40 million of us lived in households that experienced food insecurity, and an overlapping 40 million people lived in poverty. *Almost nothing on this scale occurs in other wealthy countries.* In his 2018 report to the United Nations on poverty and human rights in the United States, Philip Alston says US citizens "live shorter and sicker lives compared to those living in all other rich democracies" and have "the highest youth poverty rate," the "world's highest incarceration rate," and "the highest rate of income inequality among Western countries." He reports that "the United States is alone among developed countries in insisting that [human rights] do not include rights that guard against dying of hunger, dying from a lack of access to affordable health care or growing up in a context of total deprivation." Alston calls the persistence of poverty "a political choice made by those in power. With political will, it could readily be eliminated."[19] A national poll shows that 86 percent of Americans agree with the statement, "In the United States of America, no one should go hungry."[20] So why don't we end hunger and the poverty that surrounds it?

In the 1960s and 1970s our country made remarkable gains against hunger; but since then we have lagged behind other countries in reducing it further. The 11.8 percent rate of our food insecurity in 2017 was almost identical to the 11.9 percent rate in 1995 when it was first measured.[21] Going back to the 1960s, however, we see that the official US *poverty* rate was cut in half from 22 percent in 1960 to a record low of 11 percent in 1973. Forty-four years later it was 12.3 percent.[22]

In the previous paragraph I switched from "hunger" to "poverty." I did so because official statistics on hunger in this country were not even gathered and published until 1995—a telling commentary on political leaders who argued for years that we lacked solid evidence ("It's only anecdotal") of widespread hunger, and then blocked efforts to document it.[23] This hardly reflected a commitment to reduce hunger or even acknowledge it. As a result, for the years prior to 1995 we turn to the nation's official *poverty* rates, which have been almost the same as the rate for food insecurity since 1995, so there is reason to believe that the sharp reduction of poverty during the 1960s reflects a similar reduction in hunger. The link between poverty and hunger is not surprising, because the official poverty threshold is set at three times the cost of an economy food diet, a diet never meant to extend beyond emergencies. For many, however, the emergency goes on and on.

By 1960 it had become increasingly apparent that postwar prosperity was leaving a large segment of the US population, white as well as black and indigenous, impoverished. Two monumental gains occurred during that decade. (1) The civil rights movement prodded the nation to declare an end to legal racial segregation as well as some aspects of racial discrimination, and to guarantee voting rights for African Americans. (2) The nation also cut poverty in half, while easing poverty for others.

While campaigning for the presidency in 1960, John F. Kennedy was shocked by the severity of poverty among West Virginia coal miners. The day after his inauguration in his first official act as president, Kennedy issued an executive order for a food stamp program as a pilot project.[24] It was expanded and then became permanent under President Lyndon B. Johnson.

Shortly before his death Kennedy began to consider a special initiative to reduce poverty. Johnson quickly seized this embryonic idea and in his 1964 State of the Union address (two months after Kennedy's assassination) he announced a "War on Poverty" for the country. A flurry of initiatives followed, including Head Start, Volunteers in Service to America (VISTA), Job Corps, community action programs, aid for schools in low-income areas, Medicare, Medicaid, Model Cities, and the expansion of

Social Security. Despite controversy and shortcomings in some of these programs,[25] the safety-net for struggling families was strengthened. Poverty declined and kept declining at a restrained pace at least into the early 1970s.

In 1967 a team of physicians reported widespread and sometimes severe malnutrition in various areas of the country, including instances of actual starvation. Senator Robert F. Kennedy led a widely publicized follow-up investigation. A 1968 CBS television documentary, "Hunger in America," rang an alarm. One viewer was Senator (earlier Congressman) George McGovern, who saw a boy being interviewed in a school cafeteria while watching other kids eat. The boy was asked how he felt about being hungry. "Embarrassed," he said, looking like he had just stubbed his toe. McGovern was shaken. "I am the one who ought to be embarrassed. Politicians like me should be embarrassed," he thought. "We live in the richest country in the world, and children are hungry."[26] He and Senator Bob Dole soon became a bipartisan team in Congress for getting legislation on domestic and international hunger.

But not without political resistance.

The Food Research and Action Center (FRAC), founded in 1970, filed lawsuits in twenty-six states that led to compliance with federal law that every state, in every county, must make either a food stamp or a food surplus distribution program available to poor people. In two FRAC lawsuits the US Supreme Court prevented the exclusion of thousands of participants from the food stamp program. FRAC's litigation also led to the release of funds for the WIC program (supplemental nutrition for Women, Infants, and Children)[27] that were appropriated by Congress but held back by the Nixon administration.[28] FRAC's work, and soon a growing network of advocates, helped make federal nutrition programs an indispensable core of the nation's safety-net, at a time when both political parties were responsive to hunger and poverty.

The team of physicians that in 1967 shocked the nation with evidence of extreme malnutrition, especially in the South, returned to the same areas ten years later and reported: "Our first and overwhelming impression is that there are far fewer grossly malnourished people in this country today than there were ten years ago. Malnutrition has become a subtler problem." They wrote that living standards were as bad as ever—with one exception: federal nutrition programs. Food Stamps, school lunch and breakfast programs, the nutrition aspect of Head Start, and the WIC program had made the difference.[29]

Rapid Progress—for a While

The rate of poverty declined sharply during the 1960s, as the nation's safety-net for poor people was greatly enlarged. Gains against poverty continued for a while into the 1970s. Since then, however, poverty has had periods of growth and periods of decline. Persistent and sometimes successful efforts to weaken the nation's safety-net have compelled citizen advocates to defend and try to strengthen it. Advocates had to do so even when the Great Recession of 2007–2009 made millions of additional Americans poor, so they called for a "circle of protection" around programs that help low-income people.

The *official* US poverty rate is often criticized because it counts only cash income but omits other government benefits. However, it also fails to adjust adequately for the cost of living. So since 2012 the US Census Bureau has offered a *Supplemental* Poverty Measure (SPM) that *adds* benefits such as SNAP, housing vouchers, and tax credits, but also *subtracts* work-related expenses, taxes paid, and out-of-pocket medical costs; it also adjusts for geographical variations in the cost of housing.[30] *Visual 1* below shows the official poverty rate, as well as the SPM rate (here anchored to the year 2012 as a fixed point of reference and adjusted for inflation).[31]

The anchored SPM reveals that, during the 1960s and until recent years, poverty was much higher than the official rate indicates. The SPM also shows that poverty has *declined* since the early 1970s, not risen (as the official rate shows). The safety-net programs have done more than previously thought to reduce poverty in the 1960s and 1970s as well as the 1990s, and to restrain its rise during the early 1980s and since 2000.[32] By either measure, however, the record indicates that *within a brief period, when we made a vigorous and sustained effort, we were able as a nation to cut poverty and hunger almost in half.*

A surge in poverty and hunger during the early 1980s coincided with a recession that was accompanied by sharp reductions in federal programs for low-income people. This prompted an explosion of food banks and food pantries that were started in frantic efforts to assist growing numbers of people newly desperate for food. These charities kept many people afloat, but they were no match for cuts in food stamps (now SNAP). This happened just as the 1981–1982 recession was forcing people to scrape for necessities. The rise in hunger and poverty aroused citizens to pressure members of Congress, so some of the cut programs were restored. Poverty and hunger began sloping downward again as the economy recovered.

Visual 1
Poverty Has Fallen Significantly Since the 1960s
Under "Anchored" Supplemental Poverty Measure

Percent of people living in poverty

Official poverty measure*   ■ Supplemental poverty measure
                                  "anchored" at 2012**

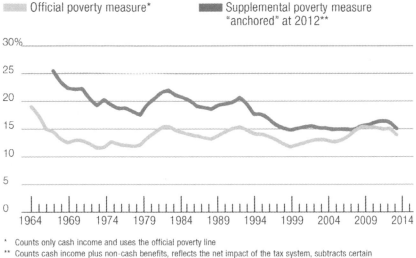

* Counts only cash income and uses the official poverty line
** Counts cash income plus non-cash benefits, reflects the net impact of the tax system, subtracts certain
   experiences from income, and uses a poverty line based on today's cost of certain necessities adjusted back
   for inflation.

Source: Christopher Wimer et al., "Trends in Poverty with an Anchored Supplemental Poverty Measure,"
Columbia Population Research Center, December 2013. For 2013–2015, CBPP analysis of Census Bureau data
from the March Current Population Survey and SPM public use files.

CENTER ON BUDGET AND POLICY PRIORITIES | CBPP.ORG

This slice of history tells us that a strong, persistent effort to improve and expand our existing federal food assistance (especially SNAP and child nutrition programs) could, along with other antipoverty initiatives, end most remaining hunger within a few years. Local communities could actively reach out to people who qualify for—but do not currently participate in—government programs that might enable them to become more food-secure and healthier. Towns, counties, and cities could go a step further and attempt to become hunger-free zones, along the lines of the Indy Hunger Network described in chapter 5 below.

War, Polarization, and Neglect

Why, in the face of sharp gains for a brief period in our own country, and promising gains globally against hunger and poverty, has the United States lagged since then?

- The War in Vietnam turned the nation's attention, as well as its resources, away from the War on Poverty. Martin Luther King Jr., in a 1967 address at New York's Riverside Church, announced his opposition to the war in Vietnam. He said he had seen "a shining moment" for both blacks and whites in the struggle against poverty. "Then came the buildup in Vietnam, and I watched this [War on Poverty] program broken and eviscerated, as if it were some idle political plaything of a society gone mad on war."[33]
- President Johnson declined as too costly the urging of Secretary of Labor Willard Wirtz, Daniel Patrick Moynihan, and others to launch a large public works program. That omission left men who were desperate for work unemployed, and the War on Poverty without job creation, the one thing that might most have helped people in collapsing neighborhoods.[34] Nicholas Lemann concludes that the War on Poverty defied logic in its "attempt to eliminate poverty in a capitalist country without giving poor people either money or jobs."[35] Although Johnson did not try to expand cash-assistance welfare, within a dozen years Aid to Families with Dependent Children tripled in size, as women with children turned increasingly to it for support rather than to job-hunting men, because able-bodied men of working age in a household—married or not, employed or not—disqualified families for support. Public opposition to welfare grew, while black men, who were excluded from many if not most jobs, were demoralized by a policy that undermined their role as a provider and was destructive of family life for women and children as well as men.
- Resentment of antipoverty measures made food stamps a prominent object of ridicule because of their visibility at checkout counters—a public humiliation for many recipients. By 1981 a *New York Times*/CBS poll could report that the food stamp program was the nation's most unpopular social welfare program by a wide margin and a prime target of President Reagan's push to reduce food assistance.[36]

- Political and racial polarization stirred resistance to government initiatives. Demonstrations for civil rights, and sometimes racial violence, prompted many whites to blame the War on Poverty rather than poverty itself for social unrest.
- Community action programs led to demands for change that brought neighborhood citizens into conflict with local officials, which led to further criticism of the War on Poverty.
- Success was also a factor. Gains made hunger less visible and less newsworthy to most of the population and thus more easily ignored.
- By 1984, "massive economic and social transformations," including access to cheap labor abroad, were imposing new hardships on America's poor.[37] Along with neglect of job creation, manufacturing began to shrink, and workers faced more competition from automation and from jobs being shipped to lower-paid workers abroad.

The political process failed to respond with adequate remedial action, so advocacy groups began a long and difficult struggle to defend and sometimes improve the safety-net, which diverted efforts from focusing on longer-term solutions through jobs and adequate wages.

As the income gap between rich and poor widened, President Reagan quipped, "In the sixties we waged a war on poverty, and poverty won!"[38] But in fact we made impressive gains for a while, then backed away. The extent to which the war in Vietnam, racial discrimination, program deficiencies, technology, globalization, or rigid political views prompted this continues to provoke debate.

Besides its lack of job creation, the War on Poverty had other serious flaws. Fast action meant that programs often gave birth to untested ideas in the complex arena of social policy. Alice Rivlin, a participant in the "war," and later (1975) the first director of the nonpartisan Congressional Budget Office, wrote (already in 1970) that "Head Start, Title I, model cities, and other federal programs *could* have been designed to produce information on their effectiveness, but they were not." The strategy, she says, was "random innovation."[39] Many ideas worked well and others did not, but there was often no way of knowing. This gave a wide opening to critics who charged the government with wasteful spending and maintained that its assistance was doing more harm than good by encouraging dependency. The government should get out of the way, they said, and let people fend for themselves, with private charity to assist those who can't fend well. And many could not.

Competing Narratives

Over the years, critics of the War on Poverty have offered two different narratives to press their case. The main one, popularized by Reagan, is that we lost the War on Poverty. House Speaker Paul Ryan's 2016 plan to scale back the federal safety-net said, "Americans are no better off today than they were before the War on Poverty began in 1964."[40] That position was abruptly reversed by the Trump administration in July 2018 with a White House report that the War on Poverty was largely over because, the report said, no more than 3 percent of Americans are truly poor (based on household purchases of nonessentials) and less than 5 percent "generally do not have to reduce food intake at any point during the year."[41] This view is at odds with widely accepted official reports,[42] but it had earlier proponents, among them political economist Nicholas Eberstadt.

For the fiftieth anniversary in 2014 of Johnson's "Great Society," Eberstadt wrote that "the long War on Poverty has indeed managed to eradicate 1960s-style poverty from our midst, or very nearly so," but in the process it financed "the rise and spread of an ominous 'tangle of pathologies' in the society whose ills antipoverty policies were intended to heal." Eberstadt's narrative, like the White House report, points to improved material well-being. Poor people today have better healthcare, education, living space, and household conveniences; so most poor Americans no longer suffer much material deprivation. Instead, he concludes, today's persistent poverty lies mainly in dependency, flight from work, and family breakdown.[43]

Eberstadt is right in seeing a substantial improvement in material conditions of poverty compared with more extreme conditions in the 1960s, and he has hit a sensitive nerve regarding "pathologies" (which we will consider in chapter 9). Better appliances, utilities, and medical care do ease poverty. However, they rarely end it. They seldom create jobs, raise wages, or put more food on the table. Moreover, poverty is not only measurable deprivation. It is also powerfully psychological, experienced as relative to its surroundings—felt internally in comparison to the living standards and expectations of the larger society.[44] "America is a vastly richer society today" than when the War on Poverty began, Eberstadt says, two and a half times more prosperous than it was in 1966, when measured by per capita after-tax incomes (adjusted for inflation), and three times more prosperous in per capita net wealth.[45]

Eberstadt's point is illuminating because America's poor shared relatively little of those prosperity gains. That makes a big difference. America's poor are not poor in India, they are poor in the United States. And today's poor are not poor fifty or a hundred years ago, they are poor today. An education that prepared people for a decent job decades ago may now prepare them for no job or a job with menial wages. Too many children, especially racial minority children but also white children, who grow up in an unsafe neighborhood with an underperforming school, high unemployment, and perhaps a troubled family, begin to think of themselves as losers in a nation of winners. If they get off to a slow start and face obstacles that seem to put dreams out of reach, they often lose hope and seek fulfillment in self-defeating ways. For reasons such as these, poverty and hunger are perpetuated on a large scale.

Eberstadt and others point out that the government is paying more than $650 billion a year in income-based antipoverty assistance, an amount that—if divided evenly among every American below the poverty line—would give each one $13,000 a year, enough to lift all of them well above the poverty line.[46] From this it would appear that our antipoverty programs are profligate, generous beyond reason. However, as Eberstadt candidly reports, Medicaid accounts for two-thirds of the $13,000; and the $650 billion in antipoverty assistance is only one slice of the $2.2 trillion in total government transfers (including Social Security and Medicare) that reach half of our population with one or more benefits. In combination these income transfers, for the nonpoor as well as the poor, make the distribution of income only "slightly less uneven," according to the nonpartisan Congressional Budget Office.[47] The biggest transfers (Social Security and Medicare) came from political decisions not to tolerate widespread poverty among retired people.

More broadly, our shared prosperity after World War II faltered, and poverty claimed or threatened many of us, writes political theorist William Galston, so "the government stepped into the breach."[48]

Low-income people are not the ones who receive the greatest share of income transfers, with Medicare and Social Security middle-class favorites. But this advantage usually goes unrecognized. On the first day of Neeraj Mehta's graduate school class on housing policy, the professor said, "Raise your hand if you have ever lived in subsidized housing." Out of forty students three or four raised their hands. "How many of you have lived in a house either you or your parents owned?" Most of the hands went up. "Congratulations," he announced. "You too have lived in subsidized housing."[49] Congress allots about $38 billion for public housing and rental vouchers; but mortgage interest tax deductions cost the government twice that much.[50] Homeowners, especially the wealthier ones, out-benefit low-income renters by a large margin when it comes to government assistance. But how many homeowners would raise their hands in response to the professor's question?

The War on Poverty helped millions of Americans rise above the poverty line and eased the harshness of poverty for others. It enabled people to eat and live at some minimal level of decency and many of them to thrive. These achievements came in part through the nation's expanding safety-net. Without social insurance and antipoverty transfers, 45 million more of us would be poor today,[51] doubling the number of Americans below the official poverty line and pushing poor people far deeper into poverty. That would reintroduce our nation to extreme hunger and hardship on a vast scale.

The War on Poverty had its liabilities, one of which was to raise unrealistic hopes, just as the conflict in Vietnam was about to put a stranglehold on the nation's budget and as big economic and cultural changes were about to widen the gap between the most prosperous Americans and the rest of the populace. The War on Poverty promised not just a *war* on poverty, but an *end* to poverty. That promise was broken. It was not able to move enough people from their disadvantages to a level where job opportunities were available, seized, and realized. That kind of empowerment turned out to be far more difficult and complex than expected. The path to such opportunities is still uneven, a subject of debate that we will take up in the second half of this book.

Poverty is concentrated in places where unemployment is high, schools struggle with low achievement rates, school dropouts are frequent, addictions and crime prevalent, and many single parents face challenges that leave them exhausted. Is Eberstadt right? Are dysfunctional habits the cause of poverty? Or is poverty the incubator of pathologies? Or is it both?

Conservatives tend to blame the poor for their poverty. They see bad choices and family breakdown as the main reasons for poverty, and government assistance as enabling bad choices. Liberals tend to see poor people as victims of circumstances beyond their control who struggle financially and socially against daunting odds, and government action as necessary to give them a hand. The result is a conceptual deadlock, a classic example of two views talking past each other. In fact, the views are not mutually exclusive, but different aspects of one complex phenomenon. There *is* something (though far from everything) to the charge that government benefits can create dependency—especially for people who see no pathway to success. Circumstances all too often prevent others from moving forward. Meanwhile the disposition of liberals and conservatives to seize opposing explanations for poverty blocks solutions that could embrace legitimate concerns on both sides.

Whatever the reasons, the nation backed away from making the end of hunger and poverty serious goals.[52] The shame is that the richest nation in history still permits this to occur on so large a scale, when other advanced nations do not. Measured by the proportion of children living in poverty, the United Nations Children's Fund (UNICEF) ranks the United States near the bottom, a disheartening thirty-six out of forty-one advanced countries.[53]

The High Cost of *Not* Ending Hunger

Improving and expanding current food assistance programs would ease poverty, because SNAP already lifts monthly income by 39 percent on average for participating households, including a 45 percent gain for households with children.[54] Doing so, however, is no substitute for longer-term solutions—the focus of the second half of this book. These longer-term initiatives should also begin now, reducing the need and cost of food assistance.

Consider that even in another deep recession it might at most require $40 billion a year more to wipe out US hunger than the $99 billion spent in 2016 on federal food assistance.[55] However, an economy with higher wages and fewer jobless people would greatly reduce the number of SNAP participants. Other antipoverty measures could also speed hunger's end, and the combination of these things could lower the cost of hunger-ending food assistance far below the current cost of food assistance that still leaves about 40 million Americans in food-insecure households.

Consider now the cost of *tolerating* hunger.

In 2014 the prevalence of hunger cost our nation $160 billion, according to research from three interconnected studies,[56] an average of about $500 for every US citizen. $160 billion is four times my highest estimate of what it might cost to eliminate most hunger in America through food assistance alone. Federal and private food assistance combined already saves our country several hundred billion dollars in preventive healthcare each year, and the research indicates a potential savings of three dollars or more for every additional dollar spent to reduce food insecurity.

One of the studies, *Hunger in America: Suffering We All Pay For*, attributes more than two-thirds of the cost of hunger to illnesses, poor health, and lost productivity. The rest includes lower educational outcomes, lower earnings, and charity costs. The report's conclusion: "The nation pays far more by letting hunger exist than it would if our leaders took steps to eliminate it."[57]

The same study reported well-tested evidence that even limited forms of food insecurity have detrimental effects.

> Malnourishment compromises the immune system, making hungry and food insecure people more susceptible to disease. For example, children . . . get sick more frequently, miss school more often, and perform worse in school. The research shows that hungry and food insecure children are more susceptible to cognitive impairment, more likely to engage in antisocial behaviors, and more in need of both medical and mental health interventions.[58]

Those are some of the consequences, which over time lead to more school dropouts, more poverty, and a higher incidence of crime, unemployment, and family dysfunction (see chapter 9). Food insecurity also leads to chronic diseases, such as diabetes, which account for seventy-five cents of every dollar spent in this country on healthcare,[59] the nation's biggest budget expense and the fastest-growing part of government budgets at every level.[60] The price of neglecting hunger looms large when you consider (to cite one example) that the government pays nearly two-thirds of the cost of treating diabetes, mostly through Medicare and Medicaid; and that the average cost of one overnight stay at a US hospital is $2,157.[61] By comparison the average daily cost of SNAP benefits for a recipient is about $4.21.[62]

ProMedica, the largest healthcare provider in northwest Ohio and southeast Michigan, found that hunger affected many of its patients, adding needless expense, for example, in hospital readmissions. So it made food security one of its top priorities, a decision that led to reduced costs and improved health. Rebranding hunger as a health issue also changed the way people think and talk about it, and removed the stigma of "welfare" from patients accepting SNAP or other forms of food assistance.[63]

Prompted in part by ProMedica's experience, Bread for the World's *Hunger Report 2016: The Nourishing Effect: Ending Hunger, Improving Health, Reducing Inequality* makes a strong case for connecting healthcare to hunger. It examines the childhood and full-life effects of hunger. It finds that social, economic, and environmental factors have more impact on health outcomes than medical care does, with good nutrition being a positive nonmedical factor. A negative factor is "toxic stress" that often accompanies poverty and hunger and makes people (children in particular) more vulnerable to physical and mental illness.[64]

Hunger Report 2016 includes publication of the third related study on the cost of neglecting hunger. It points out that public and private food assistance is a cost of *preventing* food insecurity, not a cost *of* food insecurity, without which other costs would soar. Like a vaccine that prevents disease from occurring, food assistance subtracts from, rather than adds to the cost of hunger.[65]

The Great Recession of 2007–2009 added 15 million more Americans to food-insecure households; but by 2017, in spite of a growing economic recovery, four million more of us were food-insecure than just prior to the recession.[66] Food insecurity is a health-destroyer and a budget buster. We are burying ourselves in debt in part by keeping 40 million Americans either hungry or in borderline-hungry households. A survey based on 43,000 students in sixty-six universities and colleges found that 36 percent did not get enough to eat, including one out of every ten community college students who went without eating for a full day during the previous month.[67] That is an expensive way of undermining their education and the nation's future. We are "managing" hunger, rather than ending it, and paying dearly for doing so.

Given the undeniable benefits of adequate nutrition, along with evidence that reducing hunger saves multiple times its cost, why on earth does Congress not take action to end it? Part of the answer is that ending hunger requires up-front spending, while the financial savings, modest at first, grow larger year after year. Front-end spending has to be seen as a long-term benefit. Politics and voters tend to focus on immediate costs. As a result, we already pay a high cost for our past neglect of hunger and poverty.

The leaky roof comes to mind as a way of saving money. Our children, our people, are the nation's most valuable resource by far. We neglect them and hold them back at a high cost. But the benefits—economically, morally, and socially—of helping them succeed make doing so an investment with an exceptionally high yield to all of us.

What is true about investing in a hunger-free America also holds true for investing in a hunger-free world. The real question in either case is not "Can we afford to do this?" but "Can we afford *not* to?" The answer depends on the kind of nation and the kind of world we wish for ourselves, our children, and generations to come. If we cannot even take the simple, decent step of putting food security within reach of all Americans, how can we expect to be morally attuned to deal effectively with the more complex inequalities that rumble beneath the surface of our discontent? That is why a national goal to eliminate hunger may be the big nonpartisan step that would enable us to begin addressing those deeply connected social and economic obstacles that currently undermine our democracy as well as our peace of mind.

One thing seems clear: a hunger-free country, like a less hungry world, requires a surge in citizen advocates and bold national leadership.

Right now we are driving with the brakes on.

3

We Could Help End Global Hunger and Poverty

Economic development is a lot cheaper than sending soldiers.

—Robert Gates[1]

Hunger is devastating and heart-wrenching.

Food deprivation even for short periods of time sucks strength from us. But chronic hunger does so in extremes. It assaults body, mind, and spirit. It drains people of hope. It diminishes life and ends life too soon.

Statistics report the extent of hunger, but they hide human misery because they are abstract and faceless. But chronic hunger is not a statistic. It is the face of a dying infant, the face of grieving parents, the face of a person gone blind for lack of vitamin A. It is the face of a child with odds of thriving stacked against her.

Hunger is Hagirso, an Ethiopian boy, nine or ten years old but only three feet tall. He had nearly starved to death, narrowly missed being one of the 3 million children under age five who die each year from malnutrition or causes stemming from that "single greatest threat to child survival."[2] Hagirso's parents had a tiny but once-thriving farm until they were whipsawed by the combination of an erratic market and a famine from which they barely survived. First a collapse in food prices wiped out their income, then drought ruined their next crop. Because famine caused a surge in food prices, they had to sell their cow and goats, then other possessions to avoid starvation. This left the family frail and impoverished. Hagirso escaped death, but the family's descent into poverty deprived him of school.[3]

In a Guatemalan village far away from Hagirso, five-year-old Gilma also nearly died, but for the special reason that she was a girl. With four sibling brothers, Gilma's family was precariously poor during the best of times, but in 2011 a severe drought struck, and according to custom the boys ate first, so sometimes there was nothing left for Gilma and her mother. Soon Gilma was suffering from severe acute malnutrition (SAM), her legs swollen and ulcerated. Save the Children, administering US government aid in that area, intervened to get her food and emergency medical care, so Gilma recovered and eventually returned to school.[4]

Gilma and Hagirso and their families must never be forgotten because they are among the sea of people who, if they manage to survive, often face physical and mental deprivations that follow them through life. It is for them, as well as for poorly fed Americans, that I write this book and for them that your own life can make a difference.

A *chronically* undernourished person does not get enough to eat—too few calories, thus too little energy for normal health and activity—not just occasionally but for prolonged periods of time. Stunted growth is evidence of undernutrition in children, and because children below the age of five are especially prone to future underachievement and ill health, they are considered chronically undernourished if seriously underweight. The "first thousand days" from conception to age two is the most crucial period of all for determining not only a child's chance of survival, but her lifelong mental and physical health[5]—one reason why maternal and child nutrition are key drivers of a nation's development, and one reason among many why gender discrimination sets back not only women and girls, but everyone. Efforts to reduce hunger address both calorie *and* nutrient deficiencies. But when UN food agencies report the extent of global hunger they mean *chronic undernourishment*,[6] so that is what I mean by extreme hunger in this book, a gauge that omits counting people who get enough calories but still come up short on nutrients.

Dramatic Gains

Throughout human history hunger and poverty have been frequent visitors, if not permanent guests. In 1820—just a handful of generations ago—an estimated 84 percent of the world's population lived in extreme poverty.[7] That gradually began to change, and by the 1930s it was occasionally reported that two-thirds of the world's people were hungry.[8] With one-third of our own nation declared "ill-housed, ill-clad, ill-nourished" by President Franklin D. Roosevelt during the Great Depression,[9] Americans were preoccupied with hunger and poverty here, not hunger and poverty abroad. A generation later

President John F. Kennedy said, "Half of humanity is still undernourished or hungry" but he urged us as a prosperous nation to assist them.[10]

In 2017 about 11 percent of the world's 7.5 billion people were chronically undernourished[11]—a stunning reduction from half or more of humankind in my own lifetime, despite a near quadrupling of the world's population since 1930. Yet, by wide margins, people continue to think that world hunger and poverty are increasing.[12]

Global hunger's dramatic decline in the face of rapid population growth prompted David Beckmann, president of Bread for the World and recipient of the World Food Prize, to write *Exodus from Hunger*,[13] which made the case on which I am building. That was in 2010.

By 2015 the prospect of bringing extreme hunger to a near end had improved.

- Extreme hunger fell by the rate of 44 percent in developing countries between 1990 and 2015.[14]
- Extreme poverty fell by an astonishing 70 percent during that period, reaching the UN goal of cutting it in half five years ahead of schedule.[15]

What accounts for these historic reductions? Key factors include advances in science and technology (food production and healthcare, for example), the spread of free enterprise and a global economy, decades of experience in social and economic development, and the growth and effectiveness of government and private aid agencies. Above all else, however, credit the determination and dogged work of people everywhere struggling to escape hunger and poverty. That determination became part of an international campaign to cut world hunger and poverty in half by 2015. Part cause and part coincidence, the UN Millennium Development Goals (MDGs) for 2015 preceded the fastest poverty reduction in human history.[16] The MDGs also pushed developing countries to cut in half the percentage of people without access to safe drinking water and to make impressive gains in reducing infant mortality, illiteracy, and gender inequality.

Building on that momentum, the nations of the world pledged to achieve even more ambitious UN Sustainable Development Goals (SDGs), the first two of which call for ending most extreme poverty and hunger by 2030.[17] The gains cited above suggest the *possibility* of doing so. However, reaching those goals will require extraordinary acceleration of efforts.

Can we do it?

A Very Steep Hill

Obstacles that routinely impoverish people are hard enough to surmount—joblessness, paltry wages, parcels of land too small and worn-out to yield an adequate harvest, illiteracy, lack of transportation, poor health, little or no medical care, gender abuse, and racial barriers, to name a few. Armed conflicts, the impact of global warming and climate extremes, economic recessions, inept and corrupt governments, or calamity on the scale of another HIV-AIDS pandemic could slow or even reverse prospective gains. Consider also the sobering fact that the most dramatic reductions in global hunger and poverty pertain to *percentages*. Because of population growth, the *number* of people who remain locked in hunger has been declining at a much slower rate.

By the end of 2017 poverty continued to decline, but the rate of reduction had slowed to two-thirds of the pace needed to reach the SDG poverty goal on time.[18] More troubling, the *number* of people in extreme *hunger* had actually increased for three years, from 795 million to 821 million, because of a spike in armed conflicts and climate extremes, as well as economic slowdowns.[19] Starting in 2018 it would require an average annual reduction in hunger of about 45 million a year to come even close to ending extreme hunger by 2030. (By "close" I mean no more than 3 percent chronically hungry.[20]) Such dramatic gains would have to include regions facing the most difficulty in reducing hunger and poverty, especially in sub-Saharan Africa, where the average income for people living in extreme poverty is far below the World Bank's level of $1.90 per person per day for extreme poverty.[21]

According to the World Bank, climate change introduces a special threat that could drive an additional 100 million people into extreme poverty by 2030 unless more aggressive steps begin to cushion its impact.[22] Factors such as these offer ample reason for skepticism about the chance of ending most extreme hunger and poverty by 2030.

A more promising outlook, however, builds on momentum since 2000 during which the Millennium Development Goals for 2015 accelerated international efforts.[23] Can an even stronger impact follow the Sustainable Development Goals for 2030? Maybe.

More accurate measurements of hunger and poverty, based on people's ability country-by-country to produce or purchase food, are being tested by international agencies and the US Department of Agriculture. They show gains that improve the outlook for further progress against hunger.[24]

As poverty and hunger decrease, more resources can be focused on countering the remaining number of poor and hungry people; and efforts to do so will be better informed and could be more intense. A digital revolution is occurring in Africa and elsewhere within some of the least-developed countries, enabling a rapidly growing number of people to access information and process transactions for jump-starting aspects of development. Cell-phone and iPad use, for example, is bringing remote farms and villages into contact with the rest of the world. Millions of small-scale entrepreneurs are starting new businesses and creating jobs, while many farmers are becoming better informed, more productive, and skilled in marketing. Research is leading to more nutritious crops and improved harvests. All of this takes time, of course, and there is not much of it before 2030.

In 2000 *The Economist* featured Africa as the "hopeless continent."[25] During the 1990s annual deaths of children under age five in Africa showed an upward trend that by 2015 would have led to almost 5 million such deaths. Instead the deaths dropped unexpectedly to about 3 million in 2013.[26] Was child survival an early sign of hope for Africa—the reverse of a canary in a mine? Some of Africa's countries, such as Ethiopia and Ghana, advanced so fast for a decade that by 2012 nine of the ten nations with the largest gains in the human development index were in sub-Saharan Africa.[27] However, from 2010 to 2016 sub-Saharan Africa's per capita economic growth slowed to a crawl, lagging well behind other developing countries in education, in access to electricity, and in the collection of taxes.[28] Because tax revenue is so necessary for spurring development, its lag suggests that foreign aid be conditioned on improving tax collection, not become a substitute for it.

Noting that Africa spends $50 billion a year buying food from rich countries, the Bill and Melinda Gates Foundation is backing efforts to enable Africa to feed itself by 2030. "Improving agriculture, the backbone of the African economy, can drive massive poverty reduction and improve life across the continent," the Gateses contend.[29] The Gateses' commitment adds potential heft to the flagship US global food security initiative, Feed the Future, launched in 2010 in nineteen focus countries to help small-scale farmers, especially women, increase income and improve nutrition for their children through food production.

Much depends upon policies and commitments of each country. Economic growth and even poverty reduction do not automatically bring similar gains against hunger. Between 2002 and 2010 India's economy grew twice as fast as that of Brazil, but because Brazil made eliminating hunger a top national priority it reduced hunger at a rate three times that of India, which had no such goal and was held back by exceptionally wide income dispari-ties.[30] Bangladesh, much poorer than India, passed India in reducing stunted growth among children because Bangladesh, among other gains, has pushed programs to improve child nutrition.[31]

Brazil launched a "Zero Hunger" campaign in 2003 involving all sec-tors of society. The campaign includes cash assistance to poor families on condition that their children attend school regularly, get immunized, and have regular health checkups. The school meals program is required to buy at least 30 percent of its food from local family farmers, which boosts their incomes. Local civic groups participate extensively in helping to shape and carry out Zero Hunger.[32] According to a progress report submitted to the United Nations, Brazil cut poverty from 25 percent in 2004 to 8 percent in 2014, while eliminating most child malnutrition. Political turmoil and a re-cession, however, led to an increase in poverty.[33] Other developing countries have been studying Zero Hunger for lessons they can apply. Peru, for exam-ple, cut chronic malnutrition for children under age five from 28 percent to 13 percent between 2008 and 2016,[34] but by 2018 the Brazilian scandal had also entangled Peru. Still, country leaders increasingly realize that reducing hunger and poverty can boost a nation's development—a lesson that leaders in our own country are not always quick to grasp.

Even with optimistic assumptions, however, the elimination of most extreme poverty and hunger by 2030 remains an exceedingly steep hill to climb. The Brookings Institution's World Data Lab estimated that, with more accurate measurements of household consumption, 2019 would be-gin with about 600 million people worldwide still living in extreme pov-erty. India was projected to have 50 million extremely poor people (less than 4 percent of its population). And during 2019 Africa would begin to reduce, rather than add to, the absolute number living in extreme poverty. However, a rising share (70 percent) of the world's extremely poor would live in Africa, an alarming prospect.[35]

What will the outcome be? More important: What outcome do we wish to champion?

Opportunities Slip Away

We have had previous claims that "for the first time in history" the world is within reach of ending hunger. Are we in for yet another "first time in history" letdown? In fact that record strengthens the case for backing the

SDG goals, *but it mainly underscores how essential it is that citizens doggedly push to achieve them.*

In June 1963 President John F. Kennedy told a World Food Congress, "We have the capacity to eliminate hunger from the face of the earth in our lifetime. We need only the will."[36]

A decade later, in November 1974, in the face of regional famines and alarming food shortages, the United Nations convened a World Food Conference in Rome, where US Secretary of State Henry Kissinger famously urged the conference to "proclaim a bold objective—that within a decade no child will go to bed hungry, that no family will fear for its next day's bread, and that no human being's future and capacities will be stunted by malnutrition."[37] The conference resolved, word for word, to do it. Like Kennedy, Kissinger warned that failure to do so should be attributed to "lack of political will."

Soon after the conference, President Gerald Ford commissioned the National Academy of Sciences (NAS) to advise the nation on "how our research and development capabilities can best be applied to meeting this major challenge." After fourteen study teams tapped more than a thousand specialists for advice, the NAS panel made many recommendations and offered this remarkable conclusion: "If there is the political will in this country and abroad, it should be possible to overcome the worst aspects of widespread hunger and malnutrition within one generation."[38] But political will fell short.

The 1974 World Food Conference prompted important steps forward, and one key recommendation called for helping small-scale farmers in poor countries produce more food. Toward that end the conference proposed the creation of an International Fund for Agricultural Development (IFAD), which was launched in 1977; but despite impressive work, IFAD struggled from the start for adequate funding. Other sources of official aid for small-scale farming, including US foreign aid, barely scratched the surface and soon began to decline. With respect to food production in poor countries, the elephant had given birth to a mouse.

Why this collapse of good intentions? Despite widespread public opinion in its favor, reducing hunger abroad seldom achieved the *intensity* of support necessary to become a high priority for political leaders. In our own country, citizens pushed successfully to get two major food reserves and a child survival initiative enacted—significant gains—yet too few Americans were politically vocal and passionate about helping small-scale farmers abroad. Consequently, congressional support for it wobbled in the face of other pressures.

At another level, political will faltered because the food shortages of the mid-1970s eased. Good weather brought good harvests, and so did the Green Revolution. High-yield, pest-resistant strains of wheat and rice became available, especially in South and East Asia; and corn did so in Latin America. Although the benefit to small-scale farmers was limited (because of the cost of seeds, fertilizer, and often irrigation), the Green Revolution came just in time to prevent massive famines and ease hunger in the face of rapid population growth. So, along with bumper crops, complacency set in.

US policy boiled down to this: If countries lack food, we will sell it to them and offer aid in emergencies. President Kennedy had said that "the real goal must be to produce more food in the nations that need it" and that "food deficit nations, with assistance from other countries, can solve their problem."[39] Later the Ford-commissioned NAS study (above) said, "Our most important reason for optimism is the increasing ability of many developing countries to address their own food problems."[40] But instead of helping farmers abroad produce more food, our subsidized grain exports often put cheap food on the market that undercut those farmers, driving them more deeply into poverty and debt, making them still more vulnerable to famine. As some of the poorest countries, mainly in Africa, faced growing food shortages, the United States increasingly shipped emergency food aid across the ocean, but spent less on development assistance for struggling farmers that might have prevented those countries from requiring food aid.

In *The End of Poverty*, economist Jeffrey Sachs says that the rate of food productivity more than anything else accounts for why some countries remain in poverty and others escape it. "The poverty trap is mainly a rural phenomenon of peasant farmers caught in a spiral of rising populations and stagnant or falling food production per person," he writes, and notes that aid donors have woefully underfunded efforts to improve their productivity.[41] Those donor countries, including the United States, forgot the extent to which their own prosperity was built on food production.

Persistent calls for more aid to reduce poverty and build self-reliance were resisted, as US development assistance (measured as a percentage of our national income) continued on a decades-long slide and in 1997 hit its lowest point since World War II (*Visual 2* below). With US leadership sagging, other donor nations also gave less, so during the 1990s combined development assistance from all donor nations fell by almost one-third.[42] However, international foot-dragging in the face of so great a need aroused citizens and a key nucleus of leaders to generate a call for action to reach the Millennium Development Goals of cutting hunger and poverty in half by 2015.

Visual 2
U.S. Official Developmental Assistance, 1960–2014

Total Aid Flows as a percentage of Gross National Income

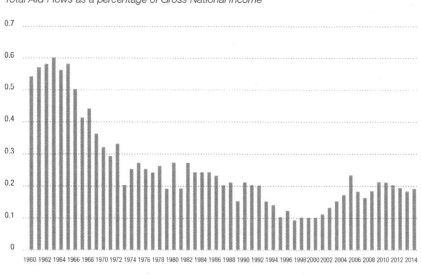

Source: Organization for Economic Cooperation and Development

A Turning Point

A small cascade of steps marked a turning point in US commitment to help reduce hunger, poverty, and disease around the world. For example:

1. The Africa Seeds of Hope Act in 1998 halted a decline in US aid for agriculture; and in 2000 passage of the African Growth and Opportunity Act opened trade and investment opportunities for a number of African countries. Both laws were urged by citizen advocates.

2. At the turn of the millennium, a new wave of advocates waged an international debt forgiveness campaign that offered a lifeline to some of the most desperately poor countries. It attracted surprising support in Congress across party lines. (More about this in chapter 4.)

3. The September 11, 2001, terrorist attacks on the Twin Towers and the Pentagon aroused the nation and the world to sense more clearly the connection between poverty and national security. Several decades of US retreat on foreign aid came to an end. Under President George W. Bush steps were taken to improve and expand poverty-focused assistance, featuring an ambitious and

highly effective Presidential Emergency Plan for AIDS Relief (PEPFAR) focused mainly on Africa.[43] Another Bush initiative was the Millennium Challenge Corporation (MCC), which makes five-year grants to countries that prove they are investing effectively in their people with projects they have identified. These competitive grants for country-led solutions have gained bipartisan support in Congress. By 2018 they were helping people in twenty-nine countries with MCC "compacts" gain traction against hunger and poverty.

4. The global financial meltdown that occurred in 2008, along with a spike in the prices of rice, wheat, and corn (the main diets for most of the world's poorest people) caused a temporary surge in hunger and created political turmoil in a number of countries. Alarmed by the prospect of long-term global food shortages,[44] President Obama and other heads of state increased efforts in 2009 to assist small-scale farmers abroad, and subsequently targeted "the first thousand days" from conception to age two for young children and their mothers during that critical period.[45]

5. By Bread for the World's estimate, US development aid that was *poverty*-focused jumped from $7 billion to $26 billion[46] during the Bush and Obama years. Some of this happened through more strategic use of funds and some with additional funding. The Obama administration created a stronger, more results-driven US Agency for International Development.

6. Rescuing development assistance from its plunge during the 1990s, traditional donor nations increased their aid and pledges to Africa by 66 percent between 2001 and 2015[47] and allocated more aid to countries needing the most help in meeting the MDG goals.[48]

7. Independent of these moves, China has become a big-time participant in Africa's development by financing infrastructure. China has clear expectations of reaping benefits in oil and minerals, business, and securing land for its future food needs.[49] It means to be a leader in connecting with the aspirations of poor countries, while enhancing its own economy.

To the extent that they build on the determination of the people and governments of developing countries themselves, these initiatives from donor countries support the hope that the world could—with enlarged public backing and good leadership—bring the worst features of hunger and poverty to a near end by 2030. Obstacles and setbacks would still leave pockets of hunger and poverty. But a growing awareness that hunger and poverty can be and is being overcome has created desire and political pressure within countries for ending them. As chronic hunger recedes, the world can concentrate on remaining pockets of both calorie- and nutrient-deficient hunger. All of this is a magnificent possibility, but its accomplishment depends in large part on translating good intentions into public policy, and for that to happen public backing in our own country is sorely needed.

What Would It Take to Eliminate Most Hunger?

The strength and health of the US economy in helping to keep the global economy humming is of underlying importance. Other nations depend upon this, and we depend upon their economic strength and health. For this reason, global cooperation on issues such as trade, climate change, and peace is essential for the entire world. Going our own way hurts everyone. For the same reason US participation in efforts to end hunger and poverty here and abroad enhances the well-being of all of us. Strong bipartisan support in Congress for US development aid in the face of President Trump's proposed cuts prevented a retreat. But more headway is necessary.

Globally we need:

1. Country-by-country commitment. Each nation and the people within it must determine its way toward ending hunger and poverty as well as achieving related goals.

2. International resolve. This calls for (a) strong US leadership (b) working in partnership with other nations, rich and poor, as well as with international agencies; and (c) special efforts to help secure peace in areas of conflict. In 2016, 60 percent of the world's hungry people and 75 percent of its stunted children lived in countries with violent conflicts, the biggest single reason for the rise in hunger that year. Uganda was such a country until armed terrorists, who uprooted almost two million Ugandans, were defeated by government forces (with outside help) and people could return to farming again. Since then Uganda has made impressive strides in reducing poverty and hunger.[50] (d) International resolve is also needed to help fragile countries address the adverse impacts of climate change, the second major cause (after armed conflicts) for the increase of hunger in the most fragile states.

3. Expansion of private enterprise (big and small) in struggling countries, spurred in part by development aid, and including public-private partnerships that promote not simply growth, but growth with equity, so that all may benefit. Otherwise private investment becomes just another form of colonialism.

4. Building on policies and practices that work. All sectors of society should participate in planning and carrying out policies. Justice and equality need to be carved into policy, plans, and action that include open accountability, full opportunity as well as education and physical protection for girls and women, a strong civil society, public safety, and other principles that promote the human rights of everyone. None of these things can be done easily or flawlessly—think of our own country—but with determination obstacles can be addressed and progress made.

5. A significant boost in poverty-focused development assistance. Aid is by no means the main path to the goal. People's determination, human rights, and trade are far more important. Aid often stumbles and invites justified criticism. But when it builds on the efforts of the people and governments of developing countries, reflects people's expressed needs, is well planned, carefully targeted, and strictly measured for results, aid can stimulate social and economic gains. Aid also indicates a level of commitment by rich nations to development goals. Outside aid, with appropriate conditions attached, can serve as a powerful incentive for needed, but politically difficult reforms. In this way the carrot of aid can help build civil society, improve and reward good governance, and promote democratic values. Such aid can pave the way for much-needed investment and market-led growth

---

One Little Child

Millions of surviving Syrians have been forced by brutal war to abandon their homes and flee. In 2015 many of them, plus others from the Middle East and North Africa, began a treacherous journey to find a better life in Europe. All of this, prominently featured in the news, prompted much hand-wringing. But the picture of a little three-year-old Syrian boy, Aylan Kurdi, washed up lifeless on a Turkish shore, touched off a tidal wave of sympathy for the plight of refugees fleeing in desperation to Europe.[1]

The suffering of millions had been widely deplored, but the sight of this dead little boy grabbed our hearts. Pictures of other victims had also jarred us, but the scale was perhaps too overwhelming to internalize, and we thought of them as distant and different from us ethnically, racially, and religiously. But this little boy was easy to imagine as our own. And his emotionally distraught father, who lost his entire family, could have been a friend or a neighbor. The endless numbers of fleeing refugees were easily ignored statistics. This lone victim was seen as ours.

So it is with victims of hunger. By the millions they are an abstraction to us, obscuring the reality that each one, like this lifeless little boy washed up on the beach, is a person, a tragic loss. One of us.

---

by helping to build roads, bridges, schools, and health clinics. It can ramp up research and extension services of the kind that would hasten a Green Revolution in Africa and greener agriculture everywhere. Aid can be the oil that makes a lot of engines hum.

How Much Would It Cost?

What would it cost donor nations to increase poverty-focused development aid enough to help countries end most extreme hunger and poverty by 2030—or even within a generation? Arriving at a figure is not a precise science; but a review of various estimates, including that of the UN Millennium Project headed by Jeffrey Sachs,[51] suggests to me that an additional global contribution from donor nations of up to $90 billion a year on top of their $137 billion in 2014[52] is a plausible target. That amount could be reached gradually, as countries are able to meet conditions that ensure adequate governance, accountability, and capacity for its use. After continuing at an appropriate level for a limited time, the aid could taper off, as countries gain their own momentum. A possible $30 billion US share of that (building gradually, say, in increments of $3 billion a year) could, if properly targeted, double our poverty-focused aid. That would bring the United States to about *half* of the development assistance goal of 0.7 percent of national income[53] for economically advanced nations—not enough to give us bragging rights, but evidence that a leading international partner is giving some of the poorest countries a realistic chance of achieving their Sustainable Development Goals.[54]

Such aid, conditioned on government policies and reforms consistent with those mentioned above, would generate increases from other donor nations and stimulate much-needed private enterprise and investment. By far the greatest commitment, of course, must come from the developing countries themselves using their own resources. Each country (including our own, we may hope) will be under the gaze of international attention for progress toward achieving its own sustainable development goals.

Too costly? Perspective, please.

The increase of $3 billion annually, even during the hypothetical peak years of a $30 billion increase in US aid, would require:

- about 8 percent of the roughly $400 billion that we *add* to our economy each year, or
- about 65 cents of every $100 in the federal budget.[55]

With it we could provide key leadership in giving the world's most impoverished people a chance to live and thrive—for less than half of the $78 billion that we spend on lottery tickets in one year.[56] Quite apart from the compelling morality of such a move, if it helped to prevent or limit only one war it would be a colossal bargain. In the words of Robert Gates, Secretary of Defense for both Presidents George W. Bush and Obama, "Economic development is a lot cheaper than sending soldiers."[57] In addition, the US effort, combined with that of other countries, would stimulate economies, boost trade, create jobs here, and help some of the poorest countries cope with the consequences of global warming. That doesn't even begin to count the benefits we and others would derive from good will and reduced suffering. US leadership in this monumental international effort would counteract a misguided "America First" mentality.

Can we in good conscience (or sound mind) shrink from so great an opportunity?

Problems are sure to be part of such an initiative. But successes show that, well-fashioned and managed, and properly engaging people in developing countries, aid can generate substantial gains. Aid reforms launched during the Bush and Obama administrations, as well as gains made on the Millennium Development Goals for 2015, indicate as much.

None of this means that ending most extreme hunger and poverty by 2030 (or soon after) would be easy. But if our nation and other nations muster the will to do it, it could be done.

With so many lives at stake, the goal of ending chronic hunger, like that of ending extreme poverty, is an immense challenge, breathtaking in scope, but not beyond the world's reach. However, America's part in its earliest possible achievement requires a new birth of national determination. In 2017 and again in 2018 President Trump and many members of Congress sought damaging cuts in foreign aid (as well as domestic antipoverty programs) but were resisted across party lines—an encouraging development. Congress held the line. But Congress will continue to fall short of backing a more aggressive US initiative against global hunger and poverty, unless more citizens insist that we do so.

Should we wait quietly and passively for leadership on this? Or should we take responsibility to join a groundswell of public support that compels leaders of both political parties to act more courageously to end hunger and poverty—unless they want to be replaced by people who will?

PART II

Speaking to Political Power Can Save Lives

4

Why We Should "Lobby" Our Members of Congress

I swore never to be silent whenever and wherever human beings endure suffering and humiliation. We must always take sides. Neutrality helps the oppressor, never the victim.

—Elie Wiesel[1]

To say that our silence kills is a disturbing accusation. But if speaking up saves and enhances lives, it follows that failure to do so diminishes others both in quality of life and length of years.

Here's how I came to understand this:

When I began serving a church on New York's Lower East Side in the 1960s, many people living there, including our own members, were struggling with poverty. Our congregation responded with meager help, often food or a little cash to buy some. It was a Band-Aid, offering only momentary relief to a handful of people. My father used to say, "It's better to build a fence at the top of a cliff than to have an ambulance at the bottom." We were driving the ambulance. But how could we build a fence? How might we nudge the nation to respond more aggressively to hunger and poverty so people could avoid the poverty trap or escape it?

Although hunger and poverty are high on the biblical agenda, and churches everywhere were offering charitable assistance, rarely were Christians being challenged to urge the nation's *decision makers* to take more effective action. So I approached a number of well-informed Catholics and Protestants to explore with me the idea of organizing a citizens' movement to influence Congress regarding hunger and the poverty that surrounds it.

That was in the early 1970s, and along the way I heard a young US senator from Minnesota and later vice-president, Walter Mondale, address a conference on international development. He deplored the lack of citizen support for foreign aid and challenged the audience to change that. He reported a conversation he and other members of Congress had with the prominent British economist, Barbara Ward. She had just returned from a meeting in the Vatican with members of a commission on justice and peace that had decided, with papal encouragement,[2] to urge Catholics everywhere to campaign for more assertive government action against hunger and poverty. She told Mondale that Catholics would soon be making their concerns known to political leaders about this. Mondale replied, "I'll call you when I get the first letter." Then, speaking to the conferees, he added, "I haven't had to make that call yet."

At the time our small group of clergy and laypeople was preparing to launch a citizens' lobby on hunger. While churches typically were assisting people locally and often collecting funds for overseas relief, the Walter Mondales in Congress were not being pressured to do more at the political level. The silence of well-meaning churchgoers was letting hunger and poverty destroy lives on a very large scale without much of a peep from any of us; and not surprisingly Congress read this as a vote for the status quo.

In May 1974 our group announced the formation of Bread for the World, a politically nonpartisan, faith-anchored citizens' lobby on hunger. In the absence of any other citizens' lobby addressing both domestic and world hunger, Bread for the World began organizing a national network of advocates from every state and congressional district. Our idea was to focus on one or more key issues each year, seeking action from Congress against hunger here and overseas. Our members would be our "lobbyists," ordinary citizens writing letters to US senators and representatives from their own state or district, and occasionally meeting with them or staff aides.

The idea took hold.

The Right to Food

Within a year 12,000 people became paying, active members, and we had encouraging signs that our efforts to alert members of Congress were having an impact. So we decided to ask Congress to pass a resolution asserting that the right of people to a nutritionally adequate diet should be a fundamental point of reference in the formulation and implementation of US policy. Our policy analysts worked with Senator Mark Hatfield (R) of Oregon (a member of our board) and Congressman Don Fraser (D) of Minnesota to frame a Right to Food resolution, which they introduced in the Senate and House.

At first, few members of Congress paid attention. Then letters from our members, from churches, and from a growing coalition of religious and secular groups, started alerting members of Congress to the resolution, which stirred interest and prompted debate. The endorsement of Catholic, Protestant, and Jewish leaders brought media coverage that included lead editorials m *The Wall Street Journal* and *The New York Times*.[3] But the driving force was a growing number of voters who sent messages to their US senators and representatives.

Kitty Schaller of New Jersey was one of those voters. She had become Bread for the World's volunteer coordinator in her congressional district, where her US representative was Millicent Fenwick, an outspoken Republican with ability to sway members of the House International Relations Committee. Fenwick not only opposed the resolution; she proposed in its place "a duty to share" resolution that urged private charity instead of government action. So Schaller challenged her position in a letter to the editor of a local newspaper. Early one morning Schaller was awakened by a phone call from Fenwick, who took issue with her. Though a little unnerved, Schaller told Fenwick she thought food was a right that entailed public responsibility, not left to the uncertainty of charity. The conversation was friendly, but each one held her ground, so Schaller redoubled her efforts to get people to contact Fenwick.

Meanwhile the State Department (led by Henry Kissinger) sent this message to Congress: "The executive branch questions both the desirability and feasibility of a worldwide right to food as a cornerstone of U.S. policy." The Department of Agriculture also opposed the resolution on the grounds that "current efforts directed at fighting hunger and malnutrition are sufficient at this time"—which drew the fire of three nationally prominent religious leaders who told a congressional panel that "it contradicts [the administration's] own position presented by Secretary of State Henry Kissinger at the 1974 World Food Conference, when he said, 'We regard our good fortune and strength in the field of food as a global trust. . . . The United States will make every effort to match its capacity to the magnitude of the challenge.'"[4]

With time running out for Congress to act, and pressure from her own party's leadership at the State Department, we feared Fenwick's opposition might stall action in the House committee. To our surprise, at the last minute Fenwick spoke out in favor of the resolution, crediting constituents for helping her see it in a different way. The committee passed the resolution, and then the full House did so by a 340 to 61 vote. The Senate approved an almost identical resolution.[5]

45

A resolution has no binding power and can easily be ignored, as this one often was. We expected that. But a resolution can educate. It made Congress aware of public support for action against hunger and showed that citizen advocacy on hunger could shape public policy and move the nation's leaders to respond. The campaign also attracted thousands of new Bread for the World members and laid a foundation for against-the-odds success in getting Congress to establish a farmer-owned, farmer-held national grain reserve, and later an emergency international grain reserve.

Fenwick became a staunch supporter of grain reserves, and a few years later was appointed by President Reagan to be the US ambassador to the UN food agencies in Rome, where she pushed for more enlightened food policies within the administration. Kitty Schaller went on to become director of the Manna Food Bank in Asheville, North Carolina.

Child Survival

In the early 1980s evidence surfaced that a few simple, inexpensive procedures[6] could save the lives of infants and children under age five who were needlessly dying. The United Nations Children's Fund (UNICEF) and the World Health Organization launched an international campaign for child survival. They reported that a staggering 42,000 children, from infancy to age five, died each day—*each day*—from malnutrition and disease.[7] In 1984 Bread for the World proposed legislation to add child survival to the nation's foreign aid program. A bill introduced in Congress got little initial attention until thousands of messages prompted Congress to enact the legislation. Modestly funded at first, child survival soon became an important part of our foreign aid program with bipartisan backing. By 2014, Rajiv Shah, head of the US Agency for International Development (USAID), could say that it spent nearly $1.5 billion annually on child survival and maternal mortality.[8] More important, many developing countries now maintain ongoing child survival programs with their own resources, and people are embracing life-saving health habits such as washing hands frequently and breastfeeding.

In 1985 the Child Survival Fund's birth caught the attention of medical doctors at Johns Hopkins School of Hygiene and Public Health. They were surprised to see an unprecedented 60 percent rise in the international health account in US foreign aid that year. How did it happen? Their investigation of this prompted an article in the *American Journal of Public Health*, which concluded that the main reason was a citizens' campaign that generated a large flow of messages to Congress. The article described in detail some of the twists and turns the legislation took at various stages in Congress, how the staff and members of Bread for the World responded, and how the legislation passed despite opposition from the Reagan administration. The article noted that previous efforts by the Carter administration, Senator Hubert Humphrey, and various organizations to increase funding for international health had failed to gain congressional support. But in this case the House and Senate together not only established the Child Survival Fund but increased USAID's international health account from $158 million to $248 million, which paved the way for further expansion. The writers concluded: "Close examination of the legislative history demonstrates that direct, focused and organized constituent pressure was almost certainly what turned congressional indifference into broad-based support."[9]

Bread for the World was not alone in this effort. The legislation was introduced and pushed in the House of Representatives by Tony Hall (D-Ohio) and Jim Leach (R-Iowa). A newer citizens lobby, RESULTS, though small, added energetic support and was especially good at garnering newspaper coverage and editorial support for child survival. A network of churches, church bodies, and other organizations, religious and secular, joined in advocating its passage.

Congressional approval gave child survival a big boost; and UNICEF's director, James P. Grant, said that it prompted other donor nations to increase their support as well. By 2016, despite an increase of more than 50 percent in the world's population since 1985, deaths among young children had been reduced to 15,000 a day. Almost half of those deaths occur during the first twenty-eight days after birth, according to the UN World Health Organization, which notes that "malnutrition is the underlying contributing factor in about 45% of all child deaths, making children more vulnerable to severe diseases."[10] Each year millions of additional children who would have died, now live. According to Bill and Melinda Gates, between 1990 and 2016 the number of children whose lives were saved had reached 122 million,[11] because global gains against hunger and poverty were accompanied by focused interventions to help children survive. Citizen advocates had an important hand in making that happen. On average, each letter written to a member of Congress in support of child survival may have saved dozens and more likely hundreds of lives. Yet people are inclined to think, "What I do won't make any difference." Today millions live because citizens were willing to urge members of Congress to act. Silence in this case would have meant death for many children. Silence would have cut their lives short.

The count of lives saved only begins to measure the benefits. UNICEF's Grant, international champion of child survival, emphasized that for every child's life that is saved, others are spared permanent disabilities that often accompany malnutrition and disease.[12] Child survival also slows population growth, because parents feel more confident that their children will be healthy, reach adulthood, and be able to care for them in old age.[13]

Child survival is an impressive, though incomplete accomplishment. It shows us what still must happen on a large scale to eliminate remaining unnecessary deaths.

WIC

A more modest form of child survival in our own country—the WIC program (the government's Supplemental Nutrition Program for Women, Infants, and Children)—assists infants and children under age five, as well as pregnant and nursing mothers, with food containing nutrients often lacking in their diets. It also includes nutrition education and provides healthcare referrals. Once again citizen advocates have gained support for this program, which serves a monthly average of more than 7 million women, infants, and children who live on low incomes.[14] They have experienced improved health and better lives because people urged members of Congress to create and sustain WIC. Silence would have cheated them of these benefits and diminished their lives. Today many prospering Americans from all walks of life report that they made it through a difficult time with the help of WIC, which now serves 53 percent of all newborns in the United States.[15] Many families who are not under the poverty line still struggle to pay their bills and are sometimes food-insecure. The WIC program assures good nutrition to babies and little children in both poor and near-poor families. Good nutrition for pregnant women, babies, and young children results in lower rates of infant mortality and childhood obesity, increased immunization rates, and better social and academic outcomes. Our entire society is better off as a result.

WIC's expansion was brought about by a coalition of committed advocacy groups and members of Congress. Coalition partners included the Food Research and Action Center, the National WIC Association, and many religious agencies. Barbara Howell, Bread for the World's domestic policy analyst during WIC's earliest decades, stayed in constant touch with her counterparts in those agencies and with congressional offices. "WIC was one of the first programs connecting nutrition with health," she says, "and in the 1980s, when opposition to 'big government' put WIC on the cutting block, Bread organized Offerings of Letters in churches around the country to expand it."[16] Bread's special strength on this and other issues has been its ability to generate tens of thousands of letters to members of Congress, and often pinpoint last-minute appeals to key legislators.

Jubilee Debt Relief

The Jubilee 2000 debt relief campaign shows how people can move nations and Congress to act against hunger and poverty. Following the oil crises of the 1970s many of the world's poorest countries, desperate to develop, began unsustainable borrowing, largely at the misguided urging of Western governments, international agencies, and banks.[17] By the late 1990s many heavily indebted poor countries were spending more to pay interest on their debts than they could spend on education and healthcare combined—like a family having to cut back on meals or medicine in order to pay the rent. The World Bank and the International Monetary Fund began to reduce their debt obligations, but not by much.

The ancient biblical year of Jubilee, which called for granting debt forgiveness and restoration of land to its original owners,[18] prompted a few British citizens to launch what became the Jubilee 2000 debt forgiveness campaign to get donor nations and international agencies to cancel debts of the poorest and most heavily indebted countries. It caught fire in England and soon became an international movement that attracted religious and other nongovernmental organizations. It gained the strong backing of leaders (such as Pope John Paul II) and entertainers (such as rock star Bono, who became one of its best-informed lobbyists) and attracted extensive media coverage abroad.

In the United States a wide coalition of religious and secular groups pushed it. Bread for the World's role was to focus on getting legislation introduced in Congress and—more difficult—help in getting Congress to approve it. That mattered, even though the US cost was relatively small, because without congressional approval other donor nations and agencies could be expected to lag in their support. Congress, however, was in a cost-cutting mood, and approval seemed beyond reach. In the words of Jeffrey Sachs, backers of the proposal "were told, in no uncertain terms, that debt cancellation could not pass the U.S. Congress."[19]

That negative assessment overlooked two things. First, the Jubilee campaign in the United States departed from international partners who were pushing for unconditional debt cancellation for all low-income countries. That would have killed the proposal in Congress. As Bread for the World's David Beckmann put it, we wanted a jubilee for poor people, not just debt reduction for their governments. The solution was "debt reduction for countries *with credible poverty reduction strategies*" (his italics).[20] That gave the legislation its intended impact, and the resulting policy changes in recipient countries gave them enduring benefits. As a bonus, the idea of linking assistance to poverty reduction plans has gained wide acceptance.

The second thing overlooked by pessimism regarding Congress was mounting public support for the Jubilee proposal, evident, for example, by the way in which it secured the backing of two key Republican congressional leaders. One was Spencer Bachus, a staunch conservative from Birmingham and the new chairman of the House subcommittee that had initial jurisdiction over the proposal. Fortunately, several Bread for the World members in Birmingham had developed a good relationship with Bachus a few years earlier, so they were well positioned to visit him and have an extended discussion about the debt reduction proposal. Bachus listened, asked questions, and later read the more detailed printed information given to him. As a result, Bachus not only endorsed the legislation but began actively persuading colleagues to join him.

The morning of October 9, 1999, *The Washington Post* printed a large picture of Bachus with a lengthy feature titled "GOP's Bachus Makes Debt Relief His Mission."[21] The article reports that he surprised his colleagues in the House of Representatives by championing this supposedly liberal cause. Bachus, a devout Southern Baptist, had become convinced that debt reduction was not only economically sound but morally right, the kind of thing his faith compelled him to support. Soon other conservatives lined up. Treasury Secretary Lawrence Summers later told Beckmann that Bachus's support convinced him to urge President Clinton to back it as well, which he did.

Meanwhile a group of Bread for the World members got an appointment to see Congressman Jim Leach, chairman of the House Financial Services Committee, in Iowa City, where he invited Tom Booker from the Bread delegation to ride with him to the airport, which gave them an opportunity to talk about the Jubilee proposal. Following up on that, Beckmann met with

Leach in his office on Capitol Hill, where Leach surprised everyone, most of all his own staff aide, by offering on the spot to sponsor the legislation.

There were other obstacles and surprising ways in which key figures came to support the legislation, including Senator Phil Gramm of Texas, who chaired the Senate Banking Committee and strongly opposed the bill. A meeting in the White House prompted Pat Robertson to reach Gramm through his *700 Club* television viewers.[22] But the eye-catching breakthroughs were possible because of swelling support from people across the country who alerted their members of Congress to its importance. After its passage Beckmann was asked to speak at the bill's signing ceremony, where President Clinton paid tribute to Spencer Bachus, saying, "Without your leadership, we wouldn't be here today." Beckmann in turn thanked the Birmingham advocates who had exercised the high privilege of citizenship by inviting Bachus to consider a unique opportunity to lead in helping some of the world's poorest people.

The Jubilee campaign of 2000 started an ongoing process that has led indebted countries to increase their investment in basic health, nutrition, and education. As one result, school attendance surged for African children. A push in 2005 to help poor countries make headway on their Millennium Development goals led to additional debt cancellations. By the end of 2015, donor nations and international agencies, as well as some commercial creditors, had written off (or down) a total of $119 billion in debts, which gives the thirty-six qualifying countries a substantial boost each year for poverty reduction. Half of the thirty-six countries had been spending more on debt service than on health and education combined, but now the picture is reversed and all thirty-six of them invest far more in health and education.[23] Debt relief has directly and indirectly helped countries end a downward slide and build stronger economies.

At a meeting of large-donor country leaders President Bill Clinton proposed that they also link debt reduction to poverty reduction. In addition the World Bank and the International Monetary Fund decided that countries receiving their financial support would be required to develop acceptable Poverty Reduction Strategies. In these ways the Jubilee campaign has helped to increase humanitarian and development assistance, make it more effective, and attract more bipartisan support.

The Jubilee campaign illustrates the leverage citizens can have in advocating gains at the highest political level for people who lack such leverage. Time and money so invested often reaps benefits for them beyond calculation. It multiplies what people can do through charitable efforts alone. In addition, speaking up in this way gives people a genuine sense of satisfaction no less real than the satisfaction of charitable giving. It is the satisfaction of feeling empowered to make a difference for people who are struggling, of being shapers and social healers rather than helpless observers of injustice.

The Jubilee debt campaign is a model of what could happen on a much larger and more sustained scale: an outcry of citizens so big and persistent that the President and the Congress will set goals and put in motion plans for ending hunger in our country, and for taking leadership to help end it worldwide. It shows us how action at the political level can arouse national will and gain unexpected bipartisan traction. It serves as a lens of hope.

"Circle of Protection"

Because the Great Recession threatened to become a total economic collapse in 2008, it triggered a sudden outbreak of bipartisanship. President George W. Bush and incoming President Obama consulted each other agreeably during the presidential transition, and Congress began passing emergency recovery measures that sent the nation's deficit for 2009 soaring to a height not seen since World War II. The recovery's strategy disproportionately favored corporations, but it also offered emergency assistance to many struggling citizens, for example, by extending unemployment insurance, giving limited job assistance, and expanding SNAP.[24]

Once a complete collapse was avoided, however, old partisan certainties returned to rescue people from their lapse into reasonable compromise. The 2010 elections brought a large number of self-proclaimed fiscal-hawk conservatives to the House of Representatives. The House (but not the Senate) passed a budget resolution that proposed deep cuts in a wide array of programs that help people in need—though poor people did not cause the recession or the mounting deficits.

Seventy-four prominent church leaders representing a broad denominational spectrum—Catholic, Evangelical, mainline Protestant, African American, and Latino—issued a public statement calling for a "circle of protection" around hungry people, asserting that government programs to protect them were solidly in keeping with Christian faith. The idea came from John Carr of the US Catholic Bishops Conference. Carr, David Beckmann of Bread, Jim Wallis of Sojourners, and key members of church-related offices on government policy began organizing the campaign. The statement called upon members of Congress "to resist budget cuts that undermine the lives, dignity, and rights of poor and vulnerable people" and "to protect and improve poverty-focused development and humanitarian assistance to promote a better, safer world."[25]

The appeal was a direct message to political leaders, but also a way of rallying people within and beyond the churches to advocate for the nation's and the world's most vulnerable people. "Circle" leaders met with President Obama, then Republican leaders John Boehner and Paul Ryan, and obtained bipartisan support for exempting SNAP, WIC, and Medicaid, not from all cuts, but from automatic across-the board budget cuts that were on the immediate horizon.

The push for deep cuts continued in subsequent years in the face of budget crises and threats to shut down the government. The "circle of protection" held firm, despite marginal setbacks. The strongest threats came in 2017 and 2018, when President Trump's proposed budgets called for large reductions in domestic and foreign assistance, and his conservative base in Congress was fired up to enact them. But throughout 2017 Republicans focused almost singularly on a failed attempt to repeal the Affordable Care Act (which extended healthcare coverage to millions of low- and moderate-income Americans) and cut Medicaid for poor and near-poor people. Surprisingly, however, Congress in 2017 and again in 2018 gave bipartisan support for domestic and international antipoverty programs. The "circle" played a large role in this, and both the nation and the world are better for it.

The Story Is Complex

To be candid, I have cherry-picked the above stories to illustrate the impact of advocacy. That may mislead you in three ways.

First, the experience of advocacy groups is not that of moving from one heroic victory to another. On the contrary, these and other gains have come only with enormous effort and over a period of years. I have said little about setbacks that also occur, making it necessary for advocates to wage defensive battles at crucial points, struggling to fend off or limit painful cuts to programs such as SNAP or development aid to poor countries. There is nothing exotic about playing defense, but it is no less important to hungry people than the gains that occur. Despite setbacks, over the years anti-hunger advocates have made substantial headway on a number of domestic and international policies, without which many more people would be poor and hungry.

A second limitation of the above examples is that they barely begin to acknowledge the courage and commitment of many members of Congress and their aides, as well as various administration officials, sometimes including presidents. They have often paved the way against the odds for better policies and practices. They are decision-makers and advisors who care deeply about people who are typically bypassed by a government that usually tilts toward money and powerful self-interests.

Because this report draws on my own experience with Bread for the World, a third way in which it may mislead you is that it does not give enough credit to other groups. Bread works in partnership with others because combined strength multiplies impact. Partners include religious denominations and civic groups such as African American and Latino organizations, international aid agencies, think-tanks, food banks that speak out on public policies, and groups that may focus on hunger as it relates to children, immigrants, or others who face discrimination. Hunger has tentacles that reach everywhere, so coalitions that emerge in support of (or opposition to) specific policy proposals embrace a great range of organizations, and participation changes from issue to issue. These allies strengthen Bread for the World's effectiveness, and in turn Bread's partnership strengthens theirs.

David Beckmann has been effective in building partnerships. Before leading Bread for the World, he was an innovative and rising young economist at the World Bank, who convinced the Bank to work with nongovernmental groups throughout the world, and then led that effort. In doing so he nudged the Bank toward addressing human needs more effectively at the local level. One of his first aims at Bread for the World was to urge organizations engaged in the charitable side of the anti-hunger movement to help "transform the politics of hunger" by addressing hunger's political causes and cures. Religious bodies across denominational lines are an important part of that anti-hunger network, and Beckmann's background as a clergyman-economist made relating to them and other organizations a natural fit. To widen the network Beckmann also persuaded Bread to start a related but independent organization, the Alliance to End Hunger, in which companies, universities, foundations, and other nonprofits collaborate to influence government action against hunger in ways that are appropriate to each.

Over the years advocacy groups that comprise the nation's "anti-hunger lobby" have grown to be a respected and significant voice on Capitol Hill for poor people. By working together, hunger coalition partners have been able to bring significant benefits to people in the United States, for example by boosting child and family nutrition programs, strengthening the nation's safety-net, and expanding earned income tax credits and child tax credits for low-income workers. Regarding global hunger, advocacy allies have helped to reform and expand US poverty-focused foreign aid; pushed self-help development, trade and investment assistance to small-scale farmers (especially in Africa), gender equality, and good nutrition with a special focus on "the first 1,000 days." They have also helped lay a solid foundation for future assistance with passage of the Global Food Security Act that was extended for five years in September 2018 with strong bipartisan support in both houses of Congress.[26]

Advocates have learned (1) that people can leverage change for poor and hungry people far out of proportion to their numbers; (2) that gains require persistence; but (3) that to get a genuine national commitment to end hunger in our own country, and to do our part as a nation in helping to end it abroad, many more citizens need to speak up.

Pushing Forward

The goal of putting an end to chronic hunger around the world, as well as widespread food insecurity in our own country, should prompt our nation to make it a high priority, not merely in half-hearted political rhetoric, but in aggressive leadership from the President and action by the Congress. That is not likely to happen until a host of citizens catch the importance of clamoring for further action against hunger and economic injustice. Many already do so through charitable assistance but remain silent before the nation's policymakers—a costly omission.

Political scientist Peter Dreier writes that a group once met with President Franklin D. Roosevelt to urge support for some bold reform. He listened carefully to their arguments and then said, "You've convinced me. Now go out and make me do it."[27] Good leaders need the backing of public support to lead well.

Because the path toward the goal of ending hunger includes resisting setbacks, advocates backed the "circle of protection." They not only succeeded at that, they also helped Congress achieve a remarkable level of bipartisanship on international assistance that augurs well for the prospect of future advances against hunger and poverty.

Steps forward can gradually narrow the hunger gap. For example, instead of buying grain in this country for emergency food aid and shipping it abroad on US flagships, most of it could be purchased near where emergencies occur. Local procurement is less costly, gets relief to people faster, and assists more people. Such purchases also boost the incomes of struggling farmers in the affected area. In the 2014 farm bill Congress allowed some of our aid to be used that way, and subsequent expansion of this cash-based food assistance has enabled many more people to survive life-threatening hunger.

Gains and prospective gains such as these can accomplish far more than the advocates who lobbied for them could achieve through private charity, and in fact such gains enhance rather than diminish the mission of charities. In the process citizens are being trained to advocate and press for further reforms. Step by step, the movement to erase hunger is being built with bipartisan traction.

My emphasis has been on "grass roots" advocates, typical citizens who usually remain voiceless but can exercise power by speaking out (mainly in writing) to members of Congress. But there is also an important role for people who, because of personal ties, position, or disposition can have special influence with one or more key leaders. A few years ago, David Douglas, president of the nonprofit Waterlines, started Water Advocates, a "grass tops" organization with a deliberate five-year life span. The project focused intensively on getting the support of a few key members of Congress to expand the work of the US Agency for International Development in bringing water for safe drinking and sanitation to more villages and communities. The outcome was a "Water for the World Act"[28] that annually funnels several hundred million dollars of assistance for carefully targeted, life-giving water initiatives. In this and subsequent efforts Douglas has effectively complemented "grass roots" advocacy.

Another "grass tops" advocate is Peter England of Miami, also a grassroots activist. In March 1992 Bread for the World was pushing Congress to pass the Horn of Africa Recovery and Food Security Act, a bill that urged a major peace initiative along with humanitarian aid, both of which achieved measurable success. But despite broad support in Congress, the bill was languishing in the House Foreign Affairs Committee—stuck there as part of a larger foreign aid bill that hit a policy roadblock. So England visited the editor of *The Miami Herald*, which responded with an editorial, "Pass the Horn of Africa Bill," calling on Miami's Dante Fascell, who chaired the Foreign Affairs Committee, to bypass the foreign aid bill and move the "Horn of Africa" forward as a separate free-standing bill.[29] That got Fascell's attention, and a few days later the committee sent the bill to the full House for approval.

The Senate also acted, and the bill became law. England is quick to say that his success did not occur in a vacuum, for he is part of a large Catholic parish that each year gets a thousand or more of its members to write handwritten letters to their members of Congress as a special offering after each of seven masses. They did it in 1992 and were still doing it in 2018. Meanwhile, the legislation redirected US policy on the Horn of Africa from Cold War purposes to the promotion of peace, development, and democracy—helping Ethiopia make immense gains in all three of those areas.

Religious leaders often play an important "grass tops" role both in representing and influencing a significant following. Bono did so in the Jubilee debt campaign. Bread for the World policy specialists do so by interacting regularly with policymakers in the nation's capital. But neither religious leaders nor policy analysts can substitute for the influence of voters from a legislator's home state or district. Voters who speak up, not big money interests, can be the movers and shakers who get Congress to act. But if voters concerned about hunger keep silent, money and self-interest will prevail. Silence will ensure that.

The most effective advocates are often people who are struggling to feed their families and can report their own real-life experience with hunger and poverty. They may do this by letter or with a group visiting the office of a member of Congress, and sometimes in testimony before a legislative committee at the state or national level. It's not easy to brush hunger aside when you see and hear it in person from someone who has suffered from it. Some, like David Obey (chapter 3 above), apply their experience with hunger later on in a leadership capacity.

Sharon Thornberry does that. She grew up on a farm but faced harsh times after a dissolved marriage left her supporting two young children. She got a job in a grocery store, surrounded by food she could not afford until Food Stamps pulled her family out of hunger. Because of the stigma attached to the program, her boss told her she would be fired if she used food stamps to buy food at his store. (It might make *him* look bad.) Later she moved with her family to Oregon as a VISTA volunteer and is now the community food systems manager of the Oregon Food Bank, with an exceptional grasp of the problems facing the rural poor and keen insights in finding solutions. Sharon is now a persuasive advocate for government action to end hunger and has testified before committees in Congress and in the Oregon state legislature. She also persuades people in the food bank network to advocate as well.[30]

By whatever name—advocacy or citizen lobbying—speaking up to political leaders is a bargain. We may deplore the way that big money has become so politically powerful in our country. Corporations invest large sums in election campaigns, but they spend thirteen times more on lobbying, according to *New York Times* pundit Nicholas Kristof. He reports that the healthcare industry has five times more lobbyists than there are members of Congress—a shrewd investment, he says, because drug companies prevented Medicare from getting bulk discounts on drugs, worth about $50 billion a year in extra profits to the pharmaceutical industry.[31] Citizen advocates can't begin to compete with that kind of money. But we *can* compete with their lobbying by becoming unpaid citizen-lobbyists, making our opinions clearly known to our members of Congress regarding hunger and related issues. Our opinion as voters to whom they are accountable can be more powerful than money. It can also help restore a sense of promise to our struggling democracy.

A New Moral Challenge

Hunger is not new. What is new is that hunger is no longer inevitable, and its demise is within grasp. This changes the moral equation for us. Remaining passive while hunger ravages people has always disturbed consciences. Now that we have the opportunity to end or nearly end it, ramping up efforts to do so and speaking out as citizens are ethical imperatives.

There is a reality called passive killing, such as declining to rescue someone who is drowning or not calling for help. The late West German Chancellor Willy Brandt observed, "Morally it makes no difference whether a human being is killed in war or is condemned to starve to death because of the indifference of others."[32] Indifference kills. Silence (often a form of indifference) can kill. It may seem benign, but it can be malignant. For that reason, it was anchored in ancient Hebrew law: "You shall not . . . stand idly by when your neighbor's life is at stake."[33]

UNICEF's James P. Grant drew the world's attention to the massive daily toll of infants and young children dying from hunger and disease. He called it "a silent holocaust." Grant stopped using that phrase, he told me, because the holocaust stands by itself as a violation of humanity. But the connection that fits both the holocaust and childhood deaths is the silence of citizens. Most Germans chose to watch passively while Hitler brought a brutal regime to power, launched the slaughter and destruction of World War II, and systematically exterminated six million Jews. The silence of ordinary, respectable, and often religious bystanders allowed this to happen. So it is today, when our silence permits millions of people to stay locked in poverty and face premature death.

I have given you only a handful of examples to show what can be accomplished when citizens become advocates. The importance of speaking out against hunger applies with special force to Americans, because our nation is uniquely situated to provide global leadership. That puts each of us in a strategic position to use our power as voters to influence members of Congress and the White House. The privilege of living in the United States includes both a responsibility and an opportunity, seen by many as a gift of God. If it is that, we are accountable to God as stewards of that gift. Jesus said the faithful and wise steward is the one who has been put in charge of the master's household to give everyone their portion of food at the proper time (Luke 12:42). He also said, in the same breath, "To whom much has been given, of him will much be required" (Luke 12:48).

Religious or not, we have been given much, and much is required of us. If we think of the household as a metaphor for the nation or the world, each of us has some measure of responsibility to enable others to receive their portion of food. Charity is one important way of doing so. An even more powerful way is to use our influence as citizens to seek justice for them.

But we don't have to choose between the two.

We can do both.

59

5

Charity Is Essential but Limited

No country has so many cheerful givers as America.
—Gunnar Myrdal[1]

Imagine eight shopping bags full of groceries, and suppose they represent all the organized food assistance for people in our country. How many of those bags do you think show the contributions of private charity and how many come from government programs?

When I ask people that question, they usually guess that private charity accounts for most of the bags, and by a wide margin. They are surprised to learn that only one bag represents the contribution of private charities. Seven bags come from government programs, primarily SNAP (food stamps) but also WIC, school meals, and a handful of smaller programs.

As *Visual 3* (below) shows, all private US charitable agencies combined (including food banks, pantries, soup kitchens, and other private agencies) contribute about $14 billion worth (13 percent) of the nation's food assistance. Government programs, however, account for $91 billion (87 percent) of it.[2] Charities provide limited food assistance to about 56 million people.[3] But to put food on the table day after day, when their own ability to do so falls short, struggling Americans depend primarily not on private charity but on federal food assistance. *Visual 3* shows food value, not operating costs (see endnote 2).

Visual 3 offers a useful starting point for examining two overarching reasons that explain why charity is not nearly enough to end hunger:

1. Charities cannot respond to hunger on a sufficiently large and comprehensive scale.

2. Charities cannot make national policy.

This chapter examines the first of those two points, mainly as it relates to the nation's food safety-net. Chapter 6 will address the second point—that charities lack the *authority* to make policies that often determine whether or not people go hungry. There I will focus on our response to global hunger, with specific reference to overseas relief and development assistance.

Charity is essential but limited. It is essential because it gives needed assistance and because it helps us become more loving and caring. Concerned people who engage in charity often (but not always) give more personal attention than government programs, affirming and encouraging struggling recipients. But the kindness of charity can obscure the need for justice, which is kindness applied on a large scale to address needs and secure rights for everyone. Because charity cannot do this, it is limited. Charity builds on justice but cannot replace it. Charities should be champions of justice, not a substitute for it.

An Instinctive Impulse

Charity is the instinctive response of Americans who are moved by the suffering of others and want to help. Is someone drowning? Throw a lifeline or call a lifeguard! Are people hungry? Help in a soup kitchen, stock a food pantry, or write a check!

Doing these things enables a person to see, or at least visually imagine, some concrete benefit to others. Millard Fuller, founder of Habitat for Humanity, used to say that if you take a picture of someone swinging a hammer, you can attract support. But it is hard to take a picture of government policy. Habitat is an outstanding charity, but no substitute for better government housing policies. A similar logic applies to hunger.

Great and small works of charity have sprung up because people saw a heart-wrenching need and were moved with compassion. They helped, and then began mobilizing others to do the same so that help could be given on a large scale. Think of relief agencies, such as CARE, that emerged from the chaos of World War II. Or Bob Pierce, who saw desperate children orphaned by the Korean War and began begging others to support them—an experience that led to the founding of World Vision. Or look at the soup kitchens, food pantries, and food banks that surged in numbers during the 1980s. These charitable efforts have attracted millions of American donors and volunteers.

New York Times columnist Nicholas Kristof writes about Dr. Stephen Foster, a missionary surgeon who has worked in a rural hospital in Angola for almost four decades under some of the most dangerous and rudimentary circumstances, once ordering gunmen off the property when they fired

Visual 3
Private vs. Federal Food Assistance

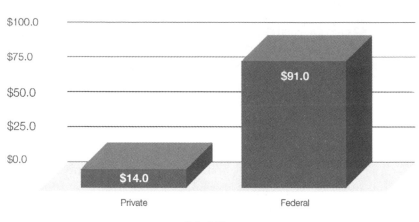

$ in billions

AK-47 rounds near his feet while trying to kidnap twenty-five male nurses. One of his sons contracted polio, a daughter survived cerebral malaria, and his family nearly starved during a prolonged civil war. But faith and compassion for suffering Angolans keeps Foster and a cohort of evangelical medics persevering.[4] You have to admire that.

Charities dealing with hunger and poverty draw heavily from people of religious faith.[5] The Bible is rife with appeals and admonitions to assist people who are poor or hungry, along with widows, orphans, and foreigners (immigrants). The Hebrew Scriptures (Old Testament) also stress the obligations of the political and economic order to pursue mercy and justice. Jesus and the early Christians lived under the firm rule of the Roman Empire, where organizing to change government policies was not an option. Although the apostle Paul used his Roman citizenship to great advantage,[6] he and fellow believers engaged in charitable assistance, as his collection of money from gentile churches for the impoverished believers in Jerusalem illustrates.[7] Emerging from the Jewish tradition of almsgiving (which became one of the Five Pillars of Islam), charity has deep roots and has greatly impacted the wider society. Over the centuries it has benefited people in numbers beyond calculation.

One reason for charity's appeal is the satisfaction it gives the givers. Richard Stearns, president of World Vision, writes, "Frankly, giving things to the poor does much more to make the giver feel good than it does to fundamentally address and improve the condition of those in need."[8] Stearns is not discouraging charity, but arguing that when possible it should be done in a way that empowers people to think and act as agents of change.

Charities have special strengths. Staff members or volunteers may develop strong personal ties with people being assisted and gain personal exposure to their needs, in this way giving and receiving far more than material benefits. Charities are sometimes (but far from always) quick, innovative, and more durable than government programs that may come and go.

Given the extent of US charity today, it surprised me to learn that from the colonial era until the latter half of the nineteenth century organized charity was often restricted, a path sketched by Ken Stern's book, *With Charity for All*.[9] Puritans, he writes, celebrated *individual* acts of compassion, not charitable institutions. The most prominent charity in post-revolutionary New York, the Society for the Prevention of Pauperism (SPP), was formed by leading citizens who successfully lobbied the city and state to *reduce* support for the poor and urged other charities to eliminate direct relief. Instead the SPP advised poor people to adopt sober, clean, industrious, and well-mannered behavior. However, the SPP's sober, clean, industrious, and well-mannered leaders were not eager to visit poor neighborhoods to teach those values, so their efforts quickly faded—while their Darwinian survival-of-the-fittest views lived on.

Widespread interest in organized charity began to emerge in the latter part of the nineteenth century, when brutal conditions imposed on industrial workers, viewed against the wealth amassed by industrial giants, was brought to the public's attention by the "muckrakers," the investigative journalists of the day. Some of those giant industrialists, such as Andrew Carnegie, John D. Rockefeller, and Henry Ford, became philanthropic pioneers, though the methods of philanthropists in obtaining wealth often contributed to the need for charity.

Charity grew by leaps as a result of (1) the Depression, (2) World War II, (3) 1954 tax legislation with incentives and loopholes favoring charitable gifts, and, counterintuitively, (4) the growth of government-sponsored assistance to ward off hunger and poverty. The government began to contract private service organizations to carry out some of its work, so it became "the largest single funder of the charitable sector," writes Stern. President Reagan's push to scale back government funding of antipoverty assistance created a bigger load for private charities—but government funding for charities also decreased, so, in order to survive, many of them began to charge clients or increase their fees for the service provided. Those fees replaced lost income, but poor clients could not make up for reductions in government funding. The winners, says Stern, were charities in the fields of health, education, and the arts that could attract an affluent clientele, and the losers were those serving "poor customers." The nation's 12,000 or so nonprofit organizations in 1940 had grown to more than 1.5 million by 2013, probably the country's fastest-growing business segment during that period. In the process we have privatized many public functions on the largely unexamined (and often erroneous) assumption that charities can do things better and more efficiently than the government can.[10]

In 2016 Americans made private contributions of $390 billion to the great range of US nonprofits that receive tax-deductible gifts for activity in the United States. However, only $47 billion (12 percent) of that went toward human services for low-income people; and food-and-nutrition is only one of ten human service areas, which include legal assistance, housing and shelter, recreation and sports, and six other categories.[11] Combined charitable efforts to assist hungry Americans totaled about $14 billion in food value in 2017 (*Visual 3* above). Of course, person-to-person help that people offer to neighbors, friends, or strangers never shows up on annual reports, so is literally of immeasurable value.

In addition to efforts aimed at domestic hunger, in 2014 US private voluntary organizations (PVOs) contributed $15.4 billion for relief and development work abroad,[12] but that understates the extent of poverty-focused private aid because it omits the broader category of philanthropy from corporations, religious groups, foundations, and universities, which covers a range of purposes.[13] *Giving USA* reports $22 billion in 2016 for "giving to international affairs," which includes disaster assistance and human rights groups.[14]

Private and official efforts often reinforce one another in beneficial ways. Rotary International, for example, has helped in the near-eradication of polio, which, a few decades before the Salk vaccine, crippled and killed thousands of people each year, most of them children. Rotary contributed $1.4 billion spread over several decades, along with volunteers, toward ending polio. As an association of business people, Rotary is a nonprofit organization that acts as a charity by amplifying the work of the World Health Organization, UNICEF, governments, and various private organizations. A mailed update from Rotary contains this appeal: "Let your *government* know that you support the allocation of *public* resources to protect children from polio."[15] Rotary understands both the strength and the limitations of charity.

A number of local innovators are combining government, business, and charitable efforts in hopes of achieving hunger-free communities.[16] The most comprehensive effort that I am aware of is the Indy Hunger Network (IHN), headed by David Miner, a retired executive and avid anti-hunger advocate, which aims to make Indianapolis hunger-free. David's wife Robin gathered data on all the major sources of food assistance, then made charts that enabled people to visualize quickly the sources and needs. The IHN documented the need for 27 million additional meals per year in Indianapolis, then brought representatives from charities, churches, government agencies, and businesses together to figure out how to close the gap. With the support of Mayor Greg Ballard (R) and Congressman Andre Carson (D), it increased children's participation in the federal summer meals program. Multiple other initiatives followed, and the meals gap was reduced to zero in 2013. Then the recession-induced expansion of SNAP expired, which cut SNAP benefits prematurely, so in 2014 the IHN was once again working to eliminate the meals gap and still doing so four years later in 2018, while also seeking easier access to food and better nutrition.[17] Its efforts to combine public and private initiatives help us understand that, in our current economy, without the expansion of SNAP Indianapolis is unlikely to become hunger-free. Meanwhile the IHN experience gives us an eye-opening demonstration of the difference that an increase—or a cut—in SNAP can make.

In the future, credible charities may contribute even more toward the ending of hunger, though not necessarily by expanding current programs. A crucial part of that work should be to upscale the advocating of government policies to meet the requirements of ending hunger. This engagement with advocacy is already under way in many charitable agencies, with Feeding America and InterAction (the main umbrella agency for relief and development aid abroad) encouraging it.

Banking on Food

In giving food to hungry people, charities fill an essential need; but they cannot come close to doing so on the scale and scope necessary to erase hunger in our country. Fair-minded conservatives acknowledge this limitation. If the Feeding America network's share (roughly $11 billion) of the nation's charitable food assistance were divided equally among the 46 million recipients within that network, each would receive about $239 worth of food a year, an average of 66 cents a day or 22 cents a meal. Arthur Brooks, head of the American Enterprise Institute, writes that "private donations cannot guarantee anywhere near the level of assistance that vast majorities of Americans across the political spectrum believe is our moral duty."[18] Even when the economy is strong, food banks, soup kitchens, food pantries, and social agencies act only as a backstop to our insufficiently funded federal nutrition programs. Government programs, though inadequate, offer far more complete coverage than the much smaller charitable network.

Smaller, however, does not mean inconsequential. Even if our government did its part completely well—extending coverage to all who are food-insecure and improving the amount and nutritional level of food assistance—charities would still be necessary for emergency help, though the need for it would recede. In that case more people could exercise their compassion in other creative ways of helping children and families find their footing in the face of adversity, still focusing their efforts on what they do best: person-to-person assistance.

Consider the work of regional food banks and the vast network of local pantries and agencies that assist Americans who need more food than they can afford. St. Mary's Food Bank of Phoenix started in 1967 and within a decade food banks had emerged in eighteen cities. This loose collection organized nationally as Second Harvest in 1978, then changed its name to Feeding America in 2008. Food banks and local agencies offering food assistance surged during the 1980s because a recession, cuts in the federal budget for assisting poor people, and global economic changes were making more Americans hungry. Desperation had become the mother of charitable invention to address the crisis. With two hundred affiliated regional food banks and 48,000 agencies that relate to them, this network now accounts for most of the organized private hunger relief throughout the United States.[19] Feeding America helps to support, supply, and coordinate the work of regional food banks that in turn help to supply food pantries, social service agencies, and other local programs that distribute food.

This is how it works in the Chicago area (Cook County):

The Greater Chicago Food Depository began in 1979, one of the earliest and largest of the nation's food banks and a founding member of what is now Feeding America. The Chicago food bank and more than 650 pantries, soup kitchens, shelters, and other programs supplied by it, serve 812,000 people—one out of every six of Cook County's 5.2 million people. Recipients receive on average the equivalent of six meals a month. Without Chicago's food bank and the distributing pantries, hunger would intensify for people in the Chicago area. Those hurt would include children and adults from low-income households whose SNAP benefits run out too soon, as well as others who are not on SNAP. It would also hurt families facing unexpected setbacks; struggling veterans; children who receive 528,000 meals during the summer when school lunches are not available; people who are fed at soup kitchens, group homes, and shelters; and people in areas of high poverty who get monthly mobile food delivery because they live far from pantries and food markets. Others live in "food deserts" that lack full-service supermarkets and have to spend time and money traveling to buy food or settle for what is sold at corner stores.

In fiscal year 2016–2017 the Chicago food bank's income of $101 million came from donations of food and money—$73 million from individuals and organizations, and $26.5 million from government food and grants, placing private charity's share at three-fourths of the food bank's total. By receiving donated food or purchasing it at a discount, the food bank was able to supply $124 million worth of food to pantries and agencies that distributed the food to recipients. Operational costs (everything above food value) for obtaining, managing, and delivering that food to partner agencies accounted for $37 million (35 percent) of its expenses. The operational costs make possible a complex program that requires skilled management; a large and well-trained staff; supervision of thousands of volunteers who contributed 97,000 hours of work at the food bank; solicitation, sorting, repackaging, and delivery of 71 million pounds of food (37 percent of it fresh produce); a huge warehouse for storage; a fleet of climate-controlled trucks to pick up and deliver food to pantries and agencies; equipment, maintenance, and much more.[20]

The Chicago food bank and the network of distributing partners serve an extensive need, but as a backup, not a replacement for the government's frontline food assistance. In 2017 the SNAP program alone provided $1.4 billion in benefits to 874,000 people in Cook County, about fourteen times the food assistance given through the food bank (or twenty times the charitable part, with government's help subtracted). Including WIC, school meals, and all other federal food assistance, the government's part in Cook County food assistance would be about twenty-seven times that of private charity through the food bank.[21] However, the food bank's related pantries and agencies have additional sources for food that they distribute, and other agencies independent of the food bank network also help, so charity's share of food assistance is much larger than that of the food bank alone. These charities are catching a lot of people who fall through holes in the federal safety-net, though nationally, despite the combination of public and private safety-nets, 40 million Americans still face food insecurity.

In Maryland's Prince George's (PG) County, where I live, some of the earliest pantries started in the late 1960s by churches in response to people asking for food. Food stamp recipients commonly came up short of food before the end of the month, and others did not qualify for food stamps or simply avoided government assistance but not charity. So pantries, based mostly in churches and heavily dependent on volunteers, emerged in scattered locations, where people need help and where facilities and volunteers are available, though pantries are often not easy to reach and groceries not easy to carry by public transportation. Pantries, typically serviced by a lone volunteer, assist people during limited hours on designated days.

Most food pantries in PG County are quite small. But Bowie, a racially integrated city of 60,000 with a slender majority of African Americans, is exceptional in its low rate of poverty (3.3 percent) and in having a large centralized pantry. It started in a Presbyterian church when Bowie, a small town in 1960, was becoming a suburban-type city. The pantry grew with the city, and today most of the city's religious congregations, along with various civic groups and businesses, participate with funding, food drives, and providing more than a hundred active volunteers.

The Bowie pantry averaged 342 client visits a month in 2017, serving 310 households. It opens on Monday, Wednesday, and Friday mornings from 9:00 to 12:00 plus one hour in the evening twice a month. Besides receiving a standard list of groceries items, clients may select from fresh fruit and vegetables that are offered "as available."

Recipients are screened by the poverty line, with extra income allowed for the cost of living in Bowie. PG County residents may receive food once a month, but twice monthly if they live in the Bowie area and are senior citizens, disabled, or their household has children under the age of eighteen. "We ask our clients whether they receive SNAP and if we think they should, we suggest that they apply, but many of our clients do not qualify," said Debora Langdon, the pantry director. "Does the pantry encourage volunteers or clients to contact their members of Congress about federal food assistance programs or other poverty issues?" she was asked. The pantry does not, because "as a small nonprofit we do not want to endanger our status by too much lobbying." The fear is understandable, but the government does not restrict *advocating* for or against government policies and allows for some *lobbying* on specific legislation.[22] ("Urge Senator Blank to oppose cuts to SNAP"— no restrictions. "Urge him to oppose bill S.1234"—okay if not done too often, though I have never heard of a pantry in legal trouble for too much lobbying. The sins of pantries against lobbying appear to be entirely those of omission.)

In 2017 the Bowie pantry gave recipients $321,000 in food and grocery items, an average of $78 per client visit, plus $14,500 for nonfood emergencies. The City of Bowie contributes $37,000 toward the pantry's administrative costs as well as $8,000 for nonfood emergencies, a government contribution of $45,000 to the pantry's $396,000 budget.[23]

The difficulty people in other localities often have in using public transportation to reach a pantry is modified, at least for Bowie seniors, with a bus service for rides to and from the pantry. But even in Bowie the pantry is exactly what the charitable network nationwide claims to be: an emergency backup to the nation's federal food assistance programs, not a substitute for them. Despite Bowie's relative affluence, food insecurity is present, though, as elsewhere, largely invisible. It is hard to believe that most people there or anywhere else who seek help from pantries would go out of their way to do so, if they could afford a nutritionally adequate diet. Pantries respond to that need; but they also raise the question, why should the nation not expand SNAP to cover the need? Are we compelling millions of Americans to ask for charity so we can avoid paying the modest tax increase that could fix the problem?

SNAP operates this way: Once people have documented their incomes and been properly certified, their electronic debit cards (in place of food stamps) can be used where they normally shop for food with no hint of begging, no risk of stigma. The cards are tightly controlled, efficiency is high, overhead is low, and fraud has been reduced to near zero.[24] The program fits seamlessly into our free market system. Still, when SNAP runs out, recipients by the millions turn to charity. So do millions who are not on SNAP, though many of them would qualify for it. Meanwhile the current need for charity is undeniable.

After learning of a mother who cleaned toilets and floors while struggling to feed her family and avoid eviction, a lawyer asked, "Why doesn't she just go to a food pantry?"[25] Time, transportation, and stress may suggest some of the limitations of that advice.

Charity and Justice

The compassion of charitable givers has drawbacks as well as advantages. Richard Stearns's observation that giving to poor people does more to help the giver feel good than it does to improve the recipient's condition, underscores both a strength and a liability. Theologian Reinhold Niebuhr noticed the liability when he wrote that "philanthropy combines genuine pity with the display of power [which] explains why the powerful are more inclined to be generous than to grant social justice."[26] The late Martin McLaughlin, a specialist in overseas development, made the same point to me more bluntly: "People prefer charity to justice because they can control it."[27] It is true. We can turn our charitable giving up or down, on or off. That gives it an unpredictable quality, and it makes recipients dependent upon the good will, ability, judgment, and mood of the givers—and on the economy.

Niebuhr and McLaughlin raise two big issues that charities face. One is a money problem. Not only is there an unpredictable aspect to the giving of those who support a charity, but the needs of people served by charities tend to increase when the economy slows; and a slow economy reduces the income of most charities, whose ability to help tends to shrink just when people need more of it. The Great Recession, for example, caused a drop in overall US charitable giving from which it took seven years (from 2007 to 2014) to exceed pre-recession levels.[28] Feeding America, however, defied the trend by doubling its growth from 2008 to 2016[29] because people responded to hunger, to its extensive promotional efforts, and perhaps also to its name-change from Second Harvest to Feeding America.

The public is especially attentive to crises and to human interest stories. Disasters such as famines, floods, hurricanes, earthquakes, or unexpected waves of desperate refugees attract the most news coverage and the greatest public response. But these are only the eye-catching part of the problem, like the tip of an iceberg. We are barely conscious of the constant, day-after-day hunger and poverty that cause far more extensive suffering and death than do news-breaking catastrophes. No news means little awareness, so our response falters. In a similar way volunteers at work in a local soup kitchen on Thanksgiving Day or delivering groceries to needy families attract more public interest than do, say, the UN Sustainable Development Goals. The media require newsworthy topics to keep an audience of viewers or readers. The public in turn learns from the media, so the media and the public are caught in a cycle that may lead to poorly informed responses.

Another aspect of the money problem is the impulse of food charities to tout success by growth in public support and the amount of food, the number of meals, and the number of people served. Success might better be measured when fewer families face food insecurity and ask for assistance. If increasing numbers of people lack food and need help, that would seem to reflect a setback rather than success.

A more disturbing issue than money, for charities and for all of us, is that of justice. Does charity undermine justice? It should not, because both are needed to achieve the common good. But there is often tension between the two, because charity tends to accept a current balance of power, while justice challenges it.

Why do people so often think charity plays a bigger role than the government in determining whether or not people go hungry, when the opposite is lopsidedly the case? And why do many assume that charity is the only response worth considering? The answer in part to both questions is that people respond to what they see in newspapers, television, social media, mail, and what they are urged to do by their church. Media coverage of federal nutrition programs tends to be abstract and impersonal, buried in news or opinion articles that are largely ignored by the public. Hands-on charity is more attractive. Boy Scouts or Girl Scouts picking up food for local charities are more photogenic than budget debates about funding for SNAP. As for churches, charity gives leaders the comfort of staying in a politically neutral zone.

Add to this the widespread notion, often fed by daily news, that government does things badly, while private efforts, seldom criticized, are portrayed as efficient and humane. The result is that people misjudge the relative importance of charitable and governmental roles in dealing with hunger, and act accordingly.

Charities themselves often contribute to this misperception with their own promotional efforts. Their survival and growth depend on convincing people that their support can make a difference to children and struggling families in their hometown or in Honduras. Featuring these has emotional appeal and may give people the impression that charity is the main thing, perhaps the only thing we can do to help. Few organizations by comparison mobilize citizens for action to improve, expand, or defend government efforts to reduce hunger. Feeding America receives more than $60 million a year for major media campaigns (donated by the Advertising Council), which effectively persuade Americans that Feeding America is the way to feed America.[30] I applaud the effort and the good that it does, but regret that too many of those Americans fail to realize that the government's nutritional programs play a far larger and more central role in addressing hunger. Organizations engaged primarily in citizen advocacy have comparatively little money for promoting that cause. And getting Congress to act doesn't quite tug at the heartstrings the way a gift for a hungry family does—even though the impact on hungry families of congressional action is greater by multiples.

Although most local food charities (mainly pantries) abstain from advocating on government policies, Feeding America and many of the two hundred food banks in its network do advocate effectively, but tend to focus only on federal food assistance, while avoiding advocacy on economic injustices that foster poverty and underlie hunger, such as low wages, unemployment, and tax policies that mainly benefit wealthy Americans. This reluctance is based in large part on a defensible calculation that their work on those issues would have less impact than speaking out on programs such as SNAP, which more closely parallels the work and expertise of charities. The downside is that it feeds the impression that food assistance, not tackling injustices, is the main way to end hunger. Still, the backing of the charitable network for federal food assistance has had a strong and positive impact on legislation for it.

Moral Dilemmas

Economic injustices related to work, wages, and taxes create a dilemma for the food banking system because of its heavy dependence on corporations, especially food processors and grocery retailers. Feeding America and its member food banks received food valued at more than $2.5 billion from companies in 2017.[31] Food banks, with company representatives on their respective boards, are wary of taking policy positions that might alienate donor companies, so most of them stick to the "safe" issue of food assistance. Even within the area of food assistance, many food banks accept and distribute sweetened drinks, and they avoid urging that those products be banned from foods approved for the SNAP program, despite the alarming rise in obesity and diabetes that strikes many low-income families with special severity. Food banks face this dilemma: they back SNAP and want justice, but they do not want to oppose the companies and risk losing company support. Andrew Fisher describes these things in *Big Hunger: The Unholy Alliance between Corporate America and Anti-Hunger Groups*.[32]

Companies donate to the charitable food network, while investing billions of dollars in marketing foods that are linked to obesity and diabetes. Walmart, for example, gains valuable publicity for reducing hunger with its gifts—mostly in food—of nearly $3 billion spread over five years (about $570 million a year)—while its low-paid employees rely on taxpayers for billions of dollars annually in public benefits from SNAP, Medicaid, and other safety-net programs.[33] A 1976 Tax Reform Act, which granted additional tax deductions to food manufacturers and retailers for food contributed to certified food charities, played a big role in the growth of food banking and has drawn companies and food charities into a formidable partnership. That partnership raises the question of whether the companies are doing good for hungry Americans or good for themselves while helping, but also hobbling, food charities.

Churches, in turn, face their own moral dilemma. Heavy participation of churches in feeding programs, and church members' response to hunger appeals, show that many people care. But isn't it strange that most congregations focus all their efforts on 13 percent of the solution (one bag of groceries) and ignore the 87 percent (seven bags) made possible through government action? In doing so, do they not risk tolerating hunger more than relieving it? Urging only charity perpetuates the myth that charity is the main answer to hunger, so it is okay to ignore the government's role. Is that what churches want to convey? When 40 million Americans are not always able to put enough food on the table—and without for a moment neglecting charity—should not more effort be made to defend, improve, and expand those remarkably efficient but underfunded federal programs, SNAP in particular, that hungry people mainly depend on? And what about injustices that feed poverty and underlie hunger?

The recession and threats to cut spending on programs that assist poor people spawned the broad coalition of groups urging Congress to maintain a "circle of protection" around those programs. When the US House of Representatives passed a farm bill in 2013 with a ten-year $21 billion cut to SNAP, Bob Aiken, president of Feeding America at the time, warned that if the cuts went through, "every food bank would need to provide an additional 4 million meals each year for the next ten years, and that is just not possible." Strong communities require public and private partnerships, he said, adding, "Government must do its share to meet the need, not increase it."[34] Fortunately, the "circle of protection" held well enough to get the US Senate to restore most of the cuts made in the House. But later that year Congress failed to prevent an automatic $4.5 billion cut in SNAP benefits from going into effect, wiping out the equivalent of much of the annual US food charity effort.[35] Local officials encouraged people to seek help from churches and charities to fill the gap.[36] The message seemed to be: "Will those of you who give to charity please reach deeper into your pockets to make up for what the rest of us are no longer willing to pay for?"

Leaders within the charitable food network recognize the need for public justice and speak forcefully for it regarding food assistance. Jim Weill, president of Food Research and Action Center (FRAC), and Diana Aviv, Aiken's successor as president of Feeding America, helped lead a thousand advocates to lobby members of Congress in March of 2017, just days before the Trump administration released a proposed 2018 budget outline that called for steep cuts in programs that assist poor people. Their message to Congress: "Protect and improve federal nutrition programs." Because hunger is solvable, wrote Weill and Aviv for *The Hill*, "greater investments, not cuts, must be made." The evidence is strong that federal nutrition programs work, they said. "SNAP is our nation's first line of defense against hunger. . . . Cuts to SNAP would add unmanageable pressure and make it impossible for people who are in need to feed their families." The government should do more, not less, they contended, to help the nation overcome hunger.[37]

As I write, Feeding America is working on an "undertaking unlike any other in Feeding America's history" that includes "charting a path toward ending hunger permanently for many Americans" so that "individuals and families will have enough healthy and nutritious food and will not need charitable food assistance."[38] Does this suggest a campaign of urging the government to lead the way toward ending hunger in America? If so, it will require much more than media to promote Feeding America as the way.

According to *The Economic Cost of Domestic Hunger*, "While the charitable institutions that now exist are among the first to proclaim that their job should not exist—handouts are not the preferred way to feed families in a wealthy democracy—charitable efforts are needed until economic opportunity and public policy combine to strengthen family economic security."[39] The work of food banks and pantries has been a lifesaver for many. At the same time its necessity exposes a serious failure of public justice.

In 1998 sociologist Janet Poppendieck wrote *Sweet Charity*, a riveting description of private charity's emergency food assistance network, which had become a new second-tier food-delivery system overlaying the nation's official food assistance programs. Poppendieck admired the people and the compassion upon which this charitable network has been built. However, she concluded that it had been "a great leap backward," undermining the nation's responsibility. She found kindness in this case abetting a decline in justice, and she said it had given our political leaders a moral safety valve for reducing much-needed food assistance.[40]

But has that happened? Had food banks and pantries not sprung into being in the 1980s, would that have spurred the public to demand responsible congressional action? Perhaps, but the food-banking network emerged because the public was *not* vocal enough in demanding justice for hungry people. My guess is that we would have seen even more suffering. Still, I think Poppendieck is undeniably correct in saying we have channeled public energy into creating and institutionalizing a more complex, second-tier charitable food assistance system, and neglected our public responsibility. So her challenge to the charity network and to the churches, the media, and all of us who have shared in this neglect is well placed. More of those engaged in charity could use their experience and well-earned respect to advocate for government leadership to end hunger. If successful, there will be no less need for charitable action, but it could be invested in reaching a remnant of hungry people, such as those living where food markets are inaccessible, and discovering other ways to assist people who are struggling to survive and thrive. No visible shortages on the horizon for that.

I have focused on food assistance, but the US safety-net includes tax credits for low-income working families (Earned Income Tax Credits and Child Tax Credits);[41] Medicaid and the Children's Health Insurance Program (CHIP);[42] Temporary Assistance for Needy Families (the scaled-back "welfare" program);[43] housing assistance;[44] disability assistance;[45] and other programs that assist people with low incomes and special needs. Social Security and Medicare cover rich and poor alike, but they also serve as a safety-net for elderly people with low and moderate incomes.

Without the government's safety-net programs the number of Americans living below the poverty line would double and claim almost one-fourth of the nation. It would also make poverty more extreme for those currently poor. Eliminating the food and nutrition programs alone would push additional millions into hunger and poverty. That would send shockwaves throughout the nation and probably trigger a recession. A job for charity? Our charitable agencies, already overburdened with existing challenges, could not begin to take on responsibilities of this magnitude. Public justice requires that all of us—the entire nation—do so.

Charities do great good. Scott Pelley on CBS's *60 Minutes* did a series of interviews of children caught in the Great Recession and its aftermath in central Florida near Disney World after many parents had lost jobs and homes.[46] Some were sheltered in cheap motels, others living in their family cars. The children told him what it felt like to go hungry, some in tears. They spoke of physical stress, being embarrassed and falling behind at school, doing homework by flashlight or candlelight, parents quarreling over money, and worry or guilt over their family's predicament. In a broadcast two weeks after kids described living in family vehicles, Pelley announced that viewers had sent in or pledged more than a million dollars of help, some offering housing for the families and jobs for the parents. Three colleges made full scholarships available for two of the children. It was a deeply touching success story for those kids and their families. But what about the countless other children and families caught in similar straits but getting no attention and no similar offers of opportunities?

Charities will continue to excel in doing what they do best—pricking consciences, arousing compassion, sometimes innovating, constantly addressing at least some of the basic needs that the nation's official programs fail to meet. But not by a long shot can charity replace the need for public justice. Not even remotely is it enough to end hunger.

"Human nature is sinful, and therefore the virtue of the few will never compensate for the inertia of the many," wrote the late William Sloane Coffin Jr. "Given human goodness, voluntary contributions are possible, but given human sinfulness, legislation is indispensable. Charity, yes always; but never as a substitute for justice."[47]

"Well, I pay my taxes and that takes care of the government's part. So now I focus on contributing to charity," you may say. A big mistake here has to do with outcomes—adding a bit to the 13 percent of food assistance in our country that is charity's part, but abandoning the far more consequential responsibility we have concerning the government's 87 percent in addressing hunger. To be active in the charitable 13 percent, but to neglect the 87 percent, is to be part of the silence that allows our nation's leaders to let hunger continue on and on.

6

Charities Cannot Make National Policy

*Everyone should be charitable. But justice aims to create a social order
in which, if individuals choose not to be charitable, people still don't go
hungry, unschooled, or sick without care.*

—Bill Moyers[1]

"The past is prologue," announces the inscription carved in stone above the
entrance to the National Archives in the nation's capital. "It means things
ain't what they used to be," explains the taxi driver. Indeed, they are not.

In the early days of our country, national defense often meant reaching
for a rifle and rounding up volunteers. As the country grew, life became
more complex and so did the dangers and technology of warfare. What used
to work with volunteers now requires government action and highly trained
personnel on a large scale.

Education? At the time of the nation's birth and beyond it, formal
education was limited. Many Americans were illiterate, and others, like
Abraham Lincoln, learned to read, write, and do basic arithmetic in rudimentary schools, from relatives, or through reading on their own. College was rare. Because people placed high value on learning, public schools
became a standard for every town and village. As the country grew, universal primary and then secondary education became the norm, and even
college came within reach for those able to afford it. While private schools
flourished, public schools became the educational bedrock. The nation in-
sisted on their availability so that everyone could learn. Our unprecedented
investment in education enriched the nation in ways beyond calculation.
Today we still respect the role of private education for those who prefer and
are able to choose it, but few seriously maintain that we should eliminate
public, government-sponsored schools and turn the job over to private,
voluntary efforts.

A similar logic leads us to the second reason why charity is not enough to end hunger. Because of the growth and complexity of life in today's world, the private, voluntary sector is neither equipped nor does it have the authority to do many things that are necessary for our well-being. For that reason, charities cannot make decisions for the nation as a whole, so their impact on key matters that relate to hunger and poverty—such as foreign policy, economic policy, trade, taxation, agriculture, healthcare, education, and civil rights—is limited. Charities can help in appropriate ways. They can influence the government. They can pioneer responses to human need that may be replicated by the government. They can (and should) advocate policies they think are best. But they cannot replace government policymaking in these areas of life, all of which deeply affect everyone and often determine whether or not people are poor or prosper.

To illustrate the point I will comment on US foreign policy in this chapter, giving special attention to the nation's overseas humanitarian and development assistance. That story helps to explain why progress against global hunger has accelerated, and why the work of charity and government are both essential and mutually reinforcing. The story reflects the strengths as well as the limitations of each, but it also shows the overarching responsibility of government.

Snapshots of Early Overseas Aid

- The first official, tax-funded US foreign aid shipment assisted earthquake victims in Venezuela in 1812. Thousands died and famine threatened others.[2]
- Churches organized and financed most early and sporadic US relief efforts abroad through American missionaries. "In place after place, they were the first carriers of community development assistance," wrote Landrum Bolling in *Private Foreign Aid*.[3] Their reports alerted Americans to deprivation in distant lands and elicited private aid on a small scale by people eager to help.
- The disastrous Irish famines of 1845–1849 prompted what may be the first organized international relief effort. Catholics and Quakers led the US response, but many others also contributed. Pope Pius IX issued an encyclical urging believers throughout the world to help with prayers and gifts.[4] The US Senate approved $500,000 in relief, but President James

Polk threatened to veto the bill on the grounds that the Constitution made no mention of such aid as a proper action of the government; and the US House of Representatives twice rejected it, so the legislation failed. Polk and the Congress, however, did approve the use of two old Navy ships to carry *privately* donated food to Ireland, though that seemed to fudge the constitutional question. More than a hundred other vessels also brought US supplies to Ireland. Private charity clearly put our government to shame in this crisis.[5]

- Following Florence Nightingale's pioneering work in organizing care for sick and wounded British soldiers during the Crimean War (1853–1856), Clara Barton's similar work during the Civil War led her to serve abroad and in 1881 to found and lead the American Red Cross.

- During World War I, famine in and beyond Belgium prompted Herbert Hoover, a wealthy businessman, to create an international Commission on Belgium Relief that attracted an unprecedented stream of private aid, which gradually gained its primary support from Allied governments. After the war Hoover led the American Relief Administration, also a public-private partnership, which broadened assistance in Europe.[6] Hoover and the ARA responded to an appeal from Russia after five million Russians died of starvation. From 1921 to 1923 the ARA supplied food and medical aid to cushion the famine. By this time Hoover was widely regarded as the nation's foremost humanitarian.[7]

World War II and the Marshall Plan

After World War II broke out in Europe, the United States responded with a $50 billion Lend-Lease program of military supplies to Great Britain and other Allies from 1940 to 1945, worth more than $760 billion today.[8] The stated purpose of Lend-Lease was national defense, though it had a sizable humanitarian element: 14 percent of the aid was food. By lending (instead of selling or giving) assistance, it skirted the Neutrality Act of 1939 and contributed to the war effort of the Allies in a way that gained public and congressional support. Repayment came partly in the form of agreements to create a new international economic order after the war, which laid groundwork for the United Nations and postwar cooperation. Winston Churchill called Lend-Lease the "most unsordid act" one nation ever did for another. Without it, Britain might not have survived, and the war probably would have taken an even more threatening turn. Lend-Lease turned out to be a priceless investment for us and for the world.[9]

Private voluntary aid from the United States began on a small scale in 1939 when Germany invaded Poland, and that aid came to be seen as a partner of the government's Lend-Lease program. After the US entrance into the war in December of 1941 private aid grew rapidly, at first with a heavy ethnic slant from groups such as Bundles for Britain and the American Jewish Joint Distribution Committee. In 1945, the last year of the war in Europe, voluntary organizations sent more than $87 million in funds plus $142 million worth of food, medicine, clothes, and blankets abroad[10] (a combined value of almost $2 billion in 2015 dollars).[11] Private aid operated under the government's relief and rehabilitation work, which "vastly overshadowed the combined activities of all the volunteer agencies."[12] By the end of 1947, these private agencies had contributed 6 percent of US overseas relief under the United Nations Relief and Rehabilitation Administration (UNRRA), which was financed primarily by US tax dollars. Many of these nonprofit organizations also received funding *from* UNRRA to carry out its work.[13]

After the war public and private humanitarian aid groups, such as CARE (with its famous CARE packages)[14] and religious agencies, continued to supply food to desperate people. Many agencies also provided clothing, medical assistance, and shelter to people in Western Europe, and helped to relocate displaced persons. These timely responses from both government and private sources enabled millions to escape famine, disease, and exposure. However, it soon became evident that the crisis reached far beyond the need for relief, because Europe was not rebounding well from the devastation of the war. People were desperate.

In April 1947 Secretary of State George C. Marshall, while in Moscow, received this assessment from the State Department: "Europe is steadily deteriorating. Millions of people in the cities are starving. If things get any worse, there will be revolution." The crisis prompted Marshall to propose the granting of billions of dollars for a European Recovery Program to rescue Europe's economies and get their industries running again. James Reston got wind of the idea and wrote about it in *The New York Times*. Senator Arthur H. Vandenberg, chairman of the Senate Foreign Relations Committee, phoned Reston to tell him he must be misinformed because Congress would never approve that much money to save anybody.[15] We had just pulled out of the Depression, were deeply in debt from the war, and tired of helping foreigners, so the argument that "we can't afford it" seemed insurmountable. But President Harry S. Truman, Marshall, and others (including Vandenberg, a Republican) made a strong and sustained case for it and got a Republican Congress to approve it with bipartisan support.[16]

The European Recovery Program (known as the Marshall Plan) gave European countries $12.6 billion in assistance from 1948 to 1951, "more than all previous [nonmilitary] U.S. overseas aid combined."[17] It claimed an average of 7.4 percent of the federal budget during those years, and more than 1 percent of our total national income—worth about $216 billion as a percentage of our current national budget (adjusted for inflation) or $260 billion as a comparable share of our current national income.[18] Most of the aid was given in the form of large shipments of wheat and other food, which was sold on the market. Funds from the sales were placed in recipient country trusts and released only on US approval for long-term development projects.[19] This served an immediate need for food, which in turn supplied cash for stimulating the economy. The plan was driven in part by humanitarian concern, in part by fear that economic failure in Western Europe was pushing countries toward communism and by a sense that Europe's recovery or collapse would have an immense impact on our own future and that of the world.

Because Europe was suffering from a shortage of dollars to buy goods and materials from the United States to fuel its sputtering economy, the Marshall Plan provided cash as well as food for development. Even more important was its timing. British Foreign Secretary Ernest Bevin called it "a lifeline to sinking men. It seemed to bring hope when there was none."[20] And although Europeans had been receiving substantial US aid after the war, none of it had a broad strategic design. In contrast, the Marshall Plan was conditioned on European national leaders working out their own integrated plan for recovery, a requirement that put these quarreling countries on a path toward regional unity "for the first time since Charlemagne in the ninth century."[21]

During the four years of the Marshall Plan the average per capita income of citizens in Western Europe increased by one-third,[22] and its economies, though still struggling, were accelerating. The Marshall Plan also solidified ties between the United States and Western Europe and allowed our government to connect quickly with country leaders and industrial needs in a way that charitable agencies could not. Western Europe began to recover, and its recovery boosted a postwar economic boom in the United States.

Private aid was still sorely needed during those postwar years, and Americans continued to provide it. During the 1950s, as organizations increased their humanitarian aid, US private voluntary organizations (PVOs) "understood their role to be that of providers of supplementary assistance, with the primary role for addressing basic needs overseas going to the U.S. government," writes Rachel McCleary.[23] Private agencies also worked with the government in welcoming thousands of European immigrants to this country.

As important as this private charitable aid was in rescuing people and sustaining hopes, it was dwarfed by the Marshall Plan. A wary but charity-conditioned US public and a resistant Congress were persuaded to back this exceptional initiative, all the more remarkable for its contrast with the punitive and destructive peace that followed World War I. The Marshall Plan required the authority of a government that could speak and act for the nation as a whole and commit the nation's resources to it on a vast scale.

The common good for Western Europe turned out to be uncommonly good for us as well.

Aiding Poor Countries

With Western European countries beginning to rebound and the Cold War heating up, President Truman turned the nation's attention to impoverished countries. Many of them were newly independent, had extremely weak economies, were ill-prepared by their colonial occupiers for governing, and some were vulnerable to the seduction of communism. In "point four" of his 1949 inaugural address, just ten months into the Marshall Plan, Truman proposed "a bold new program [called the Point Four Program] for making the benefits of our scientific advances and industrial progress available for the improvement and growth of undeveloped areas," which the Senate approved a year later—by the slender margin of a single vote. As Western European countries recovered, they also became donor nations and launched aid programs, often working through UN agencies. These government and government-related international organizations pushed technical assistance and economic development, while private voluntary organizations (PVOs) continued to specialize in relief efforts and local, small-scale assistance for which they were better equipped.

In 1954 President Dwight D. Eisenhower made US food aid, later called Food for Peace, a permanent feature of our overseas aid. Soon after President Kennedy's inauguration in 1961, he established the US Agency for International Development (USAID) and launched the Peace Corps. In these and other ways humanitarian and development assistance remained an important part of US foreign aid—of little interest to many Americans but a lifeline to countless families struggling to escape poverty or recover from a famine, and a boon to US leadership abroad.

The motivation of halting the spread of communism helped overcome congressional opposition to foreign aid, but also frequently distorted its humanitarian purpose.[24] Aid was often used to reward countries ruled by corrupt autocrats for taking our side in the Cold War. Development specialists from donor countries (including our own) frequently assumed a sense of racial and intellectual superiority that led them to impose solutions on people while neglecting their human rights.[25] Colonial attitudes, it turns out, are not easily erased. Yet never before had the United States or other industrial nations attempted, through their governments, to help people in poor countries lift themselves out of poverty. Though motives and methods were flawed and the results mixed, humanitarian and development aid gave hope to many people. Over the years former aid-recipient countries, including European countries, as well as Japan and South Korea, have become aid-givers, and more countries continue to join them. Through this tangled process the world has learned a great deal about what kind of development and development assistance works and what does not.

In 1969 an international commission led by Lester B. Pearson, former Prime Minister of Canada, reported on two decades of postwar development efforts and set its sights on the 1970s as the first official UN development decade. It recommended that each aid-giving country allocate annually seven-tenths of one percent (0.7 percent) of its national income for development aid to poor countries.[26] Several European countries quickly reached that goal, but the United States never again came even close. Under the Marshall Plan US assistance (measured as a percentage of our national income) had exceeded that UN standard, but then it began a long descent.

In 1963, two weeks before he was assassinated, Kennedy addressed a gathering of church leaders and deplored the fact that our foreign aid had slipped to 4 percent of the federal budget (four times the current 1 percent of our budget). To provoke the nation by shame, he invoked T. S. Eliot's vision of people whose legacy was "an asphalt road and a thousand lost golf balls."[27] The skid continued for three and a half decades, and our development aid sank to less than one-tenth of one percent (0.1 percent) of our total economy—ten cents of every $100—in the 1990s. (See *Visual 2* in chapter 3.) Under President Bush it doubled briefly to 0.23 percent in 2005, then fell to a post-recession 0.18 percent in 2016.[28] More of it addressed poverty,[29] however, along with initiatives and reforms that improved its effectiveness. Our aid is still far greater than that of any other country in total dollar value, but as

Visual 4
Official Development Assistance 2017—Preliminary Data
As a Percent of National Income

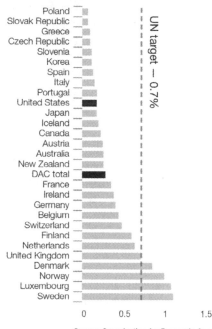

Source: Organization for Economic Cooperation and Development

Visual 4 shows, measured and compared with other countries as a percentage of national income, US aid does not look so generous.

Why Did the US Aid Decline?

In spite of the extraordinary cost of Lend-Lease, of US leadership during World War II, and of our help in preventing the collapse of Western Europe, we had leaders who helped us pivot to assist yet other countries that were struggling to escape poverty. Our aid to those countries then declined even as other, less prosperous countries we had helped surpassed us in generosity. The question is "Why?"

Among the reasons, a few stand out. First of all, exceptional circumstances prompted our aid to Europe. We had gone through the trauma of World War II together. US military service personnel had seen the terrible destruction and human suffering during and after the war and had sacrificed to defend and liberate Europe's people. As in the past, Europe's future and ours were clearly intertwined, and both the need and positive impact of our aid became quickly apparent.

Second, Europeans were "like us." We had long historical ties to Western Europe because of the flood of immigrants that populated our country from the time of the earliest white settlers. Many Americans had relatives and memories from those countries, so it was easy for them to identify with Europeans. As a result, strong support emerged for helping desperate British, Dutch, French, Germans, Irish, and Italians. But few Americans had close ties to Asian or African countries. People—perhaps all of us—tend to have difficulty relating sympathetically to the predicament of those who look different and seem "other" than ourselves, which suggests racial, ethnic, or cultural bias as a strong, if often subconscious factor. At any rate, these "others" had no natural constituency of US citizens to speak up for them.

A third reason for lagging aid was that, unlike Western Europe, which needed a big boost to recharge its economies, poor countries lacked basic requirements for quickly becoming modern industrial nations. Few of their people were well educated and technologically skilled. Their legal and economic framework was mostly undeveloped, transportation and communication woefully deficient, healthcare services severely limited, institutions for governing primitive, and they had few local nongovernmental organizations. Under those conditions, changes tend to occur slowly, almost imperceptibly, so it was often hard to tell whether our assistance was making much difference. Factors to consider are sufficiently complex that measuring what works and what doesn't work well in assistance can frustrate even trained observers. Disagreements similar to the opinions we have today about the best way to address hunger and poverty in the United States emerged. Mixed outcomes forced ongoing consideration of how to do aid effectively and even if it should be done at all.[30] US citizens, weary of problems abroad, reverted to some of their pre-war isolationist instincts. Old-fashioned selfishness no doubt had a lot to do with this as well.

Furthermore, the Cold War that dominated the nation's attention in international affairs focused us mainly on the use of military power and defense spending. That priority sucked the budget of money that might otherwise have supported aid.

As if these considerations were not enough, over the years Americans have held a wildly exaggerated idea about how much aid we were giving other countries—an impression that, strangely, still prevails more than a half-century since World War II and its aftermath. Memories of our out-sized help during the war and then of the Marshall Plan years shaped lingering myths of overflowing US generosity. Polls today indicate that, on average, Americans still think we spend from 21 percent to 28 percent of our budget on foreign aid, not the actual 1 percent.[31] So it is not surprising that more than half of us say we are way too generous.[32] When asked what percent of the budget *should* go to foreign aid, the same people who think we spend too much on it favor, on average, designating "only" 10 percent of our budget for it—ten times what we actually do.[33] Foreign aid, like food stamps, has become a favorite punching bag for politicians who find it popular to oppose spending but need easy targets, and foreign aid serves this purpose. They exaggerate its cost while ignoring its benefits in shameless pandering for votes. The result has been ill-informed citizens and shortsighted policies that both exploited and fed a strong "America first" undercurrent, which was tapped effectively by candidate Donald Trump in the 2016 presidential race and now threatens to undermine the kind of response that is needed from our country in helping the world put an end to extreme hunger and poverty.

Twists and Turns in US Aid

Various factors have shaped our approach to development aid since the Marshall Plan, especially the Cold War that pitted communism against democracy and dominated US foreign policy after World War II. North Korea's invasion of South Korea brought us into a brutal conflict (1950–1953) that intensified fear of communism and tilted the purpose of our food and development aid in that direction. A dozen years later the war in Vietnam (1965–1975) reinforced that focus. The fear of communist aggression steered military and humanitarian aid disproportionately to South Korea and South Vietnam, but also to other countries where communism was perceived as a real or potential threat. That raised the question of whether the dominant purpose of our assistance was to secure allies for the Cold War or to strengthen the economies of poor countries, and prompted the further question: Could it do both at the same time? The Cold War complicated the work of US private voluntary organizations that wanted to help people without being seen as political tools of either side, especially when local conflicts involved surrogate forces fighting (militarily or politically) on behalf of their American or Soviet sponsors.

The illusion that Western Europe's rapid economic comeback could be replicated in poor countries soon faded, but what lingered on is the tendency of development experts, educated in rich countries, to think they know best what poor countries need. Instead of listening to what the people themselves say they need, and developing in partnership plans that they embrace, donors often imposed solutions that were never truly owned by the intended beneficiaries, as well as technologies that could not be maintained.

In 1973 Congress rewrote the foreign aid bill, calling for "New Directions" that shifted the focus of our assistance to "basic human needs" such as nutrition, healthcare, and education, areas of traditional strength of private charities. This led to additional government funding of private voluntary organizations (PVOs) and made collaboration between the US Agency for International Development (USAID) and private agencies more important.[34] It also nudged the PVOs to include more longer-term development, as well as relief, in their work.

In the 1980s US development aid policy shifted direction again, this time to emphasize free enterprise over basic human needs. That matched a similar emphasis in domestic policy by the Reagan administration and led to an additional two-decade slide in US assistance to developing countries (measured as a percentage of national income). During the 1990s that assistance dropped to its lowest level since its inception in the Marshall Plan years.

Then a change in US aid began to occur near the turn of the millennium. The long downward trend of our official development assistance ended and, spurred by events and citizen advocates, official development assistance began rising again, and not just from the United States. Assistance from all traditional donor nations combined grew by 83 percent in real dollar value between 2000 and 2015.[35] Countries in Africa, the only continent that does not produce enough food to feed its populations, were primary beneficiaries.

While official US assistance sagged to new lows in the 1990s, PVOs expanded their work abroad. Those charitable agencies accounted for only 5 percent of US development aid in 1992, but for 36 percent by 2012.[36] This happened partly because private agencies had a clear and effective path to donors. PVOs can solicit charitable donations with advertising. Because they provide direct assistance to communities, they can show children who are hungry or seeking financial sponsors to give them a chance in life, or vivid examples of the impact of charitable donations—children going to school or a community with clean water. The US Agency for International Development (USAID), as part of the government, releases reports with statistics and press announcements that few read. Its work is less direct and therefore less visible and harder to explain. Without a mandate to publicize its "success stories," it depends largely on the news media and public interest groups to keep people informed. The hope is that public approval combined with the good sense of Congress will lead to generous funding for humanitarian and development assistance. Because Americans are largely unaware of the value and impact of this assistance, citizen advocates have to work hard to get Congress to act responsibly.

The Bill and Melinda Gates Foundation (which focuses on health, agriculture, and education) is not content with that. It is part of the surge in private aid and in 2012 contributed more than $2 billion for work within developing countries. That year the Gates Foundation became the fifteenth-largest donor agency in the world, the first private agency to reach that level, and is still the only nongovernment agency that reports its aid activities to the Organization for Economic Cooperation and Development.[37] Bill and Melinda Gates, however, see the foundation's work as a catalyst for greater impact through government aid, so they keep pressing leaders for a stronger response. In a report to the European Parliament's development committee Bill Gates said, "I think we can grow . . . and I think [we] have a special role . . . but in terms of the big things, really helping poor countries with health

---

Consider This Contrast

The European Union (EU) contributes about two-and-a-half times as much as does the United States in *official development assistance*, even though our country has a national income about the same as that of all EU nations combined; and the US per capita income is much larger than theirs. However, in *private assistance (charity)* it is just the opposite: The United States accounts for about 78 percent of it and the EU the other 22 percent. Because private assistance is smaller than government assistance, even after combining the two, EU aid almost doubles our own.[1] Europeans prefer to help struggling people abroad through taxes, so everybody chips in, while Americans are stingier with taxes and tend to prefer charity, so citizens can decide whether or not to help others. (One survey found that only a 54 percent bare majority of the US public rejected the idea that foreign aid "should be strictly a private matter taken care of by individuals giving donations through private organizations."[2]) The American way does not benefit as many people who need help. The Europeans outperform us. The silence of too many of us about assisting poor countries allows our policymakers to yield to other pressures.

---

and agriculture, it's government foreign aid."[38] As Gates has urged repeatedly, the predominant role belongs to governments, a view underscored by the foundation's launching of Global Citizen as an advocacy organization and its support for the ONE campaign and other advocacy groups.

You have probably received mail from charitable agencies telling you that a small contribution will feed a surprisingly large number of people. This often indicates that food and transportation are being supplied and paid for, at least in part, by our government. The government, of course, could just as legitimately report that your tax dollars feed more people because of its partnership with charitable organizations. Many private voluntary organizations working to alleviate hunger and poverty abroad receive government grants.[39] Because they implement projects at the local level, often in remote areas, collaborative arrangements can be beneficial, though not without serious tensions when purposes clash, for example as when armed conflict gives US agencies the appearance of taking sides.[40]

The $15.4 billion contribution of US private aid agencies to the reduction of hunger and poverty abroad is significant, though smaller than the $33.6 billion in official US humanitarian and development aid for 2016, and the $142.6 billion from twenty-nine donor nations, much of it channeled through international agencies.[41] Because US government aid *in total dollars* exceeds by far that of any other donor country, it influences the size and shape of government assistance that other countries give and affects private aid agencies as well.

The leverage of the US government is even more important than the dollar amounts of its assistance. It can nudge recipient countries toward more coherence in development efforts and encourage needed policy changes on matters that range from nutrition and climate change to human rights. It enabled the Marshall Plan and Western Europe's recovery to become one of history's great achievements. Today our government's partnership with recipient countries, other donor nations, international agencies, and even private companies increases our impact on hunger and poverty. US foreign aid, wisely used, can lay useful groundwork for enabling an economy to flourish. So can private charity, but not on the scale of the US government. Strong and wise leadership on our part can stir other countries to a higher level of commitment, but when we hold back we encourage those countries to do the same.

Precisely because of US leverage, President George W. Bush was able to play a leading role in getting donor nations to increase assistance to Africa at the G-8 Summit of key leaders in 2005. Our country's increase was driven mainly by the President's Emergency Program for AIDS Relief (PEPFAR), an example of how a strategic investment can produce outsized gains. It helped halt the advance of AIDS and put a brake on a pandemic that was throwing development into reverse in large areas of Africa. Effective treatment for AIDS has jumped from 50,000 to 17 million people, way beyond the resources of charity. Partly because of PEPFAR, Africa's population has experienced a sharp increase in life expectancy since the turn of the century, which translates also into economic gains and less poverty.[42]

US leverage also enabled President Obama to gain pledges from donor nations to increase investments in agriculture and brought together African nations, international donors, and private companies to assist countries willing to spend more of their own resources on food production and government reforms.[43] Private charities rarely have that kind of influence.

The Obama administration also initiated an effort to bring electrical power to more of Africa. In 2014 "Power Africa" drew African leaders, donor nations, international agencies, and private companies to a historic African Summit. To escape poverty Africa needs a large influx of private capital that can speed up development, for which electrical power is essential. So US and international agencies are combining assistance with links to African government leaders and private investors.[44] But more assistance is needed.

Unfortunately a slow post-recession recovery and a rigid congressional formula on spending caused a dip in funding for US development aid after years of rebounding.[45] However, according to Bread for the World, US *poverty-focused* development assistance remained high.[46] But that required shifting funds from other programs to pay for new African initiatives.[47] Ironically, reduced funding came just as reforms were improving the effectiveness of our assistance. USAID now has policies and practices in place that generate confidence across political lines. As a result, the United States is well positioned to increase its assistance and help lead the way globally for the world to reach the new UN Sustainable Development Goals of bringing an end to extreme hunger and poverty. But cuts hamper us. We could do our part, but only *if* we summon the will do it, which means *if* enough citizens demand it and *if* Congress seizes the opportunity.

In a rare show of bipartisanship on back-to-back days during July 2016, Congress passed two landmark anti-hunger bills urged by a wide coalition of citizens: The first one locks into place a more rigorous and open system for monitoring and evaluating our assistance programs.[48] The second, the Global Food Security Act of 2016 (reauthorized for five years in 2018), makes USAID's "Feed the Future" initiative (as well as other reforms) a permanent feature of US foreign aid. The "Feed the Future" partnership with small-scale farmers (women in particular) boosts food production, lifts incomes, and improves family nutrition, especially for women and children during the crucial "first thousand days" from conception to age two. By USAID's estimate, between 2011 and 2017, Feed the Future lifted more than 5 million families out of hunger and 23 million people above the poverty line.[49] Bipartisanship held in Congress throughout 2017 and 2018 on "circle of protection" issues, keeping hope alive that steps to end hunger could bring people across party lines despite political division on other issues.

*   *   *

I can imagine someone reading these lines thinking, "I'm for bringing hunger to an end, but I don't have much confidence in what the government does, so I'd rather write checks for charity than letters to Congress." By all means, write those checks, and write bigger ones if you can. The point of this book, however, is that the silence that kills is not the silence of heartless people, but the silence, *at the political level*, of good, check-writing people who truly want to help others escape hunger. That silence is holding back our ability to bring hunger to a merciful conclusion. But because the public has grown so skeptical about government, that skepticism warrants special consideration.

To that concern we now turn.

7

Government Must Lead

Government is not the solution to our problem;
government is the problem.

—Ronald Reagan[1]

When the subject of hunger and poverty came up for discussion at church recently, a friend of mine said, "Things were fine when people just pitched in and helped each other. Then the government stepped in and screwed things up."

It did?

This widely held point of view defies the evidence. It invokes a mythic past.

One can hardly overstate the importance of people helping each other, and charities are a way of doing that on a large scale. My friend, however, vastly exaggerated the results of people "just pitching in and helping each other." The government stepped in precisely because the help of individuals and charitable organizations fell woefully short. Too many were left hungry and destitute, too many without a job or one that could sustain a family. Not everyone could help or bothered to help, others chipped in a little, and still others helped a great deal but were soon overwhelmed by the magnitude of need. The Great Depression exposed the limitations of charities. It set charities back financially, and caused many of them to collapse.[2] Human suffering was so extensive and in such deviation from personal and public values that people saw the necessity of the entire nation ensuring a floor of justice for everyone, a role that only the government could assume.

The government is a necessary way for people to "pitch in and help each other," and it often does so where voluntary efforts fall short. Government action to counteract hunger and poverty came, not in defiance of people helping one another, but as a necessary extension of it.

The "bucket brigade" used to be the way neighbors responded when someone's house caught fire—a good example of people pitching in to help. Unfortunately, it rarely worked. Today fire departments put out fires using advanced technology and paid professionals as well as volunteers, and people do not complain that the government is doing what charity could do better and cheaper. Yet many of us still have a bucket-brigade mentality when it comes to hunger and many other public concerns.

Fran Quigley tells of a desperate woman in his state of Indiana, which, he says, provides difficult access to Medicaid, so clients with severe disabilities or illnesses are often denied help. After one of his colleague-lawyers helped her file an appeal, she faced a judge known for his negative opinion of "welfare." The judge listened to evidence of the woman's chronic pain and struggles to afford medication and therapy, then promptly denied her request for Medicaid coverage. The woman left the courtroom in tears. "It really is too bad what she is going through," the judge said to Quigley's colleague. "Isn't there some kind of program out there to help people like her?" Yes, there is, but he had just turned down her application for it, and there was no charity "out there" able to provide the expensive medical help she needed.[3]

Without government leadership in today's complex world, where people are often at the mercy of economic factors beyond their control, hunger and poverty would persist on a much larger and more destructive scale than we currently experience. Ending hunger, like ending smallpox or polio, or fending off ebola, cannot naïvely depend on free enterprise and private charitable agencies. The Centers for Disease Control and Prevention is, after all, a unit of our government; and the World Health Organization an instrument of many governments—and the public counts on these agencies to help us keep danger in check. For similar reasons, ending hunger must ultimately be expressed as the will of the nation. It requires a vocal public, a Congress to enact the necessary legislation, and a President who rallies people around that goal. Such an accomplishment would enhance rather than diminish both free enterprise and charity. But the government must do its part, which is to lead in ways that it alone has the authority and capability of doing. Its proper functioning, however, depends upon citizens being well informed and holding leaders accountable.

This positive role of government is expressed in the Declaration of Independence as equality, liberty, and justice for all. Our Constitution mandates us to promote the "general welfare" (the common good)[4] as the nation expands and life becomes increasingly complex. Think of its initiatives and its oversight in the fields of banking and commerce, transportation and communication, agriculture and education; or its responses to the Great Depression or the Great Recession; or civil rights, public safety, national defense, Social Security, and Medicare, to name just a few key areas. None of these government initiatives has happened flawlessly or without controversy. Some things (emancipation and civil rights, for example) were doggedly and even violently resisted, with remnants of resistance still deeply embedded in our culture. Despite serious flaws, our government is one for which each of us can be profoundly grateful. No other authority has been established and empowered by the people to act on our behalf "to form a more perfect union."

A genuine conservative tradition recognizes this positive role of government, as opposed to the slogan that "government is the problem, not the solution." Consider this thoughtful summary by Yuval Levin, editor of *National Affairs*:

> The promise of conservatism has always been that what matters most about society happens in the space between the individual and the state—the space occupied by families, communities, civic and religious institutions, and the private economy—and that creating, sustaining, and protecting that space and *helping all Americans take part in what happens there* are among the foremost purposes of government. (italics added)[5]

The biblical roots of Christianity affirm those who govern as "God's servant for your good."[6] For those who see it this way, governing is at once a noble and a humbling assignment. If subordinate to God, government cannot claim a person's highest allegiance; but its laws are to be obeyed and its officials, serving for the good of those governed, are to be respected. The apostle Paul, who wrote those words, had experienced brutality and injustice from governing authorities, along with the special privileges of his Roman citizenship, which he put to good use. By comparison, we are favored beyond measure to be part of a government of the people. The government about which we complain is not "it" or "they." It is "we the people," and we are responsible for shaping it.

Animosity toward Government

Why is there such a negative attitude toward government today? The reasons are many. One is that respect for all institutions and authorities has declined in recent decades, along with the weakening of many of the invaluable social connections and associations that bring people together. A "government of the people" reflects the collective weakness of human nature, including our own, so it often stumbles and deserves criticism. As the philosopher Immanuel Kant said, "Out of the crooked timber of humanity no straight thing was ever made."[7] The nation's founders, reflecting both human experience and biblical realism, recognized our innate selfishness as well as our capacity to do good; so they fashioned a government with checks and balances in recognition of both aspects. Political life, like every other human endeavor, reflects human nature. The selfish side of politics, widely publicized, tends to obscure the good that government does. Well-deserved criticism, however, can quickly become whining and then cross the line to destructive contempt, which may reflect self-contempt as well.[8]

We expect much more from government than we are willing to pay for. To get elected, candidates promise what they think voters want. People's expectations drive politicians to do this and those expectations are inevitably dashed. As the 2016 presidential campaigns showed, if voters feel sufficiently frustrated, they can react in unpredictable ways. Their disappointment in this case had multiple roots, among them economic hardship and growing inequalities, for which the public was given years of a polarized and often dysfunctional Congress with an approval rating not far north of zero.

There is enough blame in this for all of us, including both major political parties. But can we honestly ascribe an equivalence of fault to each side? Two prominent scholars, one from the conservative American Enterprise Institute and the other from the moderately left-leaning Brookings Institution, collaborated for decades on changes in Congress, and published an assessment in 2012: *It's Even Worse Than It Looks: How the American Constitutional System Collided with the New Politics of Extremism*. The extremism, they conclude, was deliberate obstructionism in Congress. They describe how the combative style of Newt Gingrich became pivotal in the 1980s and 1990s, replacing civility with confrontation in the House and Senate, which led to rigid partisanship. Senate GOP leader Mitch McConnell announced, "The single most important thing we want to achieve is for President Obama to be a one-term President."[9] Opposition to Obama became an obsession. Like every president, Obama had shortcomings, but what prompted voters to put him in the White House was his vision of a nation rising above its partisan divisions. That hope was dashed primarily by obstruction, which diminished not just Obama's legacy but the Congress and the nation, along with respect for government. One unexpected consequence: the further coarsening of civic life during the 2016 presidential campaigns and the election of Donald Trump.

Let Charity Do It?

Should charity take care of food assistance in our country?

Consider the Chicago, Illinois, food bank (described in chapter 5) and its network of pantries and agencies that offer emergency help to people. Suppose they replace the government's food assistance. To simplify, ignore school meals, WIC, and smaller federal programs. Let this charitable network only take on the $1.4 billion annual SNAP program for Cook County recipients, which accounts for about 70 percent of the cost of federal food assistance there.[1] Include also the $100 million cost of the food bank's current assistance.[2] Total cost: $1.5 billion.

"Let the church do it," people often say, so let's turn to the 3,354 religious congregations of all faiths in Cook County.[3] Dividing the $1.5 billion cost of combined food assistance among them would require an annual average contribution of $447,000 from each congregation, many of them struggling to stay afloat financially and all of them carrying out other core spiritual and social ministries. Could they do it? Not a chance. Besides, by what logic should we expect the religious segment of the population to shoulder this responsibility for everybody else?

So let's ask Cook County's 5.2 million people or, say, only those in the top two-thirds of household income, to contribute. That would mean seeking $1.5 billion from 3.5 million people, an average of about $430 per person each year.

How many people do you think would voluntarily give that much to this new charity? One out of four? That would be an astonishingly high response. But even if it happened, to make up for nongivers (many of them children) those who give would have to contribute an average per person of four times $430 for a total of $1,720. How many are in your household? Two? That would cost (on average) $3,440. Four of you? Make that $6,880.

The cost doesn't begin to address such things as the need to improve nutrition and expand outreach, or the complexity of setting up and operating this massive new food distribution system with warehouses, equipment and trucks, hundreds of large super-pantries at convenient locations, and extended shopping hours; a huge network of hard-to-find volunteers trained to carefully screen recipients; accurate and detailed record-keeping; solicitation of donated food from the food industry on a vastly enlarged scale; a big fundraising department, and much more. Of course, seeing all of this bypass our retail food stores might not be welcomed by the food industry, and having to use a dual-market system is probably not the way most people would prefer to shop for food.

Or would you rather upgrade the nation's streamlined SNAP program that enables recipients to use electronic debit cards for buying groceries?

Many faults have undermined trust in government. The Vietnam War that was President Johnson's nemesis and the Watergate scandal that brought down the Nixon administration—as well as the efforts of both men to mislead the public about these things—were big factors in souring people on government and contributed to the erosion of respect for authority during the 1960s and 1970s and beyond. As George Will has noted, since 1968 Americans' trust in government has not risen to pre-Vietnam levels.[10] The mistrust that emerged from the Vietnam and Watergate episodes gave new momentum to a culture of individualism unmoored from traditional restraints, which found startling expression in the political revolt of 2016.

Increasingly mean-spirited partisanship poisons public opinion. The practice demeans politics and government. Mark Shields once wondered on PBS News what it would do to the beer industry if companies aired commercials about their competitors' beer giving people bad breath and large bellies.

Other factors that erode trust in government include:

- Education (from home and school through college) now mainly oriented to social and financial success, but ruinously weak on responsible citizenship and civic participation.[11]
- The growing reliance of people on social media and entertainment for news and guidance.
- The corrosive impact of money in electing and influencing political leaders. More and more money in presidential and congressional campaigns puts influence increasingly in the hands of wealthy donors who expect—and usually get—special access to elected officials who subsequently tend to donors' interests. The soaring cost of political campaigns drives candidates to spend inordinate time soliciting contributions from such donors, with the result that political decisions in all three branches of government shape the rules by which our market economy operates primarily to the advantage of those with high incomes.[12]
- An army of well-paid lobbyists (on a scale unknown in any other country) who help rich corporate interests wield excessive influence over government policy. They differ sharply from organizations and people who speak up for social justice, not to advance their own financial fortunes.
- The increased number of House districts that are carved out (gerrymandered) to be predictably "safe" for one party or the other. This frequently enables candidates with the most polarized and rigid views to be nominated and elected to Congress.

- Our own unwillingness to listen respectfully to those we may not agree with and allow that they might have some insights we have neglected.

"Government is the problem, not the solution" offers a slogan in place of reason. Government is a flawed undertaking, always in need of whistleblowers and reforms. It is not the solution to everything, but it is a solution or a partial solution to many things that only the government has the authority to do or the ability to do on a large enough scale.

The key question is not "How big should the government be?" but "What unit of society can most appropriately carry out particular responsibilities?" The principle of subsidiarity is helpful here. It maintains that what can best be handled at a local level should not be assigned to a higher level. Things that a family or a voluntary association can do well should not be left to the government. Parents can instill strong moral values and a sense of purpose, give their children love, time, and attention. But parents often delegate things upward, expecting the schools to instill discipline or the church to instill faith and both to instill values, when these are neglected at home. This abdicates a vital responsibility and leaves children vulnerable to cultural influences they are not equipped to handle.

Most appropriate to the challenge of ending hunger is that the government exercise the kind of leadership it alone can provide. Part of that leadership is to guide the nation, and to help guide the world, toward a flourishing economy to which all who are able contribute, and the benefits of which all can enjoy. Because hunger and the poverty that underlies it are matters of public justice and the common good, government leadership is essential.

Regarding the nation's food safety-net, the assumption that the government does everything less efficiently and at higher cost than does the private charitable sector is mistaken. The lower cost of charity in this case is possible only because of extraordinary efforts to solicit donations of food and money as well as volunteers. As a backstop to a faltering government response, this charitable initiative is widely needed. But as a way of reducing cost or replacing the nation's responsibility for ending hunger, it is defective. The box on page 96, "Let Charity Do It?," illustrates why having charities do what the SNAP program now does would be an administrative and financial nightmare, more costly and less efficient than what the government and food markets in combination now do remarkably well, if insufficiently so.

The Role of Free Enterprise

As the driving force behind the US economy, free enterprise capitalism does far more than either the government or charity to put food on the table. Free enterprise is an astonishingly impressive engine of innovation and economic growth, and we need to build on that. However, an engine is not a steering wheel. The free market can power the economy by responding to and stimulating consumer demand; but it cannot by itself guide the economy well.

Like any other human project, free enterprise has its own weaknesses and limitations. Because it is driven by the profit motive, it is susceptible to human greed. Claims for its moral neutrality mean that it does not by itself distinguish between selling illicit drugs and selling apples or between honest and dishonest transactions. So free enterprise must be tamed by values other than its own in order to function for the common good. Unhindered, it crushes people and creates unbearable inequalities. As a result, all Western democracies have free market economies that are regulated to protect people and to modify those inequalities. Other industrialized democracies have had more success in finding a good balance in doing so than has the United States and seem happier for it.[13] All capitalisms are not the same, it turns out; some are more humane than ours. "No European city has experienced the level of concentrated poverty and racial and ethnic segregation that is typical of American metropolises," writes William Julius Wilson. Europeans are more focused on shortcomings in the broader society than on individual deficiencies and offer more support to prevent people from falling into poverty, he observes.[14] Wisdom, which entails humility, could lead us to learn things from them that we might usefully adapt, perhaps alleviating some of the downsides of capitalism that have left too many Americans behind.

The moral integrity of individuals is essential in taming the free market; but few would want to rely on that, say, in buying a house. So we ask the government to prohibit abuses and enforce contracts. Its laws protect us—and protect the free market itself—from ruthless entrepreneurs. A healthy, educated workforce, a reliable banking system, regulated transportation and communications systems, and public safety are among the many ways in which private enterprise relies on good government. Private enterprise, like the rest of us, is also among "the needy," and by far the most influential supplicant for government benefits.

It is one thing to admire the immense role of free enterprise in the development of our country and in enabling the world to make dramatic gains against hunger and poverty; but it is quite another thing to ignore its limitations and the great damage it can do when left to its own devices, all of which makes careful regulation essential. A mindset that considers free enterprise an independent source of pure good and government instinctively bad undermines both. It is not hard to see this mindset at work in our political life.

The vaunted self-regulating free market led to the Great Depression of the 1930s. It also helped trigger the Great Recession that began in 2007, and except for massive government bailouts of financial and auto industry giants, the excesses of untamed capitalism would have caused the economy to crash. "Too big to fail" brought government to the rescue, which prevented an economic catastrophe. Even so, many Americans who were not too big to fail lost jobs, homes, and savings. The intervention was necessary but lopsided.

This shows that the free market is not an autonomous sacred reality. It is, rather, a valuable human arrangement that can take many different forms, the success and fairness of which are determined to a large extent by legislation and policies of the government. Because wealthy individuals and corporations have inordinate influence in shaping those policies, they usually get the government to protect and distribute wealth in an upward direction through rules that tilt the market in their favor. One result of this has been the growing inequalities of the past four decades.[15] The government is not neutral about poverty. Its decisions have made too many people poor. Supposed neutrality, like silence, means you put your thumb on a scale that favors those who are economically prosperous.

The free market must be given all the liberty it needs so it can flourish; but it must also be governed by policies that require it to contribute to the common good and not simply feed its own appetite for higher profits. That is true regarding the economy as a whole, and it is especially true regarding hunger. People have a right to food before the rich have a right to unlimited wealth. "Our greatest national illusion is that a healthy society can be organized around the single-minded pursuit of wealth," writes Jeffrey Sachs.[16]

Have we become obsessed with greed? The problem, according to Alan Greenspan, chairman of the Federal Reserve Board from 1997 to 2006, is "not that humans have become any more greedy than in generations past," but that "the avenues to express greed have grown enormously."[17] This happens by human choices that find political expression.

A healthy society and morally attuned citizens seek the common good. There is much to applaud about free enterprise and individualism, but not when they crush people. If individualism propels us to seek only freedom from restraint, freedom to do as we please, whether in the economic or the social arena, rather than freedom for the common good, it becomes destructive. Both liberals and conservatives have deep roots in this. Consider the worsening in recent decades of crude speech and behavior in civic discourse, which Daniel Patrick Moynihan called "defining deviancy down." It has contributed to political decline and our present political crisis. We are witnessing the fruit of individualism untethered to the common good. Sociologist Daniel Bell's idea of the nation as a household is useful here.[18] Like a household, the nation flourishes when personal responsibility is combined with social responsibility. Ending the scourge of hunger calls for responsibility of both types, including that of government leadership.

The US Food System

To put this in a larger context, consider the US food system, which reflects the dominant role of private enterprise, the crucial but sometimes flawed role of government, and the more modest but necessary role of private charity. The picture that emerges is both inspiring and troubling.

US agriculture is the story of extraordinary natural resources and vast fertile lands. No other nation on earth has had so many natural advantages. That story is also the story of the remarkable achievements of farmers past and present, technological advances, and free enterprise—though the enterprise looked anything but free to slaves and native Americans. That shame aside, farming has flourished because of free enterprise as well as far-sighted government policies. The results are impressive. US agricultural exports for 2017 were expected to reach $140 billion and gave us an agricultural trade surplus that year of about $24 billion.[19] A hundred years ago it took one US farm to feed an average of about a dozen people. By 2016 one farm on average fed 165 people in the US and abroad.[20] The average amount we spend on food in our country is just under 10 percent of per capita income, and less than 6 percent is spent on food eaten at home. The poorest fifth of our population, however, has to spend an average of 36 percent on food and still faces extensive food insecurity.[21]

US agriculture is also the story of public and private partnership. It includes food assistance programs that keep millions of people here and abroad from going hungry. As it has evolved, however, our food system is rife with contradictions and incoherence regarding people's health and well-being.

Early American settlers and pioneers struggled to clear land for cultivation and produce enough in order to survive and often to thrive, though many died trying. In accomplishing this they sometimes forcibly pushed native Americans off their ancestral lands, an aspect of our history of which we need not be proud. In 1862 during President Lincoln's Republican administration Congress passed a Homestead Act that gave farmers opportunity to settle on virgin land. In the 1890s my grandfather inherited forty acres of wooded land in Wisconsin from his father and later bought an adjoining forty acres. With the help of neighbors, he gradually cleared land for farming and built both a barn and a house for his growing family. My grandparents had a small income from crops and livestock, and sometimes logs or raccoon pelts, but they also bartered for food and supplies.[22] They were able to build on the sweat of earlier settlers, and then did considerable sweating of their own. The Morrill Land Grant Act, also of 1862, set aside land for colleges to educate farmers and engineers and to keep them abreast of unfolding research and technology. Other legislation launched a network of state agricultural extension services to bring practical application of the latest and best practices to farmers in counties throughout the nation. These actions, along with the construction of railways, roads, and ports, prepared the nation for urban growth, which gave farmers a growing market and made industrial life possible. Tractors and harvesters began replacing draft animals. US agriculture became a big export trade industry as farms grew larger and larger.

From time to time many farmers went broke as weather and price fluctuations, along with economic swings, created boom-and-bust cycles. Then came the Great Depression of the 1930s, and in the middle of it dust storms that ravaged over-tilled land in the Great Plains. President Roosevelt proposed, and the US Congress enacted, emergency legislation to keep small family farms going. Government subsidies helped offset depressed prices and encouraged soil conservation practices. Sometimes subsidies paid farmers for farming less land, both to conserve it and to lift the price of crops. These actions kept many farmers afloat.

As the years went by, however, those programs were tweaked and changed by Congress and gradually lost much of their original purpose. Some payments were made on the basis of acres planted (or not planted) even when the market price of a crop was high and the farmer a flourishing millionaire. In response to growing criticism, Congress dropped those direct subsidies in the 2014 Farm Act in favor of crop insurance to protect incomes but subsidized the insurance at rates that may prove to be just as costly. Government support continues to benefit mainly the most prosperous owners of very large farms with crop insurance that applies mostly to four commodity crops: corn, wheat, soybeans, and rice.

Could We Do Better?

Despite the remarkable achievements of US farmers and the food industry, we also have food policies that are sometimes incoherent or even perverse, contributing to a public health crisis fueled by cheap calories and lack of diversity, with poor diets now a leading cause of premature death.[23] These policies are heavily shaped by financially powerful farm and food industries. The US Department of Agriculture (USDA) recommends a healthy diet that includes half fruits and vegetables, but its support for fruits and vegetables "remains a small fraction of that spent on all commodity crops."[24] It mainly supports crops that feed animals, fuel cars, or get processed into food that contributes to the national surge in obesity and diabetes,[25] subsidizing heavily the production of foods that we are advised to eat less, while offering only modest help for growing the fruits and vegetables that we are urged to eat more. Risk-conscious farmers plant accordingly.

Meanwhile the food industry, which mostly opposes the USDA's dietary guidelines, uses effective marketing techniques to promote junk food for all of us and reach eager consumers at an early age.[26] In this way the industry casts a shadow over the SNAP program, because a small portion of SNAP benefits are predictably spent on junk food and drinks. Although their use by SNAP recipients may simply reflect the buying habits of all consumers, a sensible reform would make such items ineligible for purchase with SNAP electronic debit cards. There is no point subsidizing habits that threaten the health of SNAP recipients, while undermining the reputation of a program that in other respects is a boon to their health and well-being.[27]

Issues of concern include soil deterioration; animal waste and fertilizer run-off into lakes, streams, and rivers; heavy consumption of fossil fuel that contributes to climate change; the depletion of water in underground aquifers as a result of irrigation; and food and drug safety. These matters attract financial interests and powerful lobbying. As a result, reforms that make good economic sense, serve the national interest, and relate to hunger at least indirectly are hard to achieve, which is why government leaders need well-informed pushback from citizens.

Our farm subsidies have sometimes hurt struggling farmers abroad. By stimulating overproduction, US grain exports have often been sold at artificially low prices (some of it on concessional terms or given away as part of our food aid), which can undercut the livelihoods of small-scale farmers in poor countries.[28] For a few years subsidized production of ethanol from corn and soybeans brought a surge in grain prices that caused a hunger spike in many developing countries. Congress sometimes takes actions that affect vulnerable people with little thought about the impact of these actions on them, in this way unwittingly exporting hunger and poverty.

In the 1970s Haiti imported only 19 percent of its food. In 1995 it was pressured to drop its import tariffs from 50 percent to 3 percent. Thanks to US rice subsidies and export promotion, Haiti now imports more than 80 percent of its rice from the United States, while most of its farmers have an income level of $400 a year. In 2010, while helping to address a disastrous earthquake in Haiti, President Clinton apologized for his role in signing 1996 legislation that he called a "devil's bargain." He said, "I have to live every day with the consequences of the lost capacity to produce a rice crop in Haiti to feed those people, because of what I did."[29] Many struggling Mexican farmers have also been impoverished or pushed off the land for not being able to compete with subsidized US corn and mechanized US agriculture. The work in Haiti and Mexico of all private charities combined fails to offset the damage of those policies.

International food assistance has been a vital part of US policy for generations. We have been the world's biggest food donor for more than a century. Annual spending on international food assistance has been averaging $2.5 billion and helping to feed 50 million people a year—many more now, thanks to recent reforms.[30] The Food for Peace program accounts for most of our food assistance. The smaller McGovern-Dole International Food for Education and Child Nutrition program is modeled after our US school lunch and breakfast programs.

Food assistance reforms in recent years include more grants instead of loans, more emphasis on nutrition for women and children (especially those under age two), and more purchases abroad near the location of need and less shipping of food from the United States. These reforms cost less, buy more food, deliver it more quickly, and give struggling small-scale farmers an additional market. But the reforms are incomplete, and obstacles such as the requirement that most food purchased in the US for assistance must be shipped on US vessels (the "Cargo preference") should be removed.[31]

Our international food aid is not entirely altruistic. Quite aside from the good will it has brought us, most of the countries that now purchase the largest amount of US agricultural products were former recipients of US food aid, so our humanitarian aid has been profitable, a fact that underscores the close relationship between the government and farming in the United States. US agricultural trade supports more than a million full-time civilian jobs, about three-fourths of them in the nonfarm sector.[32]

In our own country the US food system includes nutrition programs that lift millions of households above the poverty line and gives them food security, while enabling countless others to become less poor and less hungry. Despite these marvelous achievements, our economy still leaves about 40 million Americans food-insecure.

The grandeur and contradictions of our food system are driven largely by the grandeur and contradictions of free enterprise, assisted by government policies that tend to its interests. Organized charity, as a program innovator, a backup safety-net, and sometimes a delivery arm for government aid, is a significant part of this food system. Because those working in the charity network often see, face-to-face, the large impact of our food system on people, they fulfill an especially important responsibility when they call attention to its shortcomings and publicly address the need for changes in government policy and practice.

The Shame of Hunger in America

You would think that, as prosperous and as abundant with food and food exports as our country is, we would be utterly ashamed to harbor extensive hunger. Food insecurity here may be "hunger lite" compared to life-choking hunger abroad, but it is nevertheless a form of hunger that cries out in judgment against our toleration of it. The shame is ours because ending it, and reducing the poverty that fosters it, is easily within our grasp.

This reality is partly responsible for the nation's political crisis, which reflects (among other things) how deeply aggrieved much of our population is from decades of growing inequalities that have left them watching the American dream slip away, while Congress seems too polarized or self-absorbed to notice. This aggrieved public is comprised not only of poor, but middle-income people whose growing frustration reached a boiling point during the 2016 presidential campaigns. Disaffected white voters often feel themselves to be the most forgotten citizens: hard-working Americans who played by the rules, then saw their jobs vanish, their incomes shrink, and their personal status diminished. American individualism tells them it's their own fault, and they believe this.[33] At the same time, a sense of alienation makes them angry and ready to blame others.

Many Americans resent government assistance for poor people, especially if those being assisted are poor African Americans, Hispanics, or immigrants. These in turn chafe at being unfairly blamed. In this way the nation's inequalities have set people against one another, when we could combine efforts to address the cause of our disaffection. Many have been seduced by a racially and ethnically tinged promise to "make America great again" although the real problem is the inequalities that devalue life for everyone.

Many members of Congress want to help people escape poverty and create opportunity for all, but they cannot make that happen by clinging to a belief that free enterprise and rugged individualism are the answer to all economic woes. That belief, like the pride of a god in a Greek tragedy, turns those strengths into fatal flaws.

In 2016 a panel of six Republican candidates for president, moderated by Speaker of the House Paul Ryan, addressed the issue of poverty.[34] Their recognition of poverty as a serious national problem and their willingness to discuss it were steps in the right direction. The desire to move people from welfare to work contains seeds of bipartisan agreement. So far, however, those concerns about poverty have typically been accompanied by policies that favor (1) enlarging tax benefits for the rich; (2) cutting programs such as SNAP and Medicaid that assist the poor; and (3) handing those programs over to the states along with "block grants" of federal funding. But (as I contend in chapters 2 and 9) those policies would make inequalities much worse. However, Democrats who support assistance for poor people, but are

---

Blaming the Poor Bites Back

Blaming poor people for their poverty is anchored in the widespread conviction that the key to success is honest, hard work, that you reap what you sow, and that those who fail have no one to blame but themselves. You firmly believe this, then your job disappears and the only work available does not pay enough to house and feed your family. You see the American dream slipping away.

Your judgment against others turns against you. It says that you too are a failure. Self-defeating behavior may follow. You may become depressed and withdrawn or turn to substance abuse for relief, or lash out at others who stay or rise in status while your status sinks.

Individualism is a great strength, a virtue to be highly admired—in proper perspective. When idolized, however, it inspires self-righteousness and hardness of heart toward others, not a desire for the common good. American history richly documents this, and examples could be drawn from this book. Rigid individualism provokes rigid divisions, when we should listen to one another to find ways of improving life for all of us.

---

passive about helping them graduate from welfare to work and creating real job opportunities, also seem tied to a losing formula.

If Congress insists on more of the same less-regulated, trickle-down economics that led to the Great Depression, the Great Recession, and four decades of expanding inequalities, does that make sense? Sanity lies in generating support for an alternative vision that could start with the simple, decent goal of ending hunger.

Let me be clear. I am not proposing an end to hunger as a panacea, a silver bullet, a Big Idea that would solve everything. I am proposing a more modest beginning, a foot-in-the-door approach of establishing the *goal* of ending hunger as a *national goal*. First the goal has to be established by Congress, then a process, with benchmarks, has to be developed for making it happen—with our federal food assistance programs as a guarantee (but not the preferred means) of keeping us on pace for ending hunger within, say, a five- or seven-year period. That would give us a lens of hope, bolstered by presidential and growing public support. Once bipartisan leaders begin to work on this, a lot of other problems will be seen more clearly and can be tackled more effectively. Of course, such efforts would face powerful resistance, but with key bipartisan backers in Congress it could happen and would shed light on how we can work together to achieve an economy that works for everybody. It could become that decent moral center that begins to unite us.

But now I am anticipating the second half of this book.

To sum up our first seven chapters: Ending most hunger here and abroad is within reach, but our silence about it at the political level is diminishing and shortening lives. Food insecurity here and chronic hunger abroad will persist until more of us break our silence and begin to insist that our nation make ending them serious national goals. As much as we might like to believe hunger would end if people "just pitched in to help each other," the reality is that the nation as a whole must take that step. As citizens, our responsibility is to insist—against all odds, if necessary, and until the odds change—that our elected officials assert that kind of leadership.

If we can persuade our leaders to seize the clearly achievable goal of ending hunger in this country, while helping also to end it globally, such nonpartisan action could give Americans a new sense of hope for our democracy, as well as perspective for making our economy and our life together more inclusive.

The possibility of bringing about that more inclusive economy will engage us now, as we turn to the second half of this book.

PART III

We Can Make Our Economy Fair and Inclusive

8

Wrenching Inequalities

If a free society cannot help the many who are poor,
it cannot save the few who are rich.

—John F. Kennedy[1]

Like termites, economic, racial, and social inequalities are eating away at the foundation of our nation. They contradict the nation's founding promises, the center of which—Lincoln and Jefferson maintained—is equality.[2] To be sure, the claim of the Declaration of Independence that all of us are "created equal" does not propose an equality of outcomes, but it does assert a God-given inalienable right to "life, liberty, and the pursuit of happiness." That tens of millions of us face food insecurity and poverty, while others gain increasingly gargantuan shares of income and wealth undermines our sense of fairness. It has weakened the hopes of many, sets people against one another, and harms the rich as well as the poor.

In the first half of this book I have argued that most hunger and food insecurity in this country could end within a few years if we improved and expanded our current food assistance programs. It is hard to imagine a better way of doing so much good for so many people so quickly with so modest an investment. But doing it would still leave too many Americans unemployed, underemployed, and underpaid, and the nation severely torn by inequalities. Therefore a commitment to end hunger rapidly should include steps toward ending poverty and making our economy work for everybody. That is the aim of this part of the book.

To achieve that aim we need to combine insights of conservatives and liberals, not as a grudging compromise between the political left and right, but as a new way forward, starting with the morally anchored, nonpartisan goal of ending hunger and following the trails that connect that goal to the rest of the economy.

This chapter (8) deals with economic and racial inequalities;
Chapter 9 with family erosion;
Chapter 10 with taxes and deficits; and
Chapter 11 sketches a path toward a more just and inclusive economy.

These chapters propose a sense of direction rather than a fixed plan. Positive action seeks to enlist presidential leadership and legislators who (urged on by citizens) are willing to listen to one another and find enough common ground to obtain an effective majority in Congress. With the simple human decency of determining to end hunger we would have a unifying lens through which we could begin to see in proper perspective other problems that plague us.

Income Inequalities

Our nation emerged from the crises of the Depression and World War II with a strong sense of national unity, though deeply flawed racially. Having gone through those challenges to our nationhood and its ideals, most Americans (racial injustice aside) were eager to move into an age of prosperity together. A widespread assumption prevailed that as we had suffered and fought together, we would now prosper together. Then by the mid-1970s that assumption began to erode.

Today in spite of safety-nets and income-transfer programs, hunger and poverty persist in our nation in part because income inequality has been widening for several decades. Even prior to the Great Recession of 2007–2009 our income inequality rivaled that of 1928, when low income and therefore low purchasing power for workers slowed the economy and helped to precipitate the economic crash of 1929.[3] Low purchasing power did even more to *prolong* the Great Depression that followed.[4] In 2007 the United States had the highest level of income inequality and the highest poverty rate of any industrialized democracy, with the exceptions of Mexico and Turkey.[5] Then the Great Recession and its aftermath caused millions of Americans to lose their homes, their jobs, and/or much of their life savings, and large numbers turned to SNAP and other assistance programs for help. By 2019 the economy looked brisk, at least on the surface. The unemployment rate stood at 4 percent, and salaries were beginning to increase slightly. Many who lost their jobs, however, were still unemployed. Others had found jobs paying lower salaries, while still others were working part-time or juggling two or three jobs to stay afloat. Setbacks had exacted a high price on health, family, community, and nation, and left many Americans with a diminished hope for the future.

Visual 5

The gap between productivity and a typical worker's compensation has increased dramatically since 1973

Productivity growth and hourly compensation growth, 1948–2017

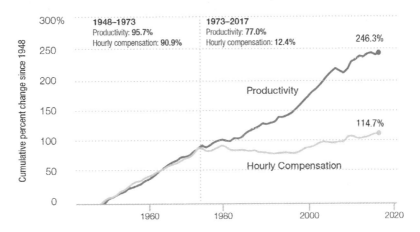

Notes: Data are for compensation (wages and benefits) of production/nonsupervisory workers in the private sector and net productivity of the total economy. "Net productivity" is the growth of output of goods and services less depreciation per hour worked.

Source: EPI analysis of unpublished Total Economy Productivity data from Bureau of Labor Statistics (BLS) Labor Productivity and Costs program, wage data from the BLS Current Employment Statistics, BLS Employment Cost Trends, BLS Consumer Price Index, and Bureau of Economic Analysis National Income and Product Accounts

Updated from Figure A in *Raising America's Pay: Why It's Our Central Economic Policy Challenge* (Bivens et al. 2014)

Economic Policy Institute

Two visuals illustrate our growing inequalities. *Visual 5* (above) shows that productivity gains and wages grew at the same rate for three decades after World War II.[6] During those years wage earners shared in rising production, as incomes rose in tandem with those gains. Then starting in the mid-1970s production continued to rise, but the wages of workers barely budged—in fact they stagnated for the next four decades. The wages shown in *Visual 5* do not include any government benefits or employer-paid health insurance. They show only the parallel growth of productivity and wages until the tide of production kept rising but quit lifting most of the boats.

Visual 6 (below) shows *average growth* in *household income after taxes*.[7] The striking thing is how incomes for the top 1 percent soared since 1979, growing fifty-nine times the average income growth of households in the bottom 20 percent.[8]

Visual 6
The incomes of the wealthy have grown
much faster than the incomes of other groups

Average Annual After-Tax Income (2015 Dollars)

PETER G.
PETERSON
FOUNDATION

Top 1%
Increase of $876,000
(+242%)

Top 20%
Increase of $109,000
(+103%)

Middle 20%
Increase of $18,700
(+41%)

Lowest 20%
Increase of $14,800
(+80%)

Source: Congressional Budget Office, The Distribution of Household Income, 2015, November 2018.
Data are for 2015. Compiled by PGPF.

Note: Increases calculated for 1979–2015.

© Peter G. Peterson Foundation

PGPF.ORG

The rates of income growth (by percent) in *after-tax* income from 1979 to 2015 show seemingly modest differences, but they result in surprisingly large dollar gaps. An 80 percent increase in income for households in the bottom fifth adds only $14,800 more annual income because they started so low. A smaller 41 percent increase for the middle fifth adds $18,700 because they started higher. The top 1 percent started so high that their increase of 242 percent adds a whopping $876,000, lifting their average income to about $1.2 million a year. The Federal Reserve reported that in 2016 the top 1 percent had reached a record high 24 percent share of US income.[9]

Visual 6 shows the moderating effect of progressive taxation, which prevents even greater inequalities. However, government transfers—primarily Social Security, Medicare, Medicaid, Earned Income Tax Credits, and SNAP—further modify income extremes. In 2015 those government benefits brought the average after-tax income of the bottom 20 percent of households to $33,000.[10] Social Security alone lifted almost 27 million Americans above the poverty line in 2015.[11]

The problem of income extremes is less the size of the gaps than what is happening to people at the bottom and many in the middle. Ben Bernanke, former chairman of the Federal Reserve, points out that since 1979, despite hefty productivity growth, the real median earnings of full-time *male* workers have actually declined.[12] How is it that our economy can generate more than 8 million millionaires and 585 billionaires,[13] while kids go hungry? These extremes signal how important it is for everyone to give back to the nation a reasonable portion of what they have gained so that everyone can prosper.

How Did This Happen?

If the data from the preceding pages were merely statistics for a class in economics, they would be of little consequence. They are disturbing because they profile the circumstances of a large number of Americans who want to be part of an American dream that seems beyond their reach. For example:

- kids from struggling homes and toxic neighborhoods who are on a pathway from underperformance in school to an impoverished adulthood;
- young men without a sense of purpose and no job, or working for a wage that puts marriage but not sex or drugs out of reach;
- mothers or fathers too stressed from work to give their children the time and attention to make them feel deeply loved, secure, and well guided.
- parents, whose upward path was reversed by the recession and stretches of unemployment, now working at lower-skilled and lower-paying or part-time jobs and worried about their future and that of their adult children.

These and others, including many in the middle class who were drawn to Trump, sense that the ground on which they stand is no longer solid and fairness a fading hope. How did we get to this point? How did an era of shared prosperity become one of growing inequalities?

Frequently cited economic reasons for this include (1) labor-saving technology that replaces workers; (2) companies moving production and jobs to countries with cheap labor; (3) the growth of lower-paying jobs—a result of numbers one and two, plus market competition; (4) tax policies that, instead of counteracting these powerful trends, have magnified them by benefiting mainly people with high incomes; and (5) the Great Recession, which wiped out decades of wealth accumulation for many Americans, caused widespread unemployment, and accelerated the trend toward lower-paying jobs. Along with these developments, social and racial disparities emerge as powerful indicators of our inequalities. Beneath *all* of these reasons, however, lie political choices the nation has made that must now be reconsidered.

Transformative changes since the mid-1970s continue to challenge us. Globalization has done enormous good in reducing hunger and poverty abroad, and access to new technologies has given us more benefits and less costly goods. But during the same period a new economic orthodoxy became widely accepted in the corporate world: that a company's only proper goal is to maximize profits for its shareholders.[14] Gone was the idea that workers and their families and community are stakeholders in the economy. Little room was left for attention to the common good. In keeping with "shareholder capitalism," executives and managers of large enterprises are now getting previously unheard-of salaries and bonuses for their success in rewarding shareholders with profits previously spent in large part on expansion and research that produced more jobs and resulted in pay raises for employees.[15] In 1965 the average total annual compensation for chief executives of large corporations was about twenty times that of the average worker, according to former US Treasury Secretary, Lawrence Summers.[16] In 2017 it was 312 times that of the typical worker, according to the Economic Policy Institute.[17]

Shareholder capitalism has shifted rewards from wages to investments, from labor to capital, from the bottom and middle to the top. In his detailed historical analysis of capitalism, economist Thomas Piketty documents the impulse of capital to grow more rapidly than the economy, which creates wealth for those near the top but leaves too many people at or near poverty. Piketty sees this happening now in what he calls "an explosion of US inequality after 1980."[18]

History offers us useful perspective. In the 1920s income inequalities reached extremes that preceded the Great Depression. Wages did not keep pace with economic growth. Low wages held back the purchasing power of most Americans, prompting companies to cut back on production and lay off workers, which made matters worse. In 1929 the unemployment rate was 3 percent, the next year 9 percent, the year after that 16 percent, then 23 percent. By 1933, when President Roosevelt was inaugurated, it reached a historic high of 25 percent.[19] The Hoover administration had faithfully adhered to the economic orthodoxy of the day: hold down government spending and allow free enterprise to make the economy bounce back. Instead the economy kept spiraling downward into the trench we know as the Great Depression. But were the Democrats swift to oppose this failing orthodoxy? Their 1932 platform called for an "immediate and drastic reduction of governmental expenditures" in order to decrease the cost of government by at least 25 percent.[20] Public trust in the magic of the free market was that complete.

In 2008 similar behavior fed a near collapse. Few saw it coming because financial institutions were allowed to buy and sell bundles of risky assets and extend easy credit to homebuyers and credit card users. The result was a financial boom and a real estate bubble that artificially lifted the economy. Many used credit to keep from slipping behind, others to advance their standard of living. As the extent of risk became apparent, giant financial institutions and the auto industry began to fail, and the real estate bubble burst. People lost jobs, homes, investments, and pensions.

The economic plunge in 2008 could easily have triggered another great depression on an even bigger scale, but the Bush and Obama administrations stepped forward to rescue failing financial firms as well as General Motors and Chrysler. The stimulus package that Obama and Congress approved also helped states, local governments, and public schools. It expanded SNAP and tax credits for low-income workers and created some jobs. Doing these things prevented the economy from going over the cliff and kept most people from going hungry.

Ironically, financial and business elites have recovered quite well, but many Americans lost homes, savings, jobs, and decent salaries. By 2018 median family income was rising again and hunger and poverty were gradually falling. But income inequalities continued, low wages still restrained consumer activity, and labor unions remained weak, while the business sector lobbied the government for tax breaks and tougher labor laws. A scissors-shaped graph shows one blade ("share of income going to the top 10%") heading upward since 1960, and the other blade ("union membership") heading down.[21]

Progressive income taxes and government benefits cushion income inequality. *Visual 6* (above) reflects this cushioning, otherwise income growth disparities would show far greater extremes. To be clear, people in the lowest fifth have made gains since 1979. However, in 2017, 40 million of us (12.3 percent of our population) lived below the official poverty line. Although the level of poverty has improved for many, home appliances and better medical care do not feed the kids. Life has become more complicated and costly over the years, and a good gauge of what it is like for those at or near the bottom is that 40 million Americans also lived in food-insecure households in 2017, most of them among the 40 million who fell below the poverty line.

We can draw two conclusions from all of this:

First, that government programs such as Social Security, Medicare, Medicaid, SNAP, and Earned Income Tax Credits have helped tens of millions of us who, without them, would be facing desperate conditions.

Second, even with that assistance, growing income inequality has led to unprecedented prosperity for some, while leaving much of the nation impoverished and many of those in between worried about what lies ahead for them and their children.

Wealth and Opportunity Gaps

Income inequality leads to wealth inequality. US millionaires and billionaires control approximately 66 percent of US wealth, according to the Boston Consulting Group. That is a far greater concentration of wealth than in any other developed country; moreover, the BCG expects the concentration to reach 71 percent by 2020. By comparison millionaires in Western Europe control 31 percent of the wealth, and in Japan 21 percent.[22] The BCG reports that wealth concentration is increasing worldwide because investment gains are outpacing growth from wages and other income, thus increasing inequalities. As wealth and its advantages are passed from one generation to the next, class inequalities become even more pronounced.

Assets are a family's private safety-net, there to tap in case of emergency. Yet in 2013 families in the bottom 25 percent of income had an average debt of $13,000 with zero net assets.[23] The government, however, mainly promotes asset building for the middle and upper classes through the mortgage tax deduction and other tax provisions. It also discourages asset building for poor people in some cases by setting limits that are too strict when determining eligibility for those who need assistance and by reducing assistance too quickly when they increase their earnings, in this way penalizing work. At the same time the government does too little to protect people from exploitation by wage theft (immigrants are most easily bilked), predatory payday lending (a $46 billion industry) or gambling (the dream of riches through an imaginary painless and harmless way of raising taxes),[24] to name but a few of the legal and illegal ways of making people poor.

The wealth gap often prevents people from seizing educational or job training opportunities for advancement. Growing up in poverty with a family burdened by debts makes it harder to overcome drawbacks, such as an unsafe neighborhood or an underperforming school. In our country 70 percent of those born in the bottom fifth of the population never reach the middle fifth or higher, according to a Pew Research Center study, which finds that having had at least some financial assets helped most people who managed to work their way upward.[25] Education offers a path toward opportunity. However, because education and training have "translated upward" for people at *all* levels, there is no evidence that education has decreased *relative* inequalities across generations, according to Thomas Piketty.[26] In fact the opposite appears to be happening from preschool to college. Lower-income people have to work harder than others at improving their education and training just to avoid falling further behind.

Schools make a difference. Evidence of this was the narrowing of racial disparities in education as a result of the civil rights movement, school desegregation, and the War on Poverty. Racial disparities remain stark, but today the educational gap between rich and poor children is almost twice as large as the gap between black and white children. The day they start kindergarten, children from low-income families are already more than a year behind children of college graduates in both reading and math. Children with the most cultural handicaps to overcome (broken homes, too little reading, too much television, fears for safety) usually attend schools with the fewest resources and teachers with the least experience.[27] The gap in spending between public schools in the poorest and the most affluent neighborhoods has steadily widened. In a recent year one of Pennsylvania's lowest-achieving school districts spent $8,700 per student, compared to $26,600 in a Philadelphia suburb.[28]

Nobel Prize economist Angus Deaton reports that the United States is "not particularly good at actually delivering equal opportunities" and ranks among the worst of highly developed countries in this respect.[29] Our country is among three out of thirty-four advanced nations surveyed by the Organization for Economic Cooperation and Development (OECD) whose schools spend more per pupil on higher-income children than on economically poor students. The other thirty-one nations allocate a higher share of national funding to poorer communities and either invest equally or disproportionately more for disadvantaged students.[30] Our neglect of such students weakens the nation and affects all of us.

Racial Disparities

Among the most deeply disturbed Americans are white working-class people, drawn to the Trump candidacy in large numbers because they see him as a champion of protest against the erosion of status and racial privileges they have cherished. Far from offending them, Trump's insults and impulsive behavior seem to capture their frustration and sense of loss. Job and income setbacks have wounded many of them, but so does a feeling that the America they cherish is slipping away from them. That feeling finds powerful expression in the slogan, "Make America great again," which draws strength from the fact that status lost can be more demoralizing than status not yet achieved. Many who feel that way are offended to see minorities (African Americans in particular) either moving ahead economically or simply being assisted by the government. We may be tempted to demean these aggrieved white compatriots as unenlightened or even bigoted. It would be more helpful, however, to respect them as persons for their pain and invite them to join other Americans, black and white, in pursuing a more opportunity-driven economy. Right or wrong, if the condescension of privileged snobs is what they feel, they are apt to resist positive alternatives even more. I want disaffected whites to know that the more equitable economy proposed in this book includes them and addresses their needs as well as the needs of rich and poor Americans.

The pain of many white Americans notwithstanding, slavery and other inhumanities have handed African Americans, American Indians, and to a lesser extent Hispanic immigrants a far more damaging legacy. Racial comparisons must be made in order to understand what is happening, but that should not lead us or aggrieved whites and colored minorities to see one another as hostile competitors. Doing so is a distraction that holds all of us back.

The nation's food insecurity and poverty rates contain many imbalances. More white people are poor and food-insecure than any other racial group. However, the poverty *rate* in 2017 for non-Hispanic whites was 9 percent, compared to 21 percent for African Americans and 18 percent for Hispanics.[31] The rates are more extreme for children, with 33 percent of black children, 26 percent of Hispanic children, and 11 percent of non-Hispanic white children in poverty.[32]

The unemployment rate has been consistently twice as high for African Americans as it is for whites, with Hispanic unemployment falling between the two.[33]

Homelessness, one of the most harmful aspects of poverty, reached a new high for children in 2013. Almost 2.5 million children (one in every thirty) were homeless for at least part of that year, up from the 2006 pre-recession 1.5 million (one in fifty).[34] But African Americans were three times more likely to be homeless than the US population as a whole. Their use of emergency shelters was seven times higher than for white families, while black children under the age of five were twenty-nine times more likely than white children to be in an emergency shelter,[35] further undermining prospects for these already-marginalized kids.

The wealth gap is even more extreme along racial lines than is the poverty gap. The median (half above, half below) net wealth of $171,000 for white households was ten times that of the $17,600 median for black households in 2016—one black dime for every white dollar.[36] A full third of black and Hispanic households had zero or minus-zero net assets during the recession.[37]

Residents in high-poverty urban neighborhoods often feel abandoned, as people, businesses, and factories moved out or failed. In 2015 the Sandtown section of Baltimore became the center of protests over police brutality and the killing of Freddie Gray, a twenty-five-year-old black man. Sandtown is marked by empty apartments and struggling schools, as well as vacant stores, cafés, and factories that once offered jobs. By one account more than 30 percent of its residents live below the poverty line, 21 percent are unemployed, about 450 are in state prison, and failing schools, drugs, and mistrust abound. A local priest, Father Ray Bomberger, sees a sense of hopelessness that his church struggles to address.[38]

The Detroit neighborhood in which neurosurgeon and now Secretary for Housing and Urban Development Ben Carson grew up shows similar signs of abandonment, with many businesses and homes boarded up. His old neighborhood had factories, shops, and restaurants that provided jobs and mentors who helped kids like Ben Carson. This once-vibrant neighborhood is plagued with drugs and violent crime—not the kind of place that would likely have set young Carson on a path toward professional and national prominence. Innate gifts, strong maternal guidance, a devout faith, and dogged determination on his part (and that of his mother) were critical ingredients in his success. But so were food stamps and other public and private forms of help.[39] If Carson had grown up there today, would he have beaten the odds?

Dealing with Racial Wounds

Our coming to terms with the nation's painful and still festering racial wounds might begin by recognizing, as President Lyndon Johnson did, that

"Negro poverty is not white poverty." Freedom is not enough, he said. "You do not take a person who, for years, has been hobbled by chains and liberate him, bring him up to the starting line of a race and then say, 'you are free to compete with all the others,' and still justly believe you have been completely fair."[40]

But that is exactly what white Americans are prone to think. Because slavery and legally enforced segregation ended, don't black people have as much chance at the starting line as whites? We fail to grasp the *current* impact on black Americans of cruelties imposed on slaves and their descendants. That history (similar in many ways for native Americans) involves massive thefts of labor, land, family, and education, as well as thefts of safety, opportunity, and respect. They and their descendants were robbed of advantages that whites have built on over many generations and now take for granted because they are engrained in our habits, assumptions, and institutions. I am the beneficiary of advantages that cushion me from seeing and feeling how different are the experiences of people who live with inherited liabilities from four centuries of slavery and post-slavery restrictions. Although that legacy is largely unseen and unacknowledged by whites, it is the source of much of the inequality that afflicts the nation today. Even the Wisconsin farm that my grandparents owned (chapter 7) had, decades before their time, been bought or taken from Indians and, because it gave my grandparents a financial foothold, it made possible my father's college education. That makes me an indirect but real beneficiary, a fact that first dawned on me as I was writing this book.

As a high school senior, Michelle Singletary wanted to go to college. Financial aid through a federal Pell grant seemed to be the only way to get there. But her grandmother, "Big Mama," refused to sign the necessary forms. "I'm not signing anything. Ain't no white man going to take my house," Big Mama said. She had experienced firsthand how African Americans could be swindled, and her fear was reinforced by the experiences of others, including her grandparents who were slaves. Fear was closing the door on Singletary. Thankfully, a high school counselor suggested that she enter a competition sponsored by the *Baltimore Sun*, which resulted in a full four-year scholarship that included room and board and summer internships.[41] Singletary is now a prominent columnist for *The Washington Post*. The legacy of racial setbacks nearly blocked her chance to advance. But what about all the other children and young people with potential that is stifled because they grow up surrounded by memories of racial barriers and closed doors?

Our history of slavery laid the foundation for racial barriers that persist. African Americans emerged from slavery only to face deep layers of hostility and discrimination embedded in our laws and practices. Consider this crippling example: In blatant violation of constitutional guarantees our government locked the nation into a pattern of racial segregation. One way it did so was to erect public housing in separate neighborhoods for blacks and whites in the 1930s. Under the New Deal it also provided insurance on mortgages for home loans through the Federal Housing Authority (FHA), which enabled a great wave of white citizens to secure homeownership in all-white, middle-class neighborhoods throughout the nation after World War II, while making it virtually impossible for black Americans to buy FHA-insured homes there. The FHA (in collaboration with bankers and real estate agents) also set conditions that prevented African Americans from obtaining bank loans on the same favorable terms as whites. Neighborhood maps throughout the nation were "red-lined" in color to show where "inharmonious racial groups" lived in order to prevent black people from living in white neighborhoods or having easy access to mortgage loans. The government, banks, and real estate firms colluded to put desirable housing off-limits to black people, compelling them to live in segregated urban neighborhoods.

This made it easy for banks and real estate firms to impose contracts on black people that allowed their homes to be repossessed without the rightful owners being entitled to a dime of equity if they missed a single monthly payment. The Veterans Administration followed the racial practices of the FHA in denying guaranteed mortgages to black veterans, many of whom served in World War II. In New York and northern New Jersey, not even 100 of the 67,000 mortgages insured by the GI Bill supported home purchases by nonwhites.[42] In these and other ways the government—federal, state, and local—erected a nationwide pattern of segregation. This did more than temporarily separate blacks from whites because, unlike discrimination in hiring or voting that can be quickly reversed, housing patterns stay in place for decades and desegregate slowly, often with resistance that is hard to surmount. Past discrimination in housing perpetuates itself far into the future, with damaging impacts on jobs, income, education, safety, and much more, including net wealth, the backbone of which is homeownership for typical households. The Fair Housing Act of 1968 forced a change in government policy, although enforcement and practice has been uneven. Richard Rothstein documents this painful history in *The Color of Law: A Forgotten History of How Our Government Segregated America.*[43]

Few white Americans know this slice of history or realize how extensively it has set back African Americans today. Consider, for example, how clueless most of us (including this writer) have been regarding what a destructive impact monuments to the champions of the Confederacy have had on black Americans. For most northern whites they are just ornaments of history. To black and many southern white Americans, however, they marked the glorifying of a racist past and continuing white supremacy. That past was buttressed in the South by harsh Jim Crow laws, the Ku Klux Klan, and the lynching of several thousand innocent African Americans who were tortured, sometimes dismembered, then hanged in public display for white people to cheer and black people to tremble. Lynching terrorized them, like public crucifixions in the Roman Empire. These things prompted an exodus of millions of black Americans from the South to northern states, where they faced extensive poverty, "free" but second-class citizens economically and socially, subjected to "Jim Crow North." The Museum of African American History in the nation's capital, as well as the National Memorial for Peace and Justice (and its affiliated Legacy Museum on lynching) in Montgomery, Alabama, are helping to correct a sugar-coated version of history by starkly displaying the nation's brutal violation of human rights. The new Gateway Arch National Park in St. Louis represents a similar effort to face our history more honestly by asking how the West was stolen, as well as how it was won, and acknowledging the awful loss of life and culture by native Americans. Owning up to this history can help us heal the nation's wounds.

A striking essay in *The Atlantic* by Ta-Nehisi Coates describes outrageous thefts of property and housing that started for Clyde Ross, a black man, during his Mississippi childhood at age ten ("You can't have that horse. We want it," the white man said). Such thefts pursued him as an adult in a Chicago neighborhood, where the laws and real estate chicanery conspired to deny, overcharge, and repossess black homes. Ross and his family were cheated in ways that continue throughout the nation today, though in more subtle form, by means legal and illegal, all of it largely unfelt and unnoticed by those of us who have inherited a culture steeped in the advantages of white supremacy.[44] White supremacy? White people tend to bristle at the thought, because we don't feel and rarely notice white supremacy, so it seems false and accusatory.

For moral, social, and economic reasons compensatory efforts are long overdue, though reparations, at least in the form of direct payments, seem beyond reach.[45] How could payments begin to be adequate or sensibly applied? Pushing payment-reparations takes the focus away from things we really *can* do. It is not too much to ask people to learn about the harm done, and to observe constitutional rights. The government and private entities at every level should work for fair housing, assured under the "equal protection of the laws" clause, as well as other constitutional guarantees; and all of us can bend personal efforts toward closing achievement gaps. As *The Color of Law* reports, by the time the 1968 Fair Housing Law was passed, the higher cost of suburban housing had itself become a barrier to many African Americans who earlier could have built up financial assets, if they had had the same FHA and VA policies working for them as white people had. A house in formerly racially restricted Levittown, New York, that cost the initial white owner about $8,000 now sells for $350,000 and up, five times higher with inflation factored in. Levittown's black population now is about 1 percent.[46]

Because of such long-lasting setbacks Ta-Nehisi Coates argues that "closing the 'achievement gap' will do nothing to close the 'injury gap,'" noting that "black job applicants without criminal records enjoy roughly the same

---

How to Save Money and Lives

A Rand study has shown that each dollar invested in prison education programs, including vocational training, saves from 4 to 5 dollars in reincarceration costs. Inmates who participate are less likely to return to prison and more likely to find employment.[1] So the idea of turning prisons, to the extent possible, into schools, colleges, and vocational training institutes is not far-fetched.[2] Would that be unfair to struggling, law-abiding citizens who need and want but cannot afford specialized training? If so, it points to the wider need of access to such opportunities for everyone, another investment with promising social and economic returns. That applies to juveniles in particular, who often face deplorable treatment[3]—and deplorable results, according to studies that show a re-arrest rate of 70 to 80 percent within a year of release. By one estimate, 66 percent of incarcerated juveniles never return to school, which reduces their prospects in the labor market—all of this, according to a Rand analysis, at a cost often ten times that of studying at a good state university.[4]

The situation cries out for preventive action to give disadvantaged young people of *any* race a hope-filled alternative to drugs and crime. When that fails, restorative justice is in most cases far more effective and less costly than punishment focused on retribution.

chance of getting hired as white applicants *with* criminal records."[47] He makes a telling point. But contrary to Coates, I think closing the achievement gap would help close the injury gap—including the example he cites. In any case, it is the least we should do, admittedly small compared to the injury inflicted, but it would be a big step forward. Closing or even narrowing most of the achievement gap would be progress that could bring new strength and health to our entire nation.

How can we make up for losses inflicted, and how can we do so in ways that are racially responsive but not racially exclusive? A weakness of race-specific policies, sociologist William Julius Wilson argues, is that "minority members from the more advantaged families profit disproportionately." The emphasis, he says, should shift to those who are truly disadvantaged in their life chances, a shift that "would not only help the white poor, but would also address more effectively the problems of the minority poor."[48]

A painful example (to extend the one cited by Coates) is our massive criminal justice system,[49] too focused on jailing and imprisoning offenders instead of helping them become useful citizens.[50] The incarceration of almost a million mostly young black men, many of them for nonviolent offenses, prevents marriages, disrupts families and neighborhoods, and robs children of a father, a loss that for boys is especially devastating. Robert Putnam points to studies showing that "more than half of all black children born to less educated parents in 1990 experienced parental imprisonment." He reports that having a dad in prison is "one of the most common themes in the lives of poor kids."[51] This in no way diminishes the responsibility of each person, young and old, on both sides of the racial divide and on both sides of the prison bars. We have been tough on crime but not smart on crime. The policy has backfired, and all of us are paying, socially and economically, for the cost of our collective irresponsibility.

Racial Perspectives

In *The American Dilemma* (1944), Swedish Nobel Prize economist Gunnar Myrdal's groundbreaking study of racial oppression in the United States, he observed this self-serving logic: "The negro is judged to be fundamentally incorrigible and he is, therefore, kept in a slum existence which, in its turn, leaves the imprint upon his body and soul which makes it natural for the white man to believe in his inferiority." Myrdal quotes George Bernard

Shaw's comment that our nation "makes the negro clean its boots and then proves the moral and physical inferiority of the negro by the fact that he is a shoeblack."[52] More than four decades later William Julius Wilson noticed the same circular argument in conservative colleagues who found the behavior of the underclass emerging from deficient cultural values rather than restricted opportunities.[53]

What makes racial understanding difficult is that all of us see reality through the lens of our own personal experience. It is instinctively hard for any of us, with the best of intentions, to shake habits and assumptions that are convenient, and put ourselves in the shoes of others. That is especially difficult if we are part of the dominant culture that is considered normative, without realizing how different and frustrating it is for those who live on the receiving end of injustices. In *America's Original Sin* Jim Wallis, founder and leader of Sojourners, writes, "We want to offer rights generously to others, but we don't see the problems rooted in our own racial identity. It becomes more about how we help people who are black and brown than how we confront our own white racial privilege"[54]—a preference for charity over justice.

Sharply different racial experiences complicate that difficulty for both black and white people. Each of us instinctively feels that others should accommodate to our own habits and experience. Both love and justice require us to recognize in each other a common human dignity—a God-given endowment, if the Declaration of Independence has it right.[55] We need to do this person-to-person but also by seeing ways in which racial advantages and disadvantages are so deeply imbedded in our culture—our policies, laws, institutions, and in our daily habits—that we perpetuate them unaware. Symphony orchestras assumed natural male musical superiority until "blind" auditions opened the way to the hiring of many more women.[56] Negative racial and gender assumptions lead to discrimination in hiring that punishes women and African Americans with reduced opportunities and lower salaries. This pushes many into hunger and poverty.[57] It also demonstrates the need for laws, institutions, and practices that encourage and often compel us to rise above our assumptions.

The national debate over immigration that has been raging also reflects a widespread inclination to regard those who are "different" as inferiors and treat them as such. This impulse runs through the nation's history, starting with the original Americans whose lands we freely and forcibly occupied (when *we* were the immigrants), and continued in our treatment of many ethnic and religious minorities who came to these shores over the years. Perhaps it is an impulse of people everywhere. During my boyhood in Oregon, a few weeks after the Pearl Harbor attack destroyed much of the US fleet, all American citizens of Japanese origin who lived on the West Coast were rounded up and shipped to prison camps ("internment camps") by executive order of President Roosevelt. Unfounded fear led to a shameful breach of human rights, but it was popular, and those who spoke against it, my father among them, were openly criticized.[58]

By 2018 immigrants, most of them of Hispanic origin and many without legal documentation, faced a spike in hostility. Many feared family breakup and life-threatening deportations. Congress had earlier failed to pass an immigration reform bill that would have restricted the flow of immigrants but also provided acceptable steps toward citizenship for those who qualify. The Senate did pass such a bill in 2013, a rare bipartisan achievement; but the House leaders refused to let the House vote on it because they were cowed by a minority of obstructionists who knew it would pass, if brought to a vote. This failure enabled Donald Trump to seize the issue in the 2016 presidential race with anti-Mexican, anti-Muslim, and anti-immigration appeals and ride them into the White House.

Racial and ethnic as well as gender inequalities are among the most deeply rooted forms of the inequalities that inhabit hunger and poverty. But charity is not a sufficient answer to any of them. The role of government in establishing justice is essential, and justice must be put into practice, embedded in our culture and in our lives. If we have thought only of helping others through private charity, it is hard for us to realize the immense good that public justice can do in liberating people from the scourges of discrimination and poverty. As a result, we are slow to see the importance of speaking up as citizens in seeking change. So we remain silent.

A few days before I wrote this, a friend of mine, Michael Smith, told me that he volunteers each week tutoring kids who are lagging in school. He knows he is offering much-needed help; but, he says, "We can't tutor our way out of poverty." Charity is not enough. But if we have the heart to see this, and if we truly care about people who bear the brunt of injustice, we should stand with them as citizen advocates.

Tutor, by all means. But not as a substitute for justice.

9

Family Erosion

Poor Americans get a new, postmodern marriage culture that works for the rich but not for them.

—R. R. Reno[1]

The inequalities that undermine our national life are intertwined with the erosion of family life, which qualifies for special attention in this book because hunger and poverty contribute to family erosion, and family erosion contributes to hunger and poverty.

The family is far more than an economic unit. Its social purpose and importance extend way beyond its impact on income levels.[2] Family erosion—the loss of family cohesion—touches a large complex of factors (mostly beyond the scope of this book) that have affected the way families function and are structured. Things that contribute to the complexity of family life include evolving gender roles and gender expectations at home and in the workplace, changes in the economy, and the impact on families of divorce or single parenting. On another level, individualism—or circumstances—may drive family members to become so engaged in separate pursuits that they spend little time conversing, playing, or working together. Fragmentation may lead to loneliness, aimlessness, or behavioral problems.

The purpose of this chapter is not to pass judgment on anyone's family circumstances, such as single parenting, but to see the special challenges that confront families living in or near poverty and consider the nation's response. Family erosion is by no means limited to low-income families, but affluent families more readily find ways to surmount or hide it. Poverty, however, exposes its effects with special severity, a point underscored by R. R. Reno in the quotation below the title of this chapter.

The signs of family erosion are often painfully evident in unfamiliar places. Listen to Jeanne Bishop, a public defense attorney in Chicago, describing a day in the courthouse lockup, a small, stuffy cell crammed with teenagers charged with burglaries. As she interviews them, a pattern emerges: perilous childhoods, neglect, and abandonment. Why, she asks one young man, were he and his siblings taken away from their birth home? "My mom chose drugs over us," he replies. Most of the others in the lockup lived with overburdened relatives or in places characterized by poverty and lack of responsible, caring adults. All were in school, often in sports, and none had a criminal background: all promising young men. Why were they being accused of stealing? One points to his tattered clothes. Another, head dropped, tells how his aunt complained bitterly that he was costing her too much and wanted him to help with expenses. Others also speak of scarcity and neglect, sometimes abuse. In the courtroom the judge sets bonds too high for any of them to post. That means jail. "After the hearing," she said, "I heard wailing from the lockup. I went to check, and saw this sight: a cell full of teenaged boys, sobbing and wiping away tears."[3]

What lies behind this heart-wrenching scene? An inner emptiness? Fear and uncertainty? A sense of despair? An aching to be loved and belong? The need for an anchor and guidance? Physical deprivation? Perhaps all of these, tied to a perception of self as born into a family that is on the losing side of life.

Family dysfunction and poverty are two sides to a coin that seems to inspire one-sided thinking. Political orthodoxies are prone to find poverty's cause and its solution either in external circumstances or in personal behavior. Historian James MacGregor Burns notes that the 1960s War on Poverty spurred those two opposing "spearhead" strategies—each with "the notion that some single solution could break through the poverty gridlock"—when in fact "both strategies were necessary."[4] Let's agree on both strategies, for unless we can see deprivation as a cause of family erosion, and the erosion of family life as contributing to hunger and poverty, our chances of taking effective action are limited. But if we combine insights, the prospect of gaining enough bipartisan support for dealing with both hunger and poverty is within reach.

Moynihan Revisited

In 1965 Daniel Patrick Moynihan, prominent then as a sociologist and later as a US senator, was accused of blaming victims after he reported an alarming 23.6 percent rate of children born to unmarried black women, compared to a 3 percent birthrate of children born to unmarried white women. The rising trend in urban ghettos of collapsing black family structure, he warned, would mean that "the cycle of poverty and disadvantage will continue to repeat itself."[5]

Moynihan was more prophetic than he realized. By 2010 unmarried women accounted for more than 41 percent of *all* US births. For white women those births, at 36 percent, far exceeded the 1965 rate for black women that so alarmed Moynihan. The rate of births for unmarried black women had risen to 72 percent, and the number of children being raised in two-parent families was 50 percent for black children and 81 percent for white children.[6] It used to be death that accounted for most single-parent American families; more recently it was divorce, but now unwed births are the most common entry point for single parenthood.[7]

Single parenthood is a feature of a larger reality that Moynihan feared: "an increasingly disorganized and disadvantaged lower class group." Moynihan saw this happening in low-income black families, but today it cuts across racial lines. Americans in large numbers are forgoing marriage, though not parenthood. Between 1960 and 2010 the percentage of adults between the ages of twenty-five and thirty-four who had never married soared from 12 to 47 percent.[8] We can add nonmarriage—especially for young, low-income adults—as an inequality that impacts other inequalities.

Drifting into Parenthood

Economic independence for women, along with the sexual revolution, has lifted much of the social stigma from becoming a single mother. Especially in low-income neighborhoods, unmarried couples may cohabit for intimacy and perhaps want a child for love and fulfillment, although they usually drift into childbearing rather than plan for it.[1] They often want to marry, but not necessarily this partner or "not yet." Beyond companionship women seek a man who is faithful and dependably kind, willing to share home and parenting responsibilities, and who adds financial security. Men usually consider a job with an adequate salary a prerequisite for marriage. As a result, joblessness and low wages affect the marriage prospects of black and Hispanic men disproportionately. According to the Pew Research Center, a far higher percentage of African Americans and Latinos than whites say that to be ready for marriage a man must be able to support a family,[2] perhaps because they have seen how marital hardships accompany poverty.

Retreat from marriage reflects not only economic, but educational and social differences. Of births to women with no high school diploma 67 percent occur out of wedlock, while only 9 percent of births occur out of wedlock among college-educated women.[9] Unintended birthrates are more than six times higher for young unmarried women below the poverty line than for affluent young unmarried women.[10] But for women in poverty, children are often the one bright spot in otherwise depressing or troubled lives.[11]

The statistical penalty for not marrying is strikingly clear. Single-parent families in 2013 had a poverty rate of 39.6 percent, five times the 7.6 percent rate for two-parent families.[12] One study concludes that "marriage is a better predictor of family income than is education, race, or ethnicity, a new class divide."[13] But if those not marrying had done so, would they all have enjoyed the same rate of success as those who did? Not likely. However, the challenges children in one-parent families face are so daunting that it makes sense to encourage and strengthen marriages as well as two-parent families. But because single parenting is widespread, undergirding single-parent families is also a matter of great importance.

The impact of growing up in poverty is not the same for both genders. Young women face a greater possibility of becoming unmarried mothers. Young men face more difficult employment prospects and lower educational outcomes than young women who are poor, especially if they grow up in a fatherless home. In a Fathers' Day speech President Obama said, "Children who grow up without a father are five times more likely to live in poverty and commit crime; nine times more likely to drop out of schools and 20 times more likely to end up in prison"[14]—a reminder that preventive action is cheaper and wiser than disaster assistance.

Two decades after Moynihan's report sociologist William Julius Wilson wrote that hostile reaction to it frightened liberal scholars, white and black, from research that might be construed as blaming the victims. The reaction of those scholars was neither wise nor racially innocent. Wilson said it left the study of inner-city social dislocations to conservative analysts who imposed their own bias on the problem, a bias that has heavily influenced public perception of an underclass with character flaws who have only themselves to blame for their place in society.[15] Regarding this perception, Martin Luther King Jr. pointed to the legacy of slavery and segregation. "No one in all history had to fight against so many psychological and physical horrors to have a family life," he said. "Our children and our families are maimed a little every day of their lives."[16]

Moynihan's Second Insight: Jobs and Income

By neglecting to pursue the evidence of growing disarray among black families, policymakers missed a rare opportunity to advance another key insight of Moynihan: the critical need for jobs. Moynihan reported that from 1951 to 1963 unemployment for black males was trending upward—as was the number of black women separated from their husbands. There were ups and downs within that trend, he said, but each time, increased black unemployment peaked a year ahead of an increase of men separated from their families, while each rise in employment led to stronger and more stable black families. "Work is precisely the one thing the Negro family head has not received over the past generation," wrote Moynihan. Using italics for emphasis, he added, "The fundamental, overwhelming fact is that *Negro unemployment,* with the exception of a few years during World War II and the Korean War, *has continued at disaster levels for 35 years.*"[17] The great need, Moynihan argued, was jobs at a decent wage, especially for black men. When jobs became more plentiful, though never adequately so, "the Negro family became stronger and more stable. As jobs became increasingly difficult to find, the stability of the family became more and more difficult to maintain."[18] As further indication that jobs, not values, were the key factor, Moynihan wrote that "the middle class Negro family puts a higher premium on family stability and the conserving of family resources than does the white middle class family."[19]

Moynihan pointed out that the American wage system in 1965 provided good incomes for individuals, but rarely adjusted to ensure that *family* needs were met. This, he said, was in contrast "almost without exception" to other industrial democracies that supplemented a worker's income to provide for the extra expenses of those with families.[20] Philip Alston's stinging 2018 report to the UN Human Rights Council[21] (chapter 2 above) shows that Moynihan's assessment still stands: the United States lags well behind other wealthy countries when it comes to assisting workers and strengthening families, a fact of significance about which the public seems almost totally unaware.

A strong case can be made that the gravest flaw in the War on Poverty and in welfare policies that preceded and followed it since then was that, unlike Roosevelt's New Deal programs, they failed to focus on creating jobs.[22] That failure generated dependency, to be sure, though not because people were lazy. Quite the opposite. It was a dependency caused mainly by limited job opportunities for people who were desperate for work, for food, and for gaining self-respect by making an honorable living and supporting a family. The old AFDC welfare program (Aid to Families with Dependent Children) and other assistance programs lifted some of our most impoverished citizens to a less punishing level of poverty. But those programs made women with children less dependent upon men for support. Unemployed men became a liability, an especially severe problem for black men who were locked in the inner city and often locked out of jobs, including many municipal and high-skill trade union positions. Marriage rates declined, while the rate of unwed births began to rise. President Reagan could tell us, "Many families are eligible for substantially higher benefits when the father is not present. What must it do to a man to know that his own children will be better off if he is never legally recognized as their father?"[23] Indeed.

The solution, however, is not to deny households with children a minimum decent level of cash support or to cut food assistance as a purported incentive to work. The solution is to prepare people for employment and to generate opportunities and rewards for work. In failing to do that, we strip an important part of life from a lot of people, especially those who have already taken a beating from history, which simply perpetuates poverty and racial injustice. With poor preparation for jobs and too few jobs available, people have been made to feel useless and rejected, trapped in a culture of despair. No wonder many turn to alcohol, drugs, crime, and violence. No wonder that children who grow up in this environment tend to perpetuate it. This happens to white as well as black people, but African Americans, especially young men, experience joblessness at a much higher rate and with more punishing consequences than do most white Americans.

An editorial in *The New York Times*, noting that young black men living in segregated, hollowed-out urban neighborhoods suffer exceptionally high rates of joblessness, cites the "catastrophic dimensions" of this situation in the city of Chicago, "where nearly half of all 20- to 24-year-old black men were neither employed nor enrolled in school in 2014." For black teenagers in Chicago, ages sixteen to nineteen, almost 90 percent had no work in 2014. It doesn't stretch the imagination to connect Chicago's high rate of joblessness to family instability and acts of violence, a connection that the *Times* explicitly underscores.[24]

The critical need for jobs to break this cycle was recognized by civil rights leaders who led the "March on Washington for Jobs and Freedom" on August 28, 1963. Martin Luther King Jr. would often say, "The Negro is not seeking charity. He does not want to languish on welfare rolls any more than the next man.ˮ[25] However, because of the urgency at that moment for securing civil rights, freedom overshadowed jobs, as it did in Martin Luther King Jr.'s riveting "I Have a Dream" speech. With this emphasis on freedom, the need for jobs never evoked the same breadth of support and intensity as did desegregation and voting rights. Later the Moynihan report's description of disintegrating black families attracted so much controversy that its strong endorsement of the need for jobs was largely ignored. Although an influential nucleus within the churches played a strong role in helping to secure enactment of civil rights laws, that nucleus did not have the same fire in its belly to promote employment for poor people, an issue that seemed less crucial and more "political." As a result, the churches and much of the general public, focusing mainly on charity and nonstructural solutions to hunger and poverty, failed to seize an opportunity to promote job creation, which might have reduced hunger and poverty as well as family disintegration and racial frustration.[26]

Welfare

With too few jobs for the unemployed poor, the nation was left with the fallback of cash-assistance welfare. By the early 1990s the public, including welfare recipients, had turned sour on welfare. Clinton's promise in the 1992 presidential campaign "to end welfare as we know it" helped him reach the White House. In his first major address to a joint session of Congress Clinton said he wanted to offer people on welfare the education, training, and child- and healthcare they needed to get back on their feet, but after a couple of years or so they would have to work "in private business if possible, in public service if necessary."[27] But failure to act promptly on that promise enabled Republicans to seize the issue, like a recovered fumble, and run with it toward gaining majority control of both Houses of Congress in 1995 by promising to replace welfare with "workfare."

As a result, in 1996 AFDC welfare assistance was replaced with Temporary Assistance for Needy Families (TANF).[28] Congress handed the implementation of TANF to the states, along with federal funding and flexibility in how the states would comply with its main goals: (1) to provide for needy families with children; (2) to move parents from welfare to work; (3) to reduce the number of unwed pregnancies and promote two-parent families; and—I am adding an unwritten but overarching goal—(4) to reduce the cost of the program.

The idea of moving people from welfare to work and out of poverty is a powerful idea, but TANF fell woefully short. Peter Germanis, a social scientist with impeccable conservative credentials, who helped craft Reagan's 1986 never-enacted welfare reform proposal, considers TANF "an unprecedented failure." It is "a safety-net with massive holes," he writes, and "its welfare-to-work programs reach only a tiny fraction of families eligible for

TANF's Failure

Reducing the welfare caseload and saving money overshadowed other TANF goals in state after state. Many families did move from welfare to work the first few years of TANF. However, shrinking caseloads, rising employment, and falling poverty began three years prior to TANF because of the economic surge of the 1990s (as well as job initiatives already under way in some states). These trends continued for several years after TANF's enactment, but before its work requirements could have had much impact. As Germanis observes, "states have pushed many eligible families off the rolls so they are not receiving assistance. The bottom line is that states are simply not investing in work programs for low-income families with children."[1]

When the economy slid into a mild recession in 2001, jobs were lost. A few years later the Great Recession caused unemployment to soar; but instead of stepping up assistance TANF moved in the opposite direction. As poverty increased, the value of block grants declined by 30 percent.[2] AFDC had assisted more than 8 million children in 1996, but in 2014 TANF helped fewer than 3 million children—just 4 percent of all US children and only 19 percent of children in poverty.[3] By 2014 the number of children on cash assistance had plummeted by two-thirds; yet the number of Americans below the poverty line increased by almost 10 million and, compared to their numbers in 1996 when TANF was enacted, more than 10 million additional Americans had become food-insecure.[4] There was no bounceback from the recovery for them, and few jobs.

A triumph? No doubt for some families it was. But what about the surge in households with children in poverty who no longer receive cash assistance? Germanis cites Wisconsin, heralded as a model of TANF's success. It had 83,000 poor families with children in 1997 when TANF began. That number rose to 114,000 in 2012. The state's average level of assistance per poor family with children fell by half from $5,637 to $2,865. Almost all (96 percent) of Wisconsin's families with children in poverty received AFDC assistance in the mid-1990s, but only 24 percent got TANF assistance in 2012.[5]

cash assistance." The root cause of TANF's problems, he says, is the block grants to the states, that "divert the funds away from core welfare reform purposes to fill state budget holes."[29]

When Work Disappears

William Julius Wilson raises the question of why crime, violence, and other evidence of dysfunctional families surged in inner-city ghettos long after civil rights gains had eliminated some of the worst features of racial discrimination. His answer is that *current* discrimination, a big enough handicap, is not nearly as destructive as the impact of *past* discrimination, which left in place economic structures that would persist even if racial prejudice disappeared. After centuries of oppression had set African Americans back, economic transformations came along to cut jobs and wages. The decline of manufacturing left a growing number of inner-city residents, especially young black men, without jobs or work experience. Emerging new jobs usually required the kind of education most of them lacked. As middle- and higher-income African Americans moved to safer neighborhoods, the inner city was left with a dwindling number of positive role models and a higher concentration of people unable to relocate, which left them more isolated socially and economically than before the War on Poverty and the civil rights victories.[30] Wilson's *When Work Disappears* maintains that joblessness, which shrank the pool of marriageable men, was more directly responsible than social and cultural trends for disproportionately high rates of crime, substance abuse, teen pregnancy, and welfare dependency. He cites a study that showed a much higher rate of violent behavior among black than among white males from adolescence to late twenties, but when the study compared only *employed* black and white males there was no substantial difference.[31]

The concentration of poverty in distinct neighborhoods brought other destructive outcomes as well. Social institutions such as schools, churches, stores, and community associations struggled, but often did not survive. Some churches stayed to serve changing neighborhoods, but often they followed members who had fled to the suburbs or just folded.

Poverty prevailed and hope faded.

The connection between joblessness and the erosion of families seems clear. The liabilities of joblessness include much more than the loss of income. Wilson writes, "Regular employment provides the anchor for the spatial and temporal aspects of daily life. It determines where you are going to be and when you are going to be there. In the absence of regular employment, life, including family life, becomes less coherent."[32]

Alarm Ringers

Two prominent sociologists who differ on policy reflect a remarkable degree of agreement in their analysis of family erosion and our growing class disparities.

Charles Murray, a libertarian political scientist with the American Enterprise Institute, who opposes government welfare programs, describes us as a nation *Coming Apart*.[33] His book features a real and a fictional Belmont (a Boston suburb) where the well-educated and affluent live, and a real and a fictional Fishtown (a Philadelphia neighborhood) for those who are neither. Belmont and Fishtown represent contrasting cultures that cut across racial lines on matters such as unmarried parenthood, industriousness, and religion. America, he says, is deeply divided between prosperous and poor people, who live apart from each other and seldom interact. The division is growing and eroding a sense of shared destiny, making it hard to agree on policies that might bring us together.[34]

There's nothing new about the existence of classes, but what is new about our current class divisions, Murray says, is that the classes diverge on core behaviors and values that previously had been widely accepted across class lines. He says that having a job, even a low-paying job, and supporting a family once made a man proud and gave him status, but now it does not.[35]

Another development he sees is increased separation by class, as prosperous Americans (the top 5 percent) choose to live in upscale neighborhoods of like-minded people. Murray sees them as increasingly isolated and growing more ignorant about the country over which they wield great influence. Newton, Iowa, where Murray grew up, was the home of the Maytag washing machine company. Fred Maytag II lived in Newton in a nice but not extravagant house, and in his neighborhood so did other professionals, white-collar workers, and factory workers. Forty years later the new company president had moved to an affluent section of Des Moines, thirty-six miles away, and other senior executives followed suit. Executives who stayed in Newton lived in upscale housing developments beyond the financial reach of factory workers and teachers. Fewer of them participated in civic activities, their spouses were less active in school and church affairs, and their children were less likely to attend Newton's public schools.[36]

Robert Putnam, in *Bowling Alone*, documented the unraveling of community life, a national trend of people doing alone things they used to do with others. Lack of social ties ("social capital") makes it hard for disadvantaged youth in particular to find their way forward.[37] It is therefore bad news that social networks have eroded in four broad areas of life (family life, workplace, religion, and community) according to a study by the congressional Joint Economic Committee.[38]

In Putnam's latest book, *Our Kids*, he tells how social capital and its loss affected his hometown, Port Clinton, Ohio, where he graduated from high school in 1959.[39] There in the 1950s people of different backgrounds lived near one another, went to school together, and looked out for each other. The kids in town, he says, were "our kids." Few adults in Port Clinton had gone to college, but half of his high school classmates have done well professionally, married, and had children and grandchildren who have done the same. Other classmates found local jobs and started families. Most of his classmates experienced "astonishing upward mobility," advancing beyond their parents in education and income. A lot of social capital was being shared.

The children of classmates who did not go to college, however, experienced no advance. The escalator, Putnam said, "suddenly halted when our own children stepped on." And many of *their* children did even less well. He now sees that "an economic, social, and cultural whirlwind was gathering force nationally that would radically transform the chances of our children and grandchildren." The manufacturing foundation of Port Clinton's prosperity began to sink, and along with it so did the working class. Factories moved or shut down, wages fell, and unemployment rose. Social norms eroded, delinquency rates, divorces, and unwed births soared. Port Clinton became a struggling town with a child poverty rate of nearly 40 percent in 2013, and people in Port Clinton no longer think of all the kids in town as "our" kids.

For about twenty miles both east and west of Port Clinton, along the shoreline of Lake Erie, an entirely different change has taken place. People of wealth discovered the beauty and charms of beaches that had previously been available to the folks in town. Now gated communities with mansions, luxury condos, golf courses, and yachts cordon off the lake from trailer parks inland. People in these communities and residents of Port Clinton are effectively separated from each other, with little chance of social capital being shared and mutual enrichment occurring.

Port Clinton exemplifies the emergence of the new segregation that Murray and others have documented: a concentration of like-minded people by class, and often by race as well—the preferred choice of people with means, while those without means usually have no alternative. High-poverty neighborhoods within ten miles of the nation's fifty-one largest cities tripled between 1970 and 2010,[40] and by 2010 there were almost as many such neighborhoods in the suburbs as in the central city,[41] although the most intensely concentrated poverty neighborhoods (with 40 percent or more poor) remain in cities. The number of people living in high-poverty neighborhoods doubled between 2000 and 2014, an alarming trend because where you grow up is a strong indication of your chances to prosper.[42] A high-poverty neighborhood imposes special liabilities on residents. In such areas family erosion is most concentrated, and parents who are cohabiting when a baby arrives have separated half the time before their child turns five.[43] Under these conditions children are apt to grow up in an unstructured atmosphere, underachieve in school, and have petty or serious behavioral problems that get passed on to the next generation and beyond. Family erosion begins to be seen as a normal, expected feature of life and therefore readily replicated. Norms, no longer normal, have eroded along with family life.

Because Americans live increasingly in like-minded neighborhoods and associate with like-minded people, it is easy for most of us to feel comfortable in our distance from Port Clinton types. Out of sight, out of mind, as they say. So we may dismiss poverty and family dysfunction as "their" problem. Such detachment puts the future of all of us in jeopardy. Consider that already half of our population under the age of ten are minority children, and by 2020 half under the age of eighteen will be, then by 2027 half under age twenty-nine, and by 2033 half under age thirty-nine. They now disproportionately face obstacles to their achievement in life, but they are ones on whom our economy, our country, and our democracy increasingly depend.[44] The Port Clinton problem is our problem too. Individualism is not a sufficient response.

Home, School, and Jobs

Children and adolescents need a home that serves as a refuge in the face of bewildering attractions and dangers. They need strong parental love and affirmation, ample time in family conversation and parental examples about life's purpose, service for others, respect for human dignity including self-respect and that of the opposite gender, the capacity to forgive and be forgiven, the courage to withstand peer pressure, and the determination to persevere in achieving goals. But the government is not designed to do these things. It takes committed parents to build families and communities in which children can thrive. If it is a religious home, it takes the faith of parents to transmit that faith to their children and reflect it authentically in their own parental lives. For many, faith is the anchor that holds them steady in the face of surrounding storms.

Education plays an essential part in preparing children for opportunities in life, so the quality of schooling makes a difference. However, public debate usually assumes that education is largely a *schools* problem (curriculum, facilities, teachers, administrators), which ignores the fact that cultural factors (home-life, reading, television, peer pressure, neighborhood safety) matter more. Most obstacles faced by kids are not caused by schools. Robert Putnam finds that what happens before children start school and what happens outside of school matters even more than what happens in school—and impacts what happens (or doesn't happen) there as well.[45]

Consider that:

- 48 percent of children from low-income families are not ready for school by age five and face a fifteen-month learning gap when compared to children from more affluent families. The gap tends to widen over the years and is generally predictive of later outcomes.[46]
- Children of highly educated parents hear an average of 2,153 words per hour, compared to an average of 616 words that children from a welfare family hear. Quality time, quality talk, and quality reading with kids are especially difficult for single parents who work, feel overwhelmed, and send stressed children to school.[47]
- Stressed parents are harsher and less attentive to their children. Putnam invokes a body of research that shows this. In his words, "Economic stress, in particular, disrupts family relations, fosters withdrawn and inconsistent parenting, and directly increases chronic stress among children."[48]
- An estimated 15 million children face unsupervised time after school before a parent returns home from work.[49]

After reading Putnam's conclusion about outside-of-school influence, I was surprised to encounter a strikingly similar one in *Equality of Educational*

Opportunity, a monumental study mandated by the Civil Rights Act of 1964 (called the Coleman report after its chief author, James Coleman). This two-volume report was released in 1966 by the Johnson administration during the July 4th weekend to attract as little attention as possible, exactly one year after release of the Moynihan report, and timed for the same reason: disturbing evidence. In this case it challenged the conventional assumption that schools could overcome cultural handicaps. The evidence pointed to environmental factors outside of the school—especially the family—as far more influential than the school itself in determining students' educational outcome. Social influences, such as the composition of the student body, showed that racial integration often helped narrow inequalities. School facilities and curriculum, however, failed to account for much gain in equality, although the influence of teachers mattered more than any other single school factor. But "a strong effect of schools that is independent of the child's immediate social environment . . . is not present in American schools," the report concluded.

> One implication stands out above all: That schools bring little influence to bear on a child's achievement that is independent of his background and general social context; and that this very lack of an independent effect means that the inequalities imposed on children by their home, neighborhood, and peer environment are carried along to become the inequalities with which they confront adult life at the end of school.[50]

Murray's and Putnam's analyses, Moynihan's report, and the Coleman report all concur in seeing the family and the social environment of people as dominant influences. That led Moynihan to urge, above all, the creation of jobs with adequate wages. Coleman's report made no recommendations, but its assessment of the problem is consistent with the argument that Moynihan and Wilson make in pointing to jobs that lift people out of poverty as a more significant remedy than better schools.

Today inadequate wages are more widespread than lack of available jobs, and the problem reaches more extensively across racial lines. Inadequate wages have ignited much of the frustration of middle- and working-class "forgotten Americans" interviewed by Isabel Sawhill. They told her they are far more concerned about their low pay and poor benefits than they are about climate change, immigration, or even health care. She concludes: "Without a robust effort to reskill America and create decently-paid jobs, we are doomed to become a second-class society," where lack of education and training, opioids, and weak family ties destroy entire communities and undermine people's faith in government.[51]

For Wilson the disappearance of work is the central problem, and high neighborhood joblessness more devastating than high neighborhood poverty. Such neighborhoods leave black adults significantly isolated from mainstream individuals and families, with jobless black females even more isolated than black males. Not surprisingly, parents who live in those neighborhoods have a much harder time guiding and controlling the behavior of their adolescent children.[52]

Wilson provides evidence that joblessness was at the core of collapsing black (and by extension also white) underclass families. Change the jobs picture—change the economic outlook for young black men in particular—he contends, then behavior will also change. He writes:

Deaths of Despair?

Family erosion is almost certainly a factor in the startling rise of "diseases of despair" that precipitate early deaths from drug overdoses among white (and to a lesser extent black or Hispanic) Americans, most frequent among young to middle-aged men with a high school degree or less. These alarming deaths have led to a decline in US life expectancy, a decline not seen in any other major developed nation. In 2015 deaths from opioid overdoses alone surpassed gun homicides for the first time, driven in part by a surge in the use of prescription painkillers. Abuse of other drugs and alcohol contributed to additional deaths, as did an increase in the suicides of white women. One-third (seventeen) of the states had more white deaths than births.[1] In 2016 deaths from drug overdoses of all kinds surged by another 21 percent, and again by 10 percent in 2017, killing more than 70,000 Americans that year. Suicides have also escalated, especially in rural counties, since 1999.[2]

Behind these deaths are the heart-rending accounts of the toll it has taken on kids, moms, dads, families, and communities. Tom Vilsack, Agriculture Secretary in the Obama administration, knows this as the child of an alcoholic and prescription-drug-addicted mother who became suicidal. "When I was a kid, I judged my mom," he said. "I thought she could just decide tomorrow to stop doing what she was doing. I had no idea it was a disease. I do now." He was fortunate enough to see her recover and become a steady, sober parent. He also knows how the opioid crisis has hit rural America with special severity.[3]

If underclass blacks have limited aspirations or fail to plan for the future, it is not ultimately the product of different cultural norms but the consequence of restricted opportunities, a bleak future, and feelings of resignation resulting from bitter personal experiences. . . . As economic and social opportunities change . . . both the patterns of behavior and the norms eventually undergo change.[53]

The converse also applies: If we leave joblessness in place, destructive behavior is sure to continue.

A Plan of Action

US public opinion is split about whether hunger and poverty are more attributable to structural inequalities or dysfunctional behavior. Which comes first? Which is more causal? For African Americans brutality began centuries ago, and its lingering impact has resulted in disproportionate joblessness and low-wage poverty. This reality (along with Myrdal's and Moynihan's research) lends credibility to Wilson's assessment. However, it is more convenient to assign blame to the personal shortcomings of others than to injustices for which we are partly responsible. Granting ourselves absolution is a constant temptation.

But rather than arguing about how the fire started, let's agree to put it out. We could tackle both structural inequalities *and* behavior rather than address only one or the other. Doing so could bring liberals and conservatives together for an effective plan of action.

Dropping out of school, having no job, and having children out of wedlock are three key indicators of future poverty and related problems. So several specialists have proposed a "success sequence" that puts (1) education, (2) job, (3) marriage, and (4) children as goals to be achieved *in that order*. Following that sequence multiplies the odds for having a stable middle-income family.[54] Ron Haskins and Isabel Sawhill maintain that if people graduate from high school, work full time, and wait until after age twenty-one to marry and have children, "only 2 percent would be poor."[55] Sounds easy, until you begin thinking about the obstacles that prevent so many young people from climbing those steps.

The government cannot begin to give children the love and guidance they need from parents. Nor can it replace "the village" of people caring for one another. The government, however, could reform the economy in ways that would help strengthen families, while addressing the nation's damaging inequalities—the focus of chapter 11. The fact that European countries do much better than the United States to include struggling children and families in their nations' social and economic life highlights an American weakness. In 2012 our country spent 19 percent of its economy (GDP) on social services for safety-net programs such as Social Security, Medicare, and SNAP. Denmark spent 30 percent, Germany 26 percent, Sweden 28 percent. Americans stand largely alone in having a sharply individualistic view of their life and being less willing to help one another through the government.[56] Would doing more to give families a boost be too costly? Far less costly than continuing to neglect our most valuable resource: people.

What about cultivating more responsible behavior—habits of the heart and mind that serve everyone's good? Acceptable norms need to be held high and celebrated. But character formation can be especially difficult for people—young people in particular—if they cannot see it as a way toward a more positive future. If cohesive families and a cohesive nation depend upon improving personal conduct on a large scale, it is hard to envision success against prevailing cultural and economic tides. However, if steps toward such change were to build on improved circumstances, such as good job opportunities that give people hope, the combination could be powerful.

Recognizing family erosion as a national crisis, a campaign for building cohesive families makes sense—if it is combined with action to end hunger and greatly reduce poverty and joblessness. Because training children and shaping habits of character are not what government does best, a campaign for cohesive families should enlist all sectors of society, public as well as private, and encompass a wide coalition of entities: businesses, civic organizations, unions, charities, religious groups, the media, and schools, with government encouragement as needed. A White House conference might be a launching or promoting event for a national campaign; but the campaign would be broadly civic, not primarily government led, and promoted in a great variety of ways. Government's leadership is mainly needed for attacking the hunger, poverty, and joblessness that contribute so heavily to family erosion.

The economic starting point plays a part in forecasting a child's outcome as an adult. Parental love, wise discipline, and a sense of purpose arguably matter even more in preparing children for adulthood. The path forward requires all of us working together on the nation's interlocking inequalities of income, wealth, opportunity, race, and family cohesion. Those inequalities feed on one another, so they beg to be addressed simultaneously through government leadership as well as individual and private-sector efforts. It is no exaggeration to say that the nation's future is at stake. The wedge issue for government leadership could be the simple, decent goal of ending hunger. The persistence of hunger and poverty in our land casts a shadow of shame that dims our vision and divides us. But a determination to work across partisan lines to lift that shadow would help us see ourselves and one another as part of a united household and could move us toward a more inclusive economy.

The silence of citizens about this in the public square will not help.

10

Taxes and Deficits

Your morality is deeply lacking if all you want is a child born but not a child fed, not a child educated, not a child housed. And why would I think that you don't? Because you don't want any tax money to go there.
—Joan Chittister, OSB[1]

In 1954 when my brother Paul (the senator, not the singer) became a newly elected member of the Illinois State Assembly from southern Illinois, the first constituent letter he received came from a city of Alton voter who listed ten requests. The first nine required more spending. The tenth urged lower taxes. Paul often spoke of this and would add, "The strange thing is, we have adopted that man's program."[2]

What do budget deficits have to do with hunger? Simply this: by piling up large annual deficits, we as a nation are squeezing ourselves out of money that should be used to address critical needs. For the sake of everyone, especially people who are struggling to get by, we should erase those deficits and reduce the national debt. A national cry to end hunger and repair our economy will not succeed if it is perceived as a wave of profligate spending.

Deficits reaching hundreds of billions of dollars annually (now poised to exceed a trillion dollars annually) suddenly became the new normal in 1981 under President Reagan. Then in 2008 the Great Recession brought the economy to the edge of collapse, compelling Presidents Bush and Obama and the Congress to take swift and drastic preventive action. Emergency measures included the rescue of sinking financial institutions and auto industries, while federal income dropped, causing the deficit to soar to $1.3 trillion in 2009.[3] The budget that year had been enacted during the Bush administration, though the Recovery Act was signed by Obama less than a month after his inauguration. The emergency fostered bipartisan responses for 2009, but partisan quarreling soon prevailed with Republicans demanding spending cuts and Democrats urging more economic stimulus, which prevented agreement on how to deal with the deficit. Public alarm that deficits seemed to be spinning out of control enabled Tea Party conservatives to gain seats in Congress and, ironically, cement Republican opposition to any increase in taxes, though an increase is essential for a sound deficit-reduction plan.

For years each party has hoped that the public would turn against the other side and give its own party a majority in Congress and control of the White House. That hope was realized by Republicans in the November 2016 elections. As President Trump and the newly elected Congress took office in 2017, the nonpartisan Congressional Budget Office (CBO) reported a budget deficit of $587 billion for the previous year (2016) with a warning that the deficit would rise in the coming years and take the national debt on the same upward path. The CBO also projected a near tripling of annual interest payments by 2027, a yearly expense that would account for more than half the cost of our soaring annual deficits.[4]

Faced with such an alarming forecast, what did deficit-denouncing Republicans do? In the waning days of 2017 they passed additional massive tax cuts that the CBO says will raise the federal deficits to an average of $1.2 trillion a year between 2019 and 2028, adding another $12.5 trillion to the national debt. That would bring the debt to about $29 trillion, 96 percent of our gross domestic product (GDP), a higher percentage of our debt than at any point since World War II and its aftermath. The pressure to accelerate the debt upward beyond 2028 would risk "serious negative consequences," including an increased likelihood of a financial crisis, warns the CBO.[5] We are already spending more than 75 percent of the federal budget (88 percent of its revenue) on just four things—health insurance, social security, defense, and interest payments[6]—and we will soon have little for other essential purposes such as public safety, research, education, and climate change, not to mention hunger and poverty. The deficit train is speeding dangerously toward out-of-control.

The 2017 tax cuts are disguised tax increases. They are tax hikes that we decide others should pay, obligations that we impose mostly on our descendants. We enlarge the problem each year by adding to the squeeze from previous decades of tax-paying neglect. Even a small fraction of the tax cuts of 2017 could have paid for the cost of eliminating hunger in the United States and providing strong leadership for helping to end it abroad as well. Instead, folly prevailed.

The 2017 tax cuts will mainly enrich people with the highest incomes—83 percent of the benefits of the tax cuts will go to those in the top 1 percent by 2027 when they are fully phased in, according to the nonpartisan Tax Policy Center.[7] As congressional conservatives anticipated ways to pay for some of the mounting deficits, Republican leaders fought tenaciously to dismantle the Affordable Care Act (Obamacare) and sought to trim programs such as Social Security, Medicare, Medicaid, and SNAP. Tax cuts for people of wealth were deemed necessary, the basic needs of low-income Americans dispensable.

Erasing Deficits the Right Way

Our impasse on how to deal with the deficit shows what happens when we lose sight of people struggling for basic necessities and opportunities. In *It's Even Worse Than It Looks* Thomas Mann and Norman Ornstein illustrate the connection between partisan obstruction in Congress and soaring deficits. They report that in 2009 the highest-ranking Democrat (Kent Conrad) and Republican (Judd Gregg) on the Senate Budget Committee jointly introduced a resolution authorizing a bipartisan eighteen-member task force to propose a long-term plan to deal with the deficit. That plan would get a straight up-or-down vote with no amendments allowed. Republican leaders in the Senate, including Mitch McConnell and John McCain, urged such a resolution and McConnell called upon President Obama to support it, which he did. In January 2010 a majority of fifty-three senators voted for the resolution, but it was killed by a filibuster backed by McConnell, McCain, and six other co-sponsors of the resolution. They killed their own proposal. Why? Because, conclude Mann and Ornstein, "President Barack Obama was for it, and its passage might gain him political credit."[8]

People are prone to substitute self-interest, bias, or party loyalty for the common good. Neither you, the reader, nor I, the writer, are immune from this disposition. Yet each of us has something to learn from those with whom we may differ on the deficit and other issues. To do so takes an open mind and a generous spirit not locked into preconceived certainties. For political leaders it takes courage to put the common good ahead of political ambition. There is a national longing to overcome partisanship, which our individual shortcomings collectively block. Columnist Michael Gerson put it this way: "Both parties could gain electoral advantages by realistically addressing their weaknesses, which would also open up the possibility of legislative progress. But everyone, unfortunately, seems to like what they see in the mirror."[9]

With that humbling thought in mind let me suggest a path toward shrinking the nation's annual deficits and, in the near future, balancing the budget. It is a path, not a roadmap, that offers a sense of direction along with a few examples to show what could be done. Because taking that path would require political compromise and undoing some of the damage of the 2017 tax cuts, it is not apt to happen quickly, and may not happen at all until we are "mugged by reality." Initial steps could be taken any time, however, and these could lead to further agreement. Meanwhile postponing the day of reckoning harms the entire nation.

Conservatives are right in asserting that the deficits are a big problem, but for decades their record on this has been worse than dismal. They have made tax cuts their main economic policy, with a dismissive attitude regarding the outsized part those cuts have had in creating our mounting deficits. They argue that cutting taxes, regulations, and spending will enable the free market to make the economy bounce back and create jobs. That instinct turned a recession into a Great Depression that began in 1929, prevented a more rapid recovery from the Great Recession that began in 2007, and contributed extensively to our present extreme inequalities. Budgets put forward by Republicans during the six Obama years in which they controlled the House of Representatives proposed that most of the spending cuts should come from programs that benefit low-income people, while the tax advantages for people of wealth should be protected. Those advantages include "tax expenditures" (loopholes) that President Reagan's former economic advisor, Martin Feldstein, has called the most wasteful part of the budget.[10]

A balanced approach to a balanced budget would include: (1) steps to improve government efficiency and performance; (2) tax reform that produces additional revenue; and (3) spending for a healthier and more equitable economy. This formula would enable us to rein in current deficits gradually, achieve a genuinely humane economy, and move us in targeted steps toward a balanced budget.

For this to happen, everything in the federal budget, both spending and income, should be scrutinized, including entitlements, defense, and taxes. Scrutiny, however, does not mean looking for political talking points or ways to penalize the poor, but sifting carefully through considered options that would improve the efficiency and quality of government while enhancing greater equality. The Government Accountability Office's 2016 report of duplication and overlap in government programs, for example, suggests potential annual savings of $125 billion.[11] It is reasonable to suppose that many of its suggestions, if implemented, would bring improvements and cut costs.

In looking for efficiencies, national defense is an especially important part of the budget. Determining what to spend on defense is a complex undertaking that attracts clashing views. Whatever the appropriate amount, we should take seriously President Eisenhower's warning that spending dollars wastefully on defense weakens our defense and is "a theft from those who are hungry."[12] The Department of Defense (DOD) is the only federal agency that, until 2018, did not comply with a 1996 law requiring annual audits of all government departments. The 2018 Government Accountability Office (GAO) audit found the DOD records riddled with deficiencies. Senator Charles Grassley (R-IA) asked, "How is it possible that the Pentagon is able to develop the most advanced weapons in the world but can't produce a workable, reliable accounting system?"[13] And how much waste does that represent?

Consider the immigration reform bill passed by the US Senate in 2013 with bipartisan support. The House of Representatives killed it. House leaders caved in to ultra-conservatives who refused to let the bill be presented to the full House for a vote because they knew it would attract enough support from moderate Republicans to pass. The bill would have saved the federal government $135 billion over a ten-year span, according to the nonpartisan Congressional Budget Office. That does not include the CBO's estimate of another possible $300 billion in deficit reduction from the impact of broader economic growth.[14] Nor does it consider the likelihood that the bill's enactment might have prevented the issue of immigration from being seized for political gain during the 2016 presidential campaigns and may have changed the outcome.

Some jobs are legally protected but unnecessary. They are the "empty calories" of employment. For example, at least before the new 2017 tax law, the Internal Revenue Service had all the data it needs for the tax returns of most taxpayers and could simply mail them the completed returns with opportunity to appeal any errors or omissions. That would eliminate a lot of work for taxpayers, as well as for many of the million or so tax preparers and thousands of IRS employees. George Will contends that tax compliance requires the equivalent of more than 3 million full-time workers,[15] though the 2017 tax law might change that estimate. Subsidizing unnecessary work is an economic liability, when the money now used for it could help to reduce the deficit or be invested in ways that generate more productive jobs that add to the quality of our lives, a point to be made in the next chapter. But think also for a moment of the toll that unnecessary work takes on public and private morale: Quite apart from its drag on the economy, what does it do to people to know that their work is not really needed?

The IRS illustrates that sometimes we can reduce the deficit by spending more. Instead of cutting thousands from the IRS payroll (to save money, of course), we could hire more people trained to catch tax evaders and avoiders. By shrinking our own collection agency, we save millions but lose billions of dollars each year in unpaid taxes (estimates range from $63 billion to $650 billion).[16] That problem may balloon, because the 2017 tax overhaul has created a new complexity of ways in which companies and people of wealth can "game" the system legally, and many may do so illegally as well.

Spending to end hunger in America is another way to save money, the case for which I sketched in the last part of chapter 2. Poverty is a big contributor to poor diets and high levels of stress in children as well as in their parents. Poor nutrition and "toxic stress" are directly implicated in low educational achievement, behavioral problems, sickness, absenteeism, and chronic diseases such as diabetes and heart disease. These contribute heavily to the escalating cost of healthcare, which is the most rapidly growing expenditure in the federal budget. In *The Nourishing Effect: Ending Hunger, Improving Health, Reducing Inequality*,[17] Bread for the World makes a detailed case for saving money by ending hunger and in the process improving the quality of life for everyone. As reported in chapter 2, the annual cost to the nation of our current level of food insecurity ($160 billion) minus the investment of ending hunger in our country could yield a potential net savings of about $130 billion.[18] In the case of healthcare, an ounce of prevention is worth a pound of revenue.

Former US Treasury Secretary Robert E. Rubin makes the same argument on a larger scale by asserting that antipoverty programs such as Medicaid and SNAP bring high rates of return to our economy. "They improve productivity and reduce social costs caused by crime, malnutrition and poor health." Having 20 percent of our children live in poverty, he writes, is "not just a moral outrage—it's a serious detriment to our economic future." Our economy would benefit, he says, "if we finally marshalled the will and resources to effectively combat poverty."[19]

These are only a few possibilities among many that illustrate what could be done. The purpose should be to fashion a budget that improves the quality and efficiency of government, responds to the nation's inequalities, strengthens the economy, and serves the common good.

Since the recession began, there has been strong public support for a "circle of protection" around safety-net programs. The "circle" coalition also supports reforms so that antipoverty programs get more bang for the buck and can be made more effective or replaced with better ones. Poor people were victims, not the cause of the recession, and it would have been both wrong and futile to make them pay for it. By extension of that logic there is a strong case for invoking the principle that, in modifying and improving our entitlement programs, we enhance opportunities for the poor, not pick their pockets. Both political parties ought to uphold that principle.

Extending the logic further, why is it okay to protect and increase tax breaks of our richest citizens while 40 million of us struggle with food insecurity and countless others feel pushed out of the American dream? Do we really want to defend such a twisted morality and invite more public frustration? If not, then Republicans should lay aside blind opposition to increased taxes. Our national debt and annual deficits today are to a surprisingly large extent the result of tax cuts and deficits acquired during Republican administrations.[20] Visual 7 below shows the connection between our presidents and the growth of our national debt.[21] The Bush II and especially the Obama years were heavily impacted by the recession. (See endnote 20 for further explanation that includes the Trump years.)

In a 1981 address to the nation near the end of his first year as President, Ronald Reagan warned that the national debt was about to reach $1 trillion for the first time in the nation's history: "One trillion dollars of debt," he announced and repeated the line to let the terrible truth sink in. Then he added, "If we as a nation needed a warning, let that be it."[22] So what did Reagan do? He left behind a peacetime debt of $2.9 trillion. Eight years under the Reagan administration almost *tripled* a debt that had taken all previous administrations two centuries to accumulate, despite the intervening costs of the Civil War, two World Wars, and the wars in Korea and Vietnam. Improvident spending is one way to produce deficits. Improvident tax cuts are another way.

Tax Fairness

The tax cuts of the Reagan and Bush II administrations, and now that of the Trump administration, tilted heavily to the advantage of our wealthiest citizens. Justice requires a simpler, more progressive tax base along with tax reform that increases revenue and modifies our inequalities. Except for the damage caused, there is an almost comical contradiction in legislators insisting on a balanced budget while cutting taxes and refusing to pay for what they spend, and then (with straight faces) deploring the government's irresponsibility in running up those deficits. Finally they choose to inflict additional damage by urging cuts in programs for poor people to help offset tax breaks they have handed the well-to-do.

Visual 7

Total Deficits or Surpluses

Percentage of Gross Domestic Product

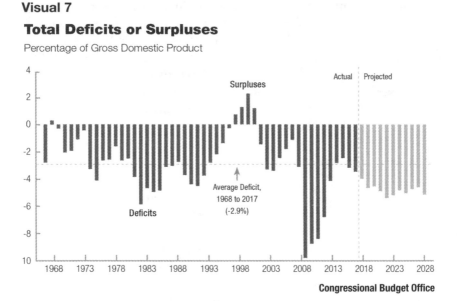

Congressional Budget Office

A strong and just economy—including a hunger-free America—cannot be achieved without tax reform and tax increases. Both should be tilted toward rewarding work and reducing our inequalities. A guiding principle should be that those who have been materially enriched by the nation should give back to it in sufficient measure so that all of us may flourish. Wealthy people have disproportionate political leverage and have used it to secure advantages that amount to welfare for themselves.[23] That makes little sense morally or economically. By taxing people the government is not robbing the public, but rather the public is investing in its own health and well-being to the benefit of rich and poor alike. The late Arthur Okun, chief economic advisor to Presidents Kennedy and Johnson, wrote that the purpose of taxing people at the top "is not to bring down the affluent but to raise up the deprived."[24] Charity is wonderful. It warms the heart of the giver while enhancing the lives of others. Paying taxes rarely leaves one with a fuzzy feeling, which belies the fact that taxes can do far more than charity to prevent suffering and enhance our lives. "Taxes are the price we pay for a civilized society," wrote Justice Oliver Wendell Holmes Jr.[25] Neglect of taxes invites an uncivilized one, and we seem determined to prove it.

The tax overhaul of 2017 was poorly timed, stimulating the economy after, rather than before, the business cycle had rebounded. And despite some positive features, it moves us in the wrong direction.[26] It can be replaced with legislation that represents tax fairness. Tax fairness would increase personal income tax rates on a sliding scale. There are many ways of crafting a tax schedule that would erase part of the deficit and help fund a more inclusive economy. It might start (my preference) with modest increases for people with incomes somewhat above the national average. But suppose we start higher than that. According to one poll, 72 percent of Americans, including 58 percent of Republicans, think that the tax rate should be increased for people earning $250,000 a year or more.[27] (A majority would likely have favored an increase at a lower level, had they been asked.) Let's say we tax a $250,000 income at 39 percent (the high rate when the poll was taken) and any income above that level by another 1 percent for each additional $50,000, going up to a maximum rate of 70 percent for someone earning almost $2 million. The 70 percent rate would hold no matter how many more millions someone earned. It is hard to imagine that such a tax schedule would impose a genuine hardship on anyone. But it could contribute substantially toward deficit reduction and a more equitable economy.

If you think that a 70 percent tax on additional income even for multimillionaires is high, compare it to the tax rates during the post–World War II era of prosperity. The top marginal rate in the 1950s and 1960s during the entire Eisenhower administration and most of the Kennedy administration was 91 percent (though loopholes lowered the effective rate). Then it was 70 percent during the Johnson, Nixon, Ford, and Carter administrations in the 1960s and 1970s. The plunge in rates came in the 1980s during the Reagan years, dropping first to 50 percent, then below 40 percent, where with variations (including 28 percent for three years under Reagan-Bush) it has stayed ever since.[28] The tax cuts coincided with other factors that were widening income inequalities, so the cuts, along with deregulation of the financial industry, boosted incomes and wealth for investors, while workers struggled to stay even.

Economists have offered a variety of possible options on personal income tax rates. Thomas Piketty, famous for his groundbreaking history and analysis of capital, suggests an optimal top rate of 80 percent for developed countries.[29] Robert Reich, former US Secretary of Labor, would increase the tax rates for the top 1, 2, and 5 percent of incomes to 55, 50, and 40 percent, but reduce the rate for most wage earners.[30] Joseph Stiglitz, Nobel Prize economist, would increase the tax rate for the top 1 percent of incomes to about 45 percent, reduce loopholes on high incomes, and broaden the tax base with a Value Added Tax, a kind of universal sales tax that would work well if accompanied by other reforms to the tax structure that Stiglitz proposes.[31]

Whatever the formula, those who have profited most from the prosperity of the nation should contribute proportionately. As billionaire Warren Buffett has urged, our tax system should never allow someone like himself to pay taxes at a lower rate than does his secretary. Even after the 15 percent capital gains tax rate for high-income earners rose to 20 percent in 2013, Buffett said he still paid a lower rate than his secretary and the rest of his office.[32] "My friends and I have been coddled long enough by a billionaire-friendly Congress. It's time for our government to get serious about shared sacrifice," he wrote in an article for *The New York Times*.[33] Higher taxes would not remove dollars from the market if they help struggling families put more food on the table. Higher taxes could also generate jobs, if properly spent on infrastructure, research, housing, healthcare, and education. They could stimulate the economy from the bottom up.

Tax *reforms* are even more important than making the tax *rates* more progressive. Reforms are needed to simplify taxes, but mostly to rectify distortions that offer high-income people unwarranted advantages that contribute to our economic inequalities. We now have a billionaire president ($3.7 billion by Forbes's estimate)[34] who has refused to make public his personal income tax returns for all but one of the sixteen years prior to his election. The 2017 tax overhaul includes a provision for tax breaks to real estate firms that could benefit President Trump by multiple millions. We also know that people of great wealth and high incomes are usually able to pay way below the official tax rate. Such "tax expenditures" are no less a redistribution of income than are SNAP and welfare benefits, but they occur on a vastly larger scale. They create, rather than correct, inequalities, and undermine rather than strengthen our democracy.

Tax reforms could be accomplished with many possible combinations, and perhaps President Trump could advise us. During the 2016 campaign he said "the system is rigged" in favor of people who tilt the laws to enrich themselves. He offered himself as an example of being smart by lawfully avoiding income taxes, but also said that, if he were elected, rich people would no longer be able to avoid paying their fair share and forgotten Americans would no longer be forgotten. His tax returns and his insights about how to ensure that people of wealth pay a truly fair share could be instructive. If he prefers to take a pass on this, there is no shortage of ideas about how to make our tax system simpler and fairer. Here are a few examples:

Deductions and exemptions. Mortgage deductions for homeowners could be limited, say, to the first $375,000 of a mortgage. The 2017 tax overhaul reduced it from a million dollars to $750,000—a nudge in the right direction. Until then, about 73 percent of mortgage interest deductions went to the top 20 percent of incomes, including 30 percent of deductions to the top 1 percent of incomes.[35] Far less housing assistance goes to low-income people, with more than 8 million very-low-income households not receiving federal housing assistance for which they qualify.[36] Families earning more than $200,000 a year have been receiving an average of four times the federal housing benefits that go to families earning less than $20,000 annually,[37] though benefits to the latter are called "welfare."

Estate and inheritance taxes. The transfer of wealth from one generation to the next is a big reason for the growing disparity of wealth. Nevertheless, the President and congressional Republicans urged elimination of the estate tax, a move that was partly enacted in 2017 by doubling the tax-exempt amount from $11 million to $22 million per couple,[38] which further increases the concentration of wealth. In 2001 Congress already exempted taxes on most large estates, so the new law helps only the nation's wealthiest millionaires, handing each of them a tax windfall that adds both to the nation's inequality extremes and to the nation's debt.[39]

Capital gains taxes. Capital gains could be taxed the same as other income, and taxes on them could be paid annually as the gains occur. Why should prosperous stockholders get a special break? One misguided law already enables a person to withhold payment of capital gains and pass the stock to an heir, who then counts only future gains as taxable. In this way people are able to die having paid zero taxes on their capital gains—another bonus for the well-to-do.

Corporate taxes. A case can be made for lowering these taxes. However, the 2017 tax overhaul that lowered the corporate rate from 35 percent to 21 percent is expected mainly to enlarge the incomes of executives and stockholders. Such a massive cut should be conditioned on recovering the revenue lost, for example, by taxing executive and shareholder income. Meanwhile US companies have fictionally "parked" $2.4 trillion ($2,400 billion) offshore to avoid paying taxes.[40] Kent Conrad, former chairman of the Senate budget committee, notes a five-story building in the Cayman Islands that claims to be "home" to more than 18,000 companies. "That and other tax scams cost our country more than $100 billion each year," he said, citing the findings of a Senate investigation.[41]

Pollution taxes. To the extent that we charge companies little or nothing when they pollute the environment, the public pays for it in poor health, medical expenses, and escalating costs connected to climate change. Taxing carbon emissions and raising gas taxes (unchanged since 1993) would slow the damage and provide the means of repairing some of it. Both types of taxes would help restrain global warming and produce revenue, some of which could be recycled to help low-income households that may be adversely affected. Meanwhile we subsidize pollution but tax labor, while wanting less pollution and more jobs. As economist Homi Kharas observes, "Get the prices wrong and the engine moves fast but in the wrong direction."[42]

Social Security. The Congressional Budget Office reports that the Social Security trust funds are on a path to be empty by 2031.[43] After that—unless Congress acts to prevent such a crisis—either Social Security benefits would drop by 29 percent (politically unthinkable) or additional payments of 29 percent legislated (further increasing the deficit and the debt by several hundred billion dollars and growing each year) or perhaps some combination of each. Social Security needs fixing now, and the longer we wait to do it, the more painful the fix. Fixing it is a political responsibility, but also a political hot potato. It shouldn't be. The fix could be done in several ways, the simplest of which would be to raise the level of income that is subject to Social Security payroll taxes, along with a cap or phasing out of benefits for retirees with an income from other sources above a specified high level. Any fix should be consistent with reducing hunger and poverty and easing our inequalities.

Restoring Public Confidence

I have sketched only a few of the possible ways in which reforms could reduce the nation's deficit and strengthen our economy. Seeing such reforms begin to take hold would help restore faith in our government and reassure investors, which would give the economy added strength. A more important purpose is to deal with the nation's alarming inequalities and make possible an economy that includes everyone. These purposes mesh nicely with the goals of reducing poverty and bringing hunger to an end.

Suppose a reordering of our national budget occurred, not a perfect reordering, but one that achieved substantial tax reform and better income distribution for the purposes suggested above. What would that look like? Suppose it had an annual trillion-dollar impact from both additional and reallocated revenue. An unreasonable sum? Consider the calculation of former US Treasury Secretary Lawrence Summers that if our country had the same income distribution it had in 1979, the bottom 80 percent of us would have $1 trillion more income (an average of $11,000 more per family) and the top 1 percent would have $1 trillion less income (an average of $750,000 less per family).[44] An actual reallocating of income, of course, might include a reduction of the deficit, plus a small percentage toward eliminating hunger, and the rest invested strategically in other forms of economic growth, job creation, and human need. Further reductions in the deficit could happen in stages. My hypothetical $1 trillion in reallocated income would shift the balance toward what we had before income inequalities began to grow. Fewer dollars would be invested in the stock market, where they tend to circulate among other well-to-do stockholders; more would be spent on bread-and-butter needs and other investments in people.

In 2018 unemployment had dropped to 4 percent, and our economy was growing at a modestly good pace, signs of a strong economy, but shadowed by its reliance on deficit spending and other underlying problems. Part-time employment, discouraged people no longer looking for work, low wages, and persisting inequalities tell us that our economy, despite its considerable strength, is faltering for many Americans.

Pessimism about our government still abounds, along with anxiety about the future. When it comes to solving really big problems, we are confused and divided, running low on hope, high on fury. What could bring us together again? Not negotiations to move us toward a balanced budget, though that should happen. Putting two sets of polarized politicians at a table to do this might yield some grudging compromises that could help us stumble from crisis to crisis much as we are doing now, perhaps doing it better. But that is no way to govern. We are the richest nation on earth, and the budget is a document that reflects what we value and indicates what kind of nation we are and want to be. If we reduce that to a fistfight or a compromise between "no new taxes" and "tax and spend," what kind of vision is that even if one side wins or they split the difference? It probably would not get us a balanced budget, but even if it did, is that a defining aspiration for a great nation? Reducing deficits and balancing the budget should be in the service of something much larger. Without a larger purpose—like a picture for a jigsaw puzzle—that helps us put the pieces of a budget together, how can we can expect to achieve something truly good and humane?

What is that larger purpose? Including everyone in the nation's well-being would enable us to rise above our divisions. Not just a dreamy notion of the common good, but a purpose that we instinctively know is right for everyone. That purpose, I submit, could begin with the ending of hunger and the reduction of the poverty and inequalities that lie behind them. Determining to end hunger could give us a focus that cuts across party lines because of its basic decency, a moral center from which to make many related decisions that should include addressing the needs of forgotten Americans in the middle who were drawn to the candidacy of Trump. The goal of ending hunger suggests a political starting point different and more promising than anything else currently being considered. We could get there in negotiated stages. But we may not get there at all unless a growing body of citizens advocates relentlessly for it.

If ending hunger helps us address our inequalities and deal with our deficits, as it should, that points us directly to the need for economic reform.

To that we now turn.

11

An Economy That Works for Everybody

What do I want? I want an education, a job, and a family.
                                   —young black man from Ferguson, Missouri[1]

A family with several children, ages four to thirteen, gathers for an announcement. The parents explain, "We have looked carefully at our finances and our plans for a generous retirement. Unfortunately, that means we will have to cut back on meals for some of you and let one of you go." Wailing and shouts erupt. "No! That's not fair! We don't want this to happen!" If such a scene strikes you as implausible, let me invoke again Daniel Bell's analogy of the nation as a household, which makes it easier to understand why a large segment of Americans feel pushed aside, while others enjoy an outsized share of the nation's prosperity.

When we appeal to our nation's leaders for an end to hunger, we are implicitly asking for a stronger and more just economy that serves the good of all. Millions of Americans, long before the Great Recession, have never felt they had a valued part in our economy and think the cards are stacked against them. Many have recovered from the recession, but others are still without work or poorly paid, or have only part-time jobs; and others, discouraged and often ill-prepared, have quit looking for work. As long as 40 million Americans live in food-insecure households, while an overlapping 40 million live in poverty and additional millions a notch or two above them struggle to stay in place, the need of a more vigorous, inclusive economy is apparent. We are far short of fulfilling one of the foremost purposes of government, articulated by Yuval Levin, of "helping all Americans take part in what happens" in the nongovernmental area occupied by families, communities, civic institutions, and private enterprise.[2]

Private enterprise is the engine of our economy and the main driver of its growth. But by itself the private economy will never be willing or able to train and employ all job-seekers at an adequate wage; nor can it be counted on to avoid creating ever greater extremes of income and wealth inequalities. For those reasons policies are needed to enhance the success of free enterprise and expand participation in it, while limiting its excesses. Such policies are determined by political choices we make, not a fatalistic, unchangeable economic law.

The nation needs to find additional ways to prepare and, when necessary, employ people for constructive work in which they contribute to the good of others and receive in return a fair wage and a measure of satisfaction. We are a rich nation. Our economy could give everyone a chance, but only if we pull together as a household and combine the hand of assistance with opportunity and personal responsibility. With that in mind I will suggest ways in which we could nudge the economy toward such an outcome. They offer a sense of direction, illustrating more than prescribing what could be done, because it will take political leaders working together to fashion solutions that can be enacted into law—and a public that insists on it.

Because the nation is deeply troubled by inequalities, the longer action to reduce them is delayed, the greater the damage, the more difficult the solution, and the more danger to our democracy. At this point in history the alternative to humanizing our economy is descent into an ever more stubbornly treacherous crisis.

Inscribed on the Thomas Jefferson Memorial in the nation's capital are these words from that morally conflicted man, speaking about a nation morally conflicted over slavery:

I tremble for my country when I reflect that God is just.[3]

It is a thought worthy of our reflection today as morally conflicted citizens in a nation still morally conflicted over severe inequalities that stem in part from its legacy of enslaving people.

Steps Toward an Inclusive Economy

We need a sense of ourselves as a national household similar to the one that emerged from World War II, but which goes further in giving everyone a fair share in the nation's prosperity. That means (1) correcting, insofar as possible, economic distortions that have accumulated since the 1970s, along with deeply rooted racial and social inequalities; and (2) aspiring as a nation to live more nearly as a family, seeking the common good and prospering or suffering together. These two marks of national health and unity are needed because we currently have no built-in combination of factors that would bring about a self-correction of our extreme inequalities. Most of the economic forces now in play will continue to produce inequality extremes and therefore more national discontent and turbulence unless we establish a sense of household unity attuned to changing circumstances. Here are a few examples:

Automation and shipping jobs abroad. If the economy is headed in the direction of more job losses than gains by virtue of blue- and white-collar employees being replaced by digital technology and robots, or industry that relocates jobs abroad, our household instincts should help us respond in ways that ensure a fair opportunity for everyone and, to the extent possible, a fair outcome. Seeking the common good means that when the economy falters, we work together to share the burden and make sure that everyone is included in securing a floor of justice.

Trade agreements. Opposition to and subsequent US withdrawal from the Trans-Pacific Partnership (TPP) was based in part on the perception that trade agreements such as the TPP and NAFTA (revised and renamed the United States–Mexico–Canada Agreement) reflect the top-heavy influence of big business with little input from labor, and as a result benefit people of wealth, while workers lose jobs and communities suffer. Protectionism, however, pulls economies down, as the Smoot-Hawley Tariff Act of 1930 did, making the Depression more severe. Trade agreements can be profitable, generate jobs, and benefit consumers with lower-priced products, but they also produce losers along with winners. If we think of ourselves as a household in such a situation, labor will need more voice in negotiating trade agreements. A precondition of an agreement could be legislation to provide adequate compensation for jobs lost, salaries reduced, and for retraining or moving people to a new location. The compensation now offered is so limited that to those who are hurt it seems more like burial assistance than job insurance.

Suppose negotiators could cut a deal that promises to create new jobs, benefit consumers, and reward management, but exacts a steep price from specific families and localities. The advantages in such a case could be recycled to include workers and communities that take an unfair hit. In trade deals, "tough luck" is not good enough. We can also get ahead of the problem to some extent by investing more in nutrition, health, and education for everyone, so people will be better able to cope with economic changes.

Public projects. The nation's backlog of projects, from bridges, highways, ports and parks, power grids, and other public facilities, begs for initiatives that could attract support across party lines. Like rural electrification during the twentieth century, internet access is now needed in remote areas and for low-income households. Modernizing our infrastructure could move us toward a stronger, more inclusive economy, and it should engage private and public partnerships, as well as state and local governments. The plan should employ many unemployed and underemployed people, not tilt toward further enriching the rich at the expense of financially strapped state and local governments and citizens of modest means.

Scientific research. Federal funding for research can spur needed innovation in areas of special importance, such as disease control and climate change. Research funding has been shrinking as we fall behind other nations in the development of pollution-free and renewable energy. If we want to lead in these areas and expand job opportunities, we have to invest in them. Poor people in developing countries, who did not create the crisis of climate change, are already disproportionately hurt by it; but our own children and generations to come will also suffer from our neglect. Because our industrial development and use of energy made us the leading contributor to global warming, we should move as rapidly as possible toward carbon-free energy to help ourselves as well as other countries adapt to the impact of climate change. Making low-income countries pay for our profligacy is a form of theft from the poor.

Healthcare is an ongoing crisis that hurts our economy and leaves millions of us uninsured. Our healthcare remains far more costly than it is in Canada or Western European countries that show equal or superior health outcomes.[4] The omission of health insurance was the most serious defect of our 1935 Social Security Act. The committee that studied and advised President Roosevelt on economic security began its work with health insurance as its primary focus. The committee concluded that sickness was the main cause of insecurity, so their report advocated a national health insurance program. Because of well-organized opposition led by the medical profession, it was dropped, with the mistaken impression that separate legislation on it would soon be introduced. That meant a lost opportunity to secure for the nation "the oldest form of compulsory social insurance in the world, one that was almost universally included in the social insurance programs of other advanced nations."[5] We need to learn from their experiences if we hope to become a nation truly seeking the common good. Our failure to do so has become a self-inflicted wound of individualism that fails to grasp the extent to which healthcare is a communal as well as a personal responsibility.[6] We are currently caught in the grip of a powerful medical-pharmaceutical-insurance complex that (with notable exceptions) resists reforms that threaten its financial interests, a resistance that does injury to all of us.

Education. A reformed public educational system and the way we finance it should—as do other prosperous democracies—devote resources and attention to disadvantaged children at least equal to those that other, more privileged children enjoy.[7] The alternative is to continue fostering inequality extremes. At another level, community colleges and the private sector need to connect more closely for job training and apprenticeships. More broadly, former US Secretary of Labor Robert Reich proposes "a world-class system of vocational-technical education" available to those for whom college is not a suitable or preferred track.[8]

Immigration. We are a nation of immigrants that needs additional immigrants, but with reasonable, enforceable limitations. We can celebrate diversity *and* strengthen our cohesiveness as a nation. Failure to reform our immigration policy left 10 million people without legal status and made it a volatile political target. In 2018 many immigrants were living in fear of deportation and additional family separations, which are especially cruel to children. We need to surmount a lurch toward nativism in favor of a more humane understanding of what we aspire to be as a national household. That should include generous, targeted aid to reduce poverty and violence in Central America so that desperate Latinos can thrive in their own country.

Work Is Good

When I graduated from Highland High School in Southern Illinois a few years after World War II, my classmates and even school dropouts could find low-skilled jobs, a typical situation for most white Americans, who usually worked their way ahead, helped form a family of their own, and felt a sense of accomplishment in realizing a piece of the American dream. Now dropouts and high school graduates, and sometimes even college graduates, may find no job or get one with a very low salary, become demoralized, and turn to behaviors that lead to a lifetime of distress. For those who come from an impoverished neighborhood or a troubled family, the statistical chances of this happening sharply increase, and those chances escalate if they are also African American or Hispanic.

The rising recognition across party lines that our nation's worsening inequalities must be addressed, and that jobs and decent wages are at the heart of figuring out how to do it, offers a ray of hope. Even in the polarized arena of electoral politics, thoughtful conservatives have worried out loud about our inequalities and the need for jobs with adequate pay.

Charles Murray, opponent of welfare assistance, stresses the virtue of American industriousness in *Coming Apart*, where he makes this observation: "Underlying the willingness to do the work was the abundance of opportunity that America offered" to people of every class. He notes that "it affected those on the bottom of American society more powerfully than those on the top."[9] *There lies the problem.* The "abundance of opportunity" beneath the industriousness that once lifted so powerfully "those on the bottom" no longer applies to many Americans—especially those at or near the bottom. In today's America they are more apt to feel like losers than achievers.

Any genuine economic renewal should help all of us celebrate a more inclusive and caring America. Doing so would attempt to bring everyone into the social and economic mainstream through jobs and adequate wages. Success in this could be at least partly defined as putting people within reach of an income that raises households well above the poverty line. That kind of success would enable us to scale back assistance programs such as SNAP, tapping it mainly for transition periods between jobs or during economic recessions.

Following the 1963 civil rights March on Washington "for Jobs and Freedom," white people who supported the civil rights movement did not have the same sense of urgency for investing freedom with meaning by creating jobs, and partly as a result, the outcome was demoralizing for those who were eager to work but still jobless. The War on Poverty established the Job Corps as a job *training* program, but not a major job *creation* program. Many newly prospering African Americans, including some who became teachers or social workers in the ghetto, found housing elsewhere.[10] Left behind were higher concentrations of people who were not well prepared to seize limited new opportunities. Hope faded and anger grew, as jobs disappeared and neighborhoods were caught in a downward spiral. Today such neighborhoods are growing more rapidly in suburbs such as Ferguson, Missouri, a flashpoint in 2015 for racial protests over a police officer shooting and killing Michael Brown.

To make matters more urgent, we have entered an era of technological changes that some call a "Fourth Industrial Revolution." Using that theme, the 2016 World Economic Forum projected a job market increasingly segregated by those in low-skill/low-pay jobs and those with high-skill/high-pay positions.[11] According to a 2014 Pew Research Center survey, the vast majority of experts agree that robotics and artificial intelligence "will permeate [and change] wide segments of daily life by 2025." Those experts were almost evenly divided, however, on whether this will lead to a net loss of jobs and possible breakdowns in the social order or a net increase in new types of work.[12] Either way, change is rapidly occurring. A detailed analysis of occupations covering 90 percent of the US workforce showed jobs with low digital skills plummeting from 56 percent in 2002 to 30 percent in 2016. Those requiring medium digital skills rose from 40 percent to 48 percent, and those requiring high digital skills from 5 percent to 23 percent.[13] The Bureau of Labor Statistics reported that in December 2017 college graduates with jobs increased by 305,000 while employment for Americans without a high school degree fell by 132,000.[14] The trend is striking. Is manufacturing following the path of agriculture, which employed half the US workforce at the outset of the twentieth century but now employs only 2 percent, and which left many small towns depopulated shells?[15] An economy in which digital technology can do many more things better and faster than humans requires extensive adaptation. How many high-tech jobs can free enterprise create? And how will those left behind support themselves and their families?

There is no reasonable way to prevent or slow this digital revolution. Economic growth and competitiveness mean that average productivity per worker per hour must rise, and that requires new technology.[16] However, many jobs, such as teaching, childcare, restaurant work, or home repair will not easily add to the nation's average hourly productivity through use of improved technology. Productivity gains through new technology need to offset jobs in the productivity plateau, along with steps to ensure adequate wages for all, including women, who are heavily concentrated in some of the "plateau" area jobs. Women face discrimination in access to a wide spectrum of other jobs, as well as in wages, which is especially hard on women who are the primary or only breadwinners. Gender discrimination in turn imposes hardship on children, including those in households with two parents working in order to make ends meet.

Growing inequalities already exceed our remedial efforts. What will we do if accelerated productivity and wealth leave still more Americans in the social and economic dust? Do we decide that additional millions of us are superfluous? Or should we figure out soon—it is already late—how it is possible for all of us to be engaged in work that will enhance the lives of one another and do so on a livable income?

Between 1990 and 2014 the US auto industry increased production by 19 percent, but with 240,000 fewer workers. By 2017 Adidas had established a shoe factory in Germany that runs almost entirely by robots, and it planned to open a similar factory near Atlanta later in the year.[17] In 2013 Facebook had slightly more than 7,000 employees, while IBM and Dell had 431,222 and 109,000 respectively.[18] As a result, says American Enterprise Institute's James Pethokoukis, "analysts on the left and right have predicted wealth redistribution rather than [wealth] creation may be the bigger challenge going forward." He quotes his AEI colleague, Charles Murray: "Massive government redistribution [of income] is an inevitable feature of advanced post-industrial societies." Murray says we ought to create "valued places for people with many different kinds and levels of ability," but have the government distribute money and leave it to individuals, families, and communities to tend to human needs charitably on a one-by-one basis.[19]

Murray would replace all forms of government welfare with a guaranteed annual income of $13,000 for every American, $3,000 of it for health insurance, leaving every adult with $833 a month of disposable income. It would be financed by eliminating Social Security, Medicare, Medicaid, SNAP, and other transfer payments. Murray argues that it would lift people out of poverty and remove a big obstacle to marriage. For example, a young man working at a low wage could marry, and together the couple would have a combined income of maybe $35,000 and substantially more if both worked. That, Murray says, would give them a new sense of responsibility.[20]

It is a breathtaking proposal, fatally flawed. It would increase income mainly for already-prospering people while putting low-income and middle-income Americans at high risk when emergencies strike or retirement arrives. Still, his proposal contributes to a discussion that should prompt conservatives and liberals alike to seek a work- and income-focused solution. Murray acknowledges that in the current system "most disadvantaged people in America have no reason to think that they can be anything else" because their prospects are so bleak. "The more fortunate members of society may see such people as obstinately refusing to take advantage of the opportunities that exist," he says. "But when seen from the perspective of the man who has never held a job or the woman who wants a stable family life, those opportunities look fraudulent."[21] Quite an admission from a man whose 1984 book *Losing Ground* persuaded many policymakers that social welfare programs cause more poverty than they alleviate, a position he still holds.

Michael Strain (another colleague of Pethokoukis and Murray) notes the impact of technology on the labor market and says that if income for those at the top increases massively (as many predict), while employment opportunities erode for most Americans, the government may have to pay over half of the salary of many workers. He thinks we may face a long and painful transition for which we need a guiding principle, and he proposes one: "Work is good." Public policy should encourage and support work, he says, and adds, "Figuring out how to do so is a great and underappreciated challenge facing our nation."[22]

Optimists are beginning to dream about the possibility of more leisure time in an economy with reduced need for work. That might allow, say, for a thirty-hour work-week and the chance to move beyond our live-to-work habits.[23] It might free many adults to split work and parenting, or allow one to earn income and the other to be a stay-at-home mom or dad. If so, that may or may not be good news for the new leisure class, but what about people who want to work and need an adequate wage? The formidable challenges of more leisure might pale compared to those of an expanding subculture of people scraping the bottom with or without jobs.

A stronger, more humane economy would help reduce hunger and poverty. It would also cut unemployment, which in 2017 still left 7 million Americans seeking work, almost 2 million of them long-term unemployed. Another 5.3 million had resorted involuntarily to part-time work,[24] and many others who would like to work had simply left the labor force—"a massive waste of economic resources," writes Michael Strain, and more importantly "a human tragedy, shattering lives on a mass scale" by way of divorces, worsened health, and long-term setbacks for children. Strain points out that the workforce rate for men twenty-five to fifty-four years old (including those unemployed but job-hunting) declined from 94 percent in 1985 to 88 percent in 2014.[25] Many of those not working were among the record number of post-recession Americans whose lengthy unemployment reduces their chances of finding work as well as the disposition to seek it. Others included fifteen- to twenty-nine-year-olds, 16 percent of whom were "disengaged" NEETs (Not in Employment, Education, or Training), though disengagement forecasts a much higher likelihood of long-term economic and social difficulties for them and their children.[26]

Changes could increase employment. For example, company workers could share reduced hours as an alternative to layoffs during a recession. Excessive licensing requirements could be scaled back so cosmetologists don't need ten times the training of an emergency medical technician. Flextime and more support for childcare would make work possible and more attractive for many. But nearly half of childcare providers need federal assistance because their median wage is $9.77 an hour, about $3 below the average for janitors.[27] The problem, however, is so big that private enterprise, even with the best of intentions and efforts, is unlikely ever to eliminate unemployment and poverty-level wages for large numbers of disadvantaged people, especially in places where industries have largely vanished.

Nicholas Eberstadt urges attention to the estimated 23 million released felons living among us. We need them to succeed as fathers, mothers, breadwinners, and citizens, he says, but we don't know how well they are doing, and we don't even bother to find out. "Some of this [gathering of data] could be done easily, quickly and at very low cost; other aspects would take more time, money and technical effort," he says. But if we really care about the poor, the sheer numbers of ex-felons and the difficulty they face in reentering society means that "the task of reintegrating reformed felons has never been more important than it is today."[28]

A related opportunity toward helping us recover from the damage of excessive imprisonment is the Sentencing Reform and Corrections Act, which passed with bipartisan approval in 2018 following the last-minute endorsement of President Trump. The federal prisoner population has grown by about 700 percent since 1980, while the US population has grown by 32 percent. Half of those prisoners committed nonviolent drug offenses, many serving excessively long sentences. This legislation allows more reasonable sentences for federal (though not the far more numerous state and local) offenders and adopts programs that would help restore prisoners to a useful and productive life when they have served their time.[29]

A century ago Henry Ford quietly hired ex-convicts at his factory and gave them assistance to help them get started. Where others saw liabilities, Ford saw assets. He said he could take a man off the street and turn him into a productive worker.[30] Ford also shocked the business world in January 1914 by announcing that he would pay his factory workers $5 a day (worth $120 in 2016), more than doubling the average wage of a worker, plus shortening the workday to eight hours—a goal long sought by the labor unions that Ford despised, but it enabled Ford to have three shifts a day. These moves led to increased production and a lot of newly employed and better-fed workers. Soon Ford employees were driving their own Model-T Fords, and other companies were raising wages to prevent workers from flocking to Ford. The economy got a boost. Everyone benefited.[31] That was a century ago, and although the economic landscape today is far more complex, we can learn from past successes if we do so carefully.

Work, Wages, and Welfare

After moving to the Lower East Side of New York as a young man in 1961, I encountered many undereducated children living in block after block of old five-story tenements in need of repair and in large public housing projects just two avenues from my apartment. Many of the residents longed for work and wages that would enable them to escape poverty. Why, I wondered, could we not begin to turn these two problems into a solution by training some of the unemployed and underpaid adults to repair housing and mentor school kids? Naïve, no doubt, considering the complexities of such a project. But not impossible. We are not good at turning problems into opportunities and treating people as treasured resources. There is almost no limit to the things people could do to improve our neighborhoods, contribute to the economy, beautify our environment, and enhance everyone's quality of living. But we need to value people and those outcomes enough to find ways of making the outcomes happen.

Jobs must be a central feature of an inclusive economy, but not jobs that leave people impoverished or nearly so. The painful truth is that low wages have left many workers and their families insecure both of food and future livelihoods. Stronger unions and a more worker-friendly culture in the business world would help lift wages. Low unemployment and a tighter labor supply can also raise wages when employers have to offer competitive salaries in order to attract and retain workers. The ideal solution would be for the free market to employ and adequately pay everyone who can and should work; but given the limitations of private enterprise, new initiatives and backup strategies are necessary.

Enforcement of labor laws would help. Wage theft of low-income workers is widely practiced by employers without adequate enforcement of penalties. According to a survey of the ten most populous states, minimum-wage workers lost an average of $3,300 a year to wage theft, almost 25 percent of their earned wages. The crime includes withholding tips, failing to pay the difference between tips and the minimum wage, overtime and off-the-clock violations, and misclassifying employees as independent contractors.[32] The Economic Policy Institute estimates the annual loss to workers nationwide at $50 billion, with few investigators attempting to enforce the wage laws.[33]

Among the ways to create jobs and increase wages, we can count improving and expanding food and nutrition assistance, healthcare, and education as sound investments in human life and productivity. Better public transportation could connect job seekers in distressed urban neighborhoods with places where jobs are available. High-speed internet service could do the same for people in many rural areas and also give them more access to education and social services. Criminal justice reforms would get more people into the job market and lift families out of poverty. The tax fairness I have proposed could pay for these things.

An initiative that requires no government funding is the raising of the minimum wage. But what is a fair level? The federal minimum wage of $7.25 an hour? Adjusted for inflation, the minimum wage of $1.60 in 1968 was worth more than $11 in 2018 dollars—roughly $4 an hour more than its 2018 level.[34] President Obama proposed setting it at $10.10 and indexing it for inflation. The argument for an increase is that it would immediately lift the income of about 28 million workers. The arguments against it are that any increase would impose a hardship on many businesses, might be inflationary, and would cause unemployment (especially for young people looking for entry-level experience) when owners find employees too costly to hire. There is a point beyond which raising the minimum wage does more harm than good, though there is no agreement on where that point is, and it varies according to local circumstances. By 2016 a small number of municipalities, counties, and states, including California, New York City, and Seattle, had voted to phase in, over several years, a minimum wage of $15 an hour, the outcomes of which will be carefully watched and assessed for guidance elsewhere.

A favorite backup strategy is the Earned Income Tax Credit (EITC) for reimbursing federal taxes to low-wage earners on a scale of need, and in many cases adding income. As an incentive and reward for work, it has extensive support across party lines. President Reagan backed the expansion of EITC in tax proposals that Congress enacted in 1986.[35] Is the EITC a subsidy to the underpaid worker or to a company for not paying an adequate wage? Either way it is a federal intervention to help address a problem that the free market by itself has either not been able or willing to solve. In 2016 the EITC lifted about 5.8 million low-income workers and family members, including about 3 million children, out of poverty, and reduced the severity of poverty for another 18.7 million people, including almost 7 million children. About 10 million of EITC's beneficiaries were children.[36] An expanded EITC could lift many more above the poverty line.

The Child Tax Credit also lifts families out of poverty and deserves to be expanded, but without giving childcare support to those above a moderate income level. Why, you may ask, should a parental responsibility such as childcare be subsidized at all by the public? The answer is that circumstances have changed. Childcare has become too costly for many parents, so without public subsidies fewer adults will have well-nurtured children, and such children are a vital public asset. As a result, William Galston argues, "child-rearing has moved from a private good to a public good" that "benefits society as a whole rather than the parents who bear most of the financial burden."[37]

Not everyone can or should work, but everyone needs enough food and a decent standard of living. Children, the ill or aged, people with disabilities, and those caring for young children or dependent adults need special support. Single-parenting situations are complex, but various combinations of work and assistance, depending on circumstances, are possible. Many persons with disabilities could qualify for certain types of full or part-time work, and are eager to have it, rather than being sidelined as totally dependent. Rehabilitation with education and job training is critically important for prisoners and substance abusers who seek reentry into society as positive contributors—the earlier the intervention, the better and less costly. Best of all, of course, is preventive action.

Many situations warrant dependency, but not the dependency of being denied the purpose and dignity of work or the dependency of becoming emotionally and mentally dwarfed from not learning to take responsibility. There is more than enough that needs to be done, most of it beyond the capability of government, and everyone needs to be part of doing it. Each of us individually and collectively as families, neighbors, communities, and nongovernmental groups of every type help shape our culture, and we should encourage one another to do this well. The government, for its part, should ensure that the most vulnerable are fully included.

Government assistance programs are an essential part of a truly inclusive economy, but we can do much better than we are now doing to make sure that such assistance does not replace work, but instead supports and prepares people for work whenever possible. The assumption that assistance routinely replaces work is badly mistaken; but the assumption that it never does is also wrong. Insisting on work for those who are able, as conservatives argue, makes sense—but only if properly advanced. Work requirements, along with education and training, must be accompanied with the real prospect of jobs and decent wages. Otherwise making demands simply crushes people. Nothing is gained and damage inflicted by shoving people off assistance in order to meet quotas or reduce costs. People needing help are not baby birds ready to be pushed out of the nest and fly. And if jobs are not available, are we going to make people destitute? Better to connect assistance to job training and/or employment of last resort—not as degrading punishment, but as a way of enabling people to contribute to the common good and helping as many as possible make the transition to sustainable employment. As Speaker of the House, Paul Ryan spoke in favor of personally tailored job training, a sensible idea but one that entails more front-end investment, not the cost-cutting that Ryan proposed.

One program that worked well briefly, as a part of the 2009 Recovery Act to help states assist disadvantaged people during the recession, was the Temporary Assistance for Needy Families Emergency Fund. It provided states with grants to place 260,000 unemployed low-income adults and youth mostly in temporary private-sector jobs. It increased their incomes, gave them work experience, and led some employers to hire them permanently. It also benefited businesses and communities, while boosting the economy.[38] But pressure in Congress for budget cuts killed the program when its two years expired. Tax advantages for a small number of rich people were seen as more important than employment opportunities for 260,000 job hunters.

Albuquerque, New Mexico, is employing homeless people through a mix of public and private funding. "It's about the dignity of work," said Mayor Richard Berry. Volunteers get $9.00 an hour plus a bag lunch in the park. The hope is to start them on an upward spiral. According to Berry, "Fines and jail time don't solve anything."[39]

Work and related assistance should be seen as a hand up, a ladder as much as a safety-net. The aim is to enable people to be or to become a contributing part of the workforce while counting rigorous job training and education as work. Fully respecting human dignity means both enabling and challenging people to live up to their potential. "Personal responsibility" is everyone's due, too honorable a virtue to let the term become captive to those who would use it as an excuse to withhold assistance from people in need or to assign work as punishment, in either case demeaning rather than helping people. As Michael Strain says, work is good.

Government as Backup Employer

The significance of work for the individual, and its impact on children, families, and communities is so great that we cannot settle for the limitations of private enterprise on a matter so important to the nation. We-the-people, through our government, can serve as employer of last resort with public service jobs for those unable to find work, as we did for millions of Americans during the Great Depression to the lasting benefit of all. Those jobs were not allowed to compete with other public- or private-sector jobs, but rather augmented them. To avoid worker displacement or substituting federal for local or state spending, William Julius Wilson favors federal administration as well as types of work currently not being done, such as more frequent cleaning of streets, picking up trash and opening of libraries, and other public services. He says the program should be open to all segments of society, not just the disadvantaged, in order to avoid stigma.[40]

By one survey, 83 percent of American adults favor work over welfare as a response to poverty; and in a related poll 61 percent of likely voters think state governments should offer minimum-wage jobs instead of welfare payments to those who have lost their jobs and have been job-hunting but unemployed for a year or more.[41] Public backing for public service jobs appears to be extensive. Done well, such a program would cost a lot more than cash assistance, but the long-term gain would far exceed the short-term cost. However, unlike a massive guaranteed-job program that would start big, cost too much, and invite failure,[42] this one could begin modestly and expand as quickly as it is tested and proven.

A program of voluntary national service should also be considered, as an addition but not an alternative to public service jobs. Voluntary national service, military or civilian, would offer adults (mainly young adults) an opportunity to give back a year or two to their country, learn skills, and experience the diversity that is an essential part of America.[43] It would better prepare them for careers and, as a reward for service (like the GI Bill), further their training and education. President Kennedy's famous inaugural line, "Ask not what your country can do for you, ask what you can do for your country," paved the way for the Peace Corps and Volunteers in Service to America (VISTA), as well as AmeriCorps during the Clinton administration—useful models, but applications for them far exceed available slots. In 1990 William F. Buckley called for a government-funded system of national service that was applauded by both Presidents Bush, Senators John McCain and Orrin Hatch, and Governors Mitt Romney and John Kasich,[44] so the idea has appeal across political lines. Meanwhile, with prominent bipartisan advisors, a nongovernmental Service Year Alliance is promoting a year of voluntary service.

We should expand service opportunities and prepare people for them so that disadvantaged Americans have the same opportunity to serve as do college graduates, with the bonus of college or vocational training for those who serve well. Volunteers could work on a great variety of social and civic problems, such as helping underperforming school kids who need personal attention. Without additional help, many of these lagging students will become dropouts and candidates for addiction or crime, or maybe part of the

20 percent of adults who are unable to read with understanding a job application form, an instruction sheet, or a newspaper.[45] Volunteers could also serve as interns in nonprofit organizations or pre-apprentices in profit-making businesses, but not replace other job-holders as lower-paid substitutes.

Within the framework of ending hunger, and as a foundational goal for full economic recovery, I have focused on employment for all who can and should work. I have avoided the term "full employment" because it is an imprecise percentage of those actively seeking work, below which the competition for workers triggers inflation.[46] The best target is widely regarded as the balance between joblessness and inflation, but it leaves many job-seekers unemployed and others too discouraged to keep looking for work—not to mention uncounted incarcerated adults. We should especially seek to include in a thriving economy those who are unemployed, accepting a small rate of temporary unemployment (perhaps near 4 percent) to allow for transition between jobs, retraining, and time for job searches.

How could we do better than we are currently doing to prepare children and youth for our changing and complex world? Good parenting, better incentives and coaching for teachers, connecting middle and high school students with apprenticeships that motivate them to find purpose in their studies, training children to serve rather than seek wealth—these things and much more are involved in nurturing a culture of citizens helping one another. But we also need to bridge the employment gap with public service jobs, training, and temporary assistance in order to face honestly the limitations of free enterprise, which bypasses millions of would-be and should-be job seekers.

A Reach Too Far?

Steps toward a more inclusive economy sketched in this chapter may strike you as politically beyond reach, but we could start the process, arouse public support for it, and begin to take steps in the direction I am urging. If we do not, we can expect to become an even more deeply divided and dangerously troubled nation, when a desirable outcome is well within reach.

We have to decide. Do we want a nation ever more polarized until we reach a breaking point, where we risk losing our democracy and facing who knows what level of chaos and violence? Or do we begin now to address our morally indefensible inequalities and cultivate a better way of including everyone in times of prosperous growth and cushioning all in times of adversity?

Three Republican presidents owe much of their greatness to the fact that they led the government to intervene actively in our economy and enhance our well-being. Lincoln for freedom from slavery, for civil rights, canals, land grant universities, and land for pioneer farming; Theodore Roosevelt for labor laws, food and drug regulation, the US Forest Service, conserving 230 million acres of land for wildlife and public use, and opposition to monopolistic practices in business; Eisenhower for our Interstate Highway system and the funding of public schools. In addition, Republican congressional leaders worked vigorously across party lines to gain acceptance for the Marshall Plan, the GI Bill, and the monumental civil rights laws of the 1960s.[47] Include also Chief Justice Earl Warren and the US Supreme Court's unanimous 1954 ruling (*Brown v. Board of Education*) that desegregated public schools. What would America be today without these bold initiatives? They were made possible through nonpartisan action that would not have occurred without foresighted leaders and citizens willing to back them.

Here lies a heritage that Republicans as well as Democrats can claim in meeting the challenges of today by working across party lines to fashion an economy that unites us and benefits the entire nation. Common ground is there for us to seize. Significant, if limited, bipartisan support has surfaced on a range of key issues such as healthcare, penal reform, immigration, and poverty-focused foreign aid, as well as defense of SNAP, and tax credits for low-income workers and childcare. These indicate that initiatives for ending hunger and humanizing our economy are not beyond reach.

Ironically, liberals and conservatives seem to have found common ground in affirming an individualistic freedom from restraint. Liberals tend to apply this to the cultural side of life, while conservatives usually apply it to economics. Both cultural and economic freedom from restraint have aggravated class disparities and made it especially hard for poorly educated and low-income people to cope. A better freedom is freedom for the common good. Combining social justice with personal responsibility would be a tonic for the nation and its citizens. Seeking an end to hunger would be an excellent catalyst for doing so.

Global Hunger and Poverty

In this chapter I have been sketching a revitalized economy for our country because the economy largely determines the extent of hunger and poverty. I have done so not to forget the greater and more extreme problem of world hunger and poverty, but for two reasons. First, what we do, or fail to do, in achieving an economy that includes everyone becomes a powerful example to other countries and an economic anchor for the world. Second, there is little chance that we will do our part to provide leadership in overcoming world hunger and poverty, if hunger and poverty here continue to divide and weaken us. "Charity begins at home," people say. So let it begin and increase here, and let it increase abroad as well. But US citizens who support charity need also to advocate for justice, not undermine justice by expecting charity to take its place.

Of all the nations of the world, ours is by far the most advantageously situated to work with people everywhere who seek to escape poverty and hunger. That is where an important part of American exceptionalism should be demonstrated, for we are blessed not only with liberty, but with natural resources and wealth beyond that of any other nation. The launching of the UN Sustainable Development Goals for 2030 gives us a rare and timely opportunity to commit ourselves and our nation to a new birth of partnership in this historic effort. Our own economic and social challenges, and those of other countries, indicate the need for a compelling vision that could unite us and give us perspective in shaping national policies. We can be guided in policymaking by our picture of what we want our nation and the world to become. Without neglecting related causes that rightly claim our time and energy, we can support the simple, utterly decent, and doable goal of ending hunger as a catalyst for bringing people together around the "clear moral consensus" that Arthur Brooks and others say is needed to unite us.[48]

An economy that addresses the alarming gaps of income, mobility, and wealth in our country provides the best long-term way of ending most hunger and poverty in the United States; but our development and the development of poor countries are intertwined. What we do (or fail to do) in efforts here and abroad will return to us in ways that surpass economic calculation. If we turn away from global cooperation, trigger a trade war, and face a global recession as a result, employment and wages are certain to take a terrible hit. The damage we do will return to haunt us. The good we do, however, has a way of surprising us with economic as well as social returns. For this to take hold, Americans across political and ideological lines need to find common ground in an instinctively ennobling cause that transcends politics. That cause could be the ending of food insecurity and most poverty in America and taking the lead in joining the nations of the world to do the same regarding extreme hunger and poverty around the globe.

The next step is crucial: to leave the comfort of silence and join the ranks of those willing to seize this compelling vision and help enact it.

PART IV

We Can Act on
a Compelling Vision

12

We Need a Compelling Vision

America is not a pile of goods, more luxury, more comforts, a better tele-phone system, a greater number of cars. America is a dream of greater justice and opportunity for the average man and, if we cannot obtain it, all our other achievements amount to nothing.

—Eleanor Roosevelt[1]

We are a great nation, a visionary nation; but we are deeply troubled, and our vision is blurred. Beneath our strength and prosperity rumbles dis-content. Confidence and trust in one another and in our institutions have eroded. Social and economic changes have handed us realities that confuse and alarm us. Problems considered in this book have left many Americans feeling powerless, fearful, often angry, and our leaders so divided that they punt some of our biggest problems into the future for others to deal with. Or they simply cling to partisan dogmas. Our ideas of who we are and what we want to be as a nation lack a unifying vision that brings us together. If a household is what we aspire to be as a nation, then "dysfunctional" is what much of our household is experiencing.

A poll by the Pew Research Center found that only 19 percent of us trust our government "always or most of the time" and only 20 percent think government programs are well run. A Gallup poll showed that the public considered government performance to be the nation's top problem in 2015.[2] No doubt the polls reflect, among other things, the gridlock that has often reduced Congress to a political version of trench warfare and extensively hobbled the governing process.

In 2016 the presidential candidates in both major political parties who departed most radically from their own party's leadership were the ones who captured the most enthusiastic following. Bernie Sanders mounted a fierce challenge to Hillary Clinton among the Democrats. On the Republican side the final two were Donald Trump, a billionaire whose impulsive boasting and thin policy credentials would normally have doomed a candidate at the starting gate, and Ted Cruz, a conservative so extreme and abrasive that he had alienated virtually all of his Republican colleagues in the US Senate. Trump and Sanders, however, tapped into the frustration of voters who were fed up with politics as usual. Demonstrations also erupted over killings by police of young black men, reminding the nation that our unresolved racial issues are a big part of the turbulence that befuddles the nation.

Because we seem to be groping in a fog, unable to move forward on problems that beg for sensible solutions and leave huge parts of our population feeling bypassed, the electorate gambled on Donald Trump. His election to the presidency was a cry of desperation from voters, as well as a revelation of how deeply conflicted we are. Trump did not cause our divisions or our racial and ethnic biases, but he exposed us to them (a favor of sorts) and has made them worse by exploiting them. In December of 2017 the conservative majority governing Congress, and elected with Trump, voted yet another huge tax cut (on money borrowed from taxpayers) that seems destined to intensify the inequalities that account for much of our national discontent.

During the 2016 campaign, columnist David Brooks noticed "a vacuum at the heart of things" among college students. "We ask students to work harder and harder while providing them with less and less of an idea of how they might find a purpose in all that work." That leaves them hungering for something "that will fulfill their moral yearnings and produce social justice."[3]

Students are not the only ones who need a compelling vision. All of us do. We need a vision that puts economics and politics in service to people, not the reverse. "The Sabbath was made for man, not man for the Sabbath"[4] is still an underlying principle. So I think of the mother and her little five-year-old boy "in kiddie garden," whom writer Jonathan Kozol met at a crowded soup kitchen in New York. "You have to remember," said one of the priests with whom Kozol shared his thoughts, "that for this little boy whom you have met, his life is just as important, to him, as your life is to you. No matter how insufficient or how shabby it may seem to some, it is the only one he has"—a comment that moves Kozol deeply.[5] I think of that little boy and his mother, and countless others like them, whose treasured lives are so fragile. They undergird my conviction that the humble, audacious goal of ending hunger is precisely the compelling vision that we as a nation and our political leaders need in order to begin finding our way through the political fog.

The right to food is basic to the inalienable right to "life, liberty and the pursuit of happiness" for which, the Declaration tells us, our government was founded. The twin goal of ending hunger in America and helping to end it globally could serve as a compass for us in guiding us through the haze of other problems as well. Because it is so essential and decent, so well within our grasp, so consistent with our founding ideals and the moral and religious beliefs that many espouse, a commitment to end hunger could give us the corrective lens for seeing our way ahead. It could bring us together and make us feel good about ourselves and our nation. It could capture our hearts and win the hearts and minds of people throughout the world.

Ending hunger would not have to be the nation's highest priority, simply a priority strong enough to make it a clear national goal with steps and benchmarks for getting from here to there. Establishing the goal of ending hunger, along with a process for achieving it, would appeal to our best instincts and could clarify our vision on a range of related issues. If policymakers start with a commitment to end hunger, they will find motivation and gain understanding to deal with the contribution of joblessness and low wages to hunger. They will see the connection between hunger and poor health, with the human and financial costs that result. They will become more attentive to the crowded path between the mass incarceration of young men and neglected kids in broken neighborhoods. In short, a determination to end hunger could lead to steps toward ending poverty and reducing inequalities that are draining too many Americans of hope.

When I was in the second grade my vision was so poor that I could no longer read what was on the blackboard, even after an embarrassing move to the front row. Fitted with eyeglasses, I was amazed at the change. People were no longer blurry. I could see individual leaves on trees and blades of grass. The world looked different, not because the world had changed, but because my vision had. As a nation we need a corrective lens through which we can see our way ahead more clearly. The blurred lens of our political bias, our pocketbook, or our anger will only trip us up. A lens that could guide us, I submit, is one that helps us focus on enabling everyone to have enough nutritious food. With that vision correction we could begin to see related issues in a surprisingly new way.

But Is It Realistic?

Because the idea of ending hunger connects us to the poverty, inequalities, and family erosion that surround hunger, an economic renewal along the lines that I have sketched in the previous chapter is necessary. But is that a fantasy? With a divided nation and a polarized Congress, it would seem a stretch.

"Let's be realistic," you say.

What is *not* realistic is to continue on the current decades-long path of expanding inequalities and divisiveness that is tearing us apart. Many in Congress seem wedded to a largely discredited top-down economics that is more the cause than the cure of the frustration that led us to this point—just as we are moving into an era of even more highly developed digital technology that threatens to accelerate inequality and social unrest. In the face of this present and gathering storm, to cling to "more of the same" is an invitation to greater loss of hope and more political danger. Resistance to change that is necessary for dealing with this crisis—*that* is the definition of head-in-the-sand unrealism.

A hunger-free America with a more inclusive economy is of course unrealistic, if relegating vast numbers of people to hunger and poverty seems acceptable. It is unrealistic, if we are guided by fear. It is, if we settle for drifting further down the stream of class extremes, social pathologies, and racial unrest. It is, if we think the status quo will do. But why do we need to accept any of those dismal assumptions? A plausible, unifying, fiscally prudent way forward that is shaped by America's founding values could be carried out by members of Congress willing to place country above partisan loyalty and work across party lines. Why should such elemental responsibility and common sense be dismissed as far-fetched?

I speak in judgment of myself as well as others, and of Democrats as well as Republicans, because all of us share in neglecting the vast body of Americans whose desperation has brought us to this point. Republicans, Democrats, and Independents—all of us—now need to bend every effort toward changing the trajectory of our political life toward ending hunger and poverty and modifying our inequality extremes. Each of us can help to improve civil discourse in political matters, cultivate friendly ties across party lines, and work together as much as possible at every level with a genuine concern for the common good, always trying to restrict damage where it is occurring and seizing opportunities for outcomes that are socially and racially healing.

It may be that our nation will continue on the path of inequality to the breaking point and to the ruin of this great democratic experiment that is the America we have loved and hoped for. On the other hand, perhaps the present course will awaken us to the folly of trusting too much in the magic of free enterprise or in our own version of untamed individualism. We are not victims of fate. We can pursue a more compelling and humane path. Sensible efforts now can lay the groundwork for that.

A February 2016 Pew Research Center survey found that 65 percent of Americans consider the US economic system to be "rigged" in favor of the rich and powerful. Only 31 percent said the system is generally fair to most Americans. The sense of unfairness holds not only for Democrats and independents, but also by a narrow margin even among conservative Republicans. The only grouping that considers the economy fair to most Americans (though only by 60 percent) is that of Republicans and Republican-leaners with family incomes of $100,000 or more.[6] Among the 38 percent of affluent Republicans who think it unfair is billionaire Charles Koch, lavish funder of conservative candidates and causes. That he and two-thirds of the US public think the economy is unfairly rigged suggests a volatile situation.

The 2016 presidential primaries and general election exposed that volatility. Public polls and voting reflected a deep, if confused desire for leadership to lift us out of our political quagmire. But we still lack a vision that can unite us. Such a vision is within reach, however, because most Americans do not want children to go hungry or live in conditions that rob them of a constructive future. Most of us also want adults who can and should work to be employed and adequately paid, and those who cannot or should not work to be adequately assisted. We want families to thrive and individuals to take personal responsibility for contributing to their own good and the good of others. As I noted in chapter 11, there is wide public resistance to "welfare" when it is seen as permitting people to avoid responsibility, but strong support for assistance that leads to work. So the main features of the hunger-ending, jobs-oriented economic renewal that I have sketched in broad strokes are in line with underlying views held by the majority of Americans, including, perhaps especially, those we think of as welfare recipients (though all of us have benefited from extensive public assistance of many kinds). People on both sides of the political divide agree with these views, despite differences on how to implement them.

Though few have ever heard of it, the report in 2015 of a bipartisan National Commission on Hunger created by Congress calls freedom from hunger in the United States "an achievable goal." The report says:

> Hunger in America is solvable. . . . Our country—with all its strength, genius, creativity, and spirit of community—has the ability to be free from hunger. America has no shortage of food, and no shortage of

food assistance programs. But those programs do not work as effectively, cooperatively, and efficiently as they should.

In addition to sound public policy, the solution to hunger in America requires an economy with broad opportunity for working age adults, robust community and corporate partnerships, personal responsibility to make good, positive choices for our families and communities, and our sincere commitment to helping others in ways that strengthen the fabric of our society.[7]

The commission calls attention to a report that of 650,000 ex-offenders released each year, 90 percent experienced household food insecurity and 37 percent reported not eating for an entire day because they had no money.[8] Imagine the impact on families of prisoners and ex-offenders who suffer, first from the absence of a family caregiver and provider, and then from their subsequent difficulty in finding employment or even food.[9]

Part of the commission's mandate was "to more effectively use existing [government] programs and funds" (always a good idea) and to encourage private-sector initiatives "to reduce the need for government nutrition assistance programs." That could suggest either a more humane economy or the ramping up of charity in order to cut SNAP and shift some of the responsibility from taxpayers to charity-givers. If the latter, it is a badly flawed reason for an otherwise welcome point of engaging more of us in efforts against hunger.[10] That caveat aside, the report makes twenty useful (if properly understood) recommendations, and I am struck by the extent to which they fit the case I have been making. The first eighteen address food assistance, but the final two recommendations call for "a White House Leadership Council to End Hunger" and specify issues that lie "far beyond the reach and effectiveness of nutrition assistance programs." Such a council would have no power to implement anything, but the idea at least implies that a President and a Congress could establish the end of hunger as a serious national goal. That possibility remains dormant until aroused citizens begin advocating a new vision for the nation. Still, the report shows the potential of agreement across party lines for ways to end hunger.

Further evidence of that potential comes from the right-leaning American Enterprise Institute and the left-leaning Brookings Institution. These two influential think-tanks selected a group of distinguished conservative and progressive policy analysts to hammer out "a consensus plan for reducing poverty and restoring the American Dream." Their 2015 report, *Opportunity, Responsibility, and Security*, deplores the fact that a large portion of our children grow up in disadvantaged, chaotic homes and neighborhoods and attend deficient schools, while their parents work for low wages. "The massive waste and loss of this human potential costs the United States in economic terms and it is a tragedy in human terms," it asserts. The group considers a growing and vibrant economy to be a top national priority and "unanimously placed employment at the center of any national strategy to reduce poverty and increase mobility." Their book-length report endorses a modest (unspecified) increase in the minimum wage, suggests helping states create more jobs, including "if necessary" government-supported jobs, but not as an entitlement. The report favors "reducing entitlement spending *for the affluent*" (italics added) as well as corporate welfare, such as agriculture subsidies, and certain types of tax breaks that "overwhelmingly benefit high-income households."[11] This report shows that conservatives and progressives can find extensive common ground when they are willing to work together to get positive outcomes.

Bipartisan congressional action on the Global Food Security Act in 2016 and 2018 and support of other global food and development assistance reforms pushed by citizen advocates during the Bush and Obama administrations[12] raise hopes for further progress and more aggressive leadership against global hunger and poverty. Those hopes were reinforced by support in Congress for both domestic food programs and foreign aid in 2017 and 2018, despite large cuts proposed by the Trump administration. To this, add earlier bipartisan agreement on Jubilee debt reduction (chapter 4) as well as Senate immigration reform that was blocked by an obstructing House minority (chapter 10), and bipartisan penal reform (chapter 11). The extent of agreement indicates the potential of public and congressional support for establishing a national goal of ending hunger in America, while pursuing a more equitable economy.

Suppose Congress adopted as a genuine commitment the goal of ending hunger here at home and doing our part toward ending it globally. That could become the centerpiece for helping us heal national wounds related to poverty, class, and race. It would give all of us a sense of hope and the satisfaction of being part of something good and great. As a significant byproduct, the United States would gain strength and luster globally as a nation to be honored for living up to its ideals. This could happen—if citizens build strong support among members of Congress from both political parties for doing so.

I am proposing that we first establish the goal and set in motion a process for getting there in defined steps and moving toward that goal through a combination of food assistance and economic initiatives. Food assistance would be the guaranteed backup to ensure that the designated annual progress toward ending hunger keeps on track if, and to the extent, that the economy otherwise falls short of enabling us to do so. While we work together in this way, the goal would serve as a lens through which we could more clearly see the connections to related social and economic problems that beg for commonsense solutions.

If federal food assistance, primarily SNAP, is to fill the gap, what might that cost?

Feeding America has estimated the additional average cost of enabling every food-insecure American to buy enough food at $823 a year for each one.[13] Allowing $1,000 as an average for each of 40 million food-insecure persons would cost a total of $40 billion on top of the current $100 billion in federal food assistance. But if we were to wipe out hunger gradually, say, in seven years, with economic reforms helping to narrow the gap, we might need the equivalent, at most, of an additional $4 billion each year for SNAP assistance (allowing for a potential maximum of $40 billion in ten years if a recession occurs) *minus* economic improvements that offset the cost. In reality, the cost would probably taper off to a small fraction of that amount as the economy improves for lower-income Americans. Evidence presented in chapter 2 shows that ending hunger would in fact save the country several times that much in a variety of ways. But even discounting such savings and considering only the most costly scenario, $40 billion extra to wipe out hunger would amount to about one penny out of every dollar in our national budget, or one penny out of every $5.00 of our total economy, for a colossal achievement. Adding a smaller but substantial amount to provide greater leadership in helping to end hunger and poverty abroad would also bring benefits that would flow both socially and economically.

The above scenario includes the "super Band-Aid" version of ending hunger in America. Food assistance is a necessary, fast, and sure way of ending that scandal, but not the best way. Far more important is economic renewal to lift all the boats so that those who are now unemployed but able to work can do so, and all who are employed can earn decent wages. This would strengthen free enterprise by including more people in it, and as the recovery takes hold it would reduce the need (and cost) of nutrition assistance and other safety-net programs.

Putting a price-tag on that kind of economic recovery depends on the details. Done well, a revitalized economy would require hundreds of billions of additional dollars annually. That prospect dooms the idea unless it is accompanied with realistic steps to rein in the deficit and reduce future deficits. Additional revenue from tax reforms would make this possible. A genuinely inclusive recovery might (or might not) delay an initial reduction of the deficit, but as recovery takes hold and the economy grows, the deficit should be phased out.

Steps that would enable us to deal seriously with the deficit include the following: (1) Bipartisan agreement on an economic package with a convincing path toward reducing future deficits and making a balanced budget a normal, but flexible expectation. Such an agreement would restore confidence in the government as well as the economy. (2) A review of all government programs, including defense and entitlements, to achieve reforms and efficiencies, while protecting those who are vulnerable. No bridges to nowhere or special subsidies for those with incomes well above average. (3) Tax reform and tax increases to reduce inequalities, provide income for a more robust economy, and help pay for reductions in the deficit.

But would *this* pass the test of realism? Or does the expectation of increased revenue echo the Reagan, Bush, and Trump-era tax cuts that were supposed to boost the economy and erase the deficits but instead increased inequalities and caused the deficits to soar? Those tax cuts did stimulate the economy to some extent, but they were a form of spending without a recovery program. Stated differently, the tax cuts *were* the recovery program, but they were accompanied by large increases in military spending for the Cold War, then the Gulf War, then wars in Iraq and Afghanistan, and now upgrading defense. Most important of all, the tax cuts heavily favored people of wealth, based on a top-down, trickle-down approach to the economy. Not nearly enough trickled down, so the tax cuts increased both the deficit and inequalities.

In contrast, the economic initiative proposed in chapter 11 would strengthen free enterprise but would do so especially by generating jobs for people who are unemployed as well as better wages for wage earners. It is a bottom-up approach for more and better-paying jobs, putting more food on half-empty tables, renovating our infrastructure, giving kids a good start and a strong finish in school, and rewarding innovative research and socially responsible technology. Prudent investments such as these get plowed back into the economy as people buy groceries, seize opportunities, and improve their living standards. The benefits could create an upward spiral for the economy. They would also address our inequalities.

Measuring Costs and Benefits

Is there reason to believe that such a program would succeed? There is, if we are willing to look at benefits as well as costs and combine courage with discretion. Consider initiatives from our own recent history that may seem, in hindsight, to have been obvious and inevitable developments, though they were anything but that at the time.

The New Deal

President Roosevelt's New Deal rescued the nation during the 1930s with targeted interventions. The business sector was prevented by a combination of fear and inability from investing money in a depressed economy. So the federal government offered emergency relief to some of the most destitute and vulnerable Americans and employed millions of others in programs such as the Works Progress Administration (WPA) and the Civilian Conservation Corps (CCC). The work they did on public projects—roads, parks, schools, libraries—continues to benefit the entire nation. In this way we invested in the nation at a time when we were least able to afford it. Or so it seemed. In fact we were least able to afford *not* doing it.

- Unemployment reached an all-time high of almost 29 percent in March 1933 (the month in which President Roosevelt was inaugurated) and averaged nearly 25 percent that year. It dropped to 14.5 percent by 1940, but not below 10 percent until 1941, when pre-war mobilization began. By December 7 of that year, when Pearl Harbor was attacked, we had shortages of skilled labor.[14]
- With the onset of the Depression revenue fell and deficits rose, causing the national debt (measured as a percentage of the nation's economy) to double during the Hoover years from 18 percent of GDP in 1930 to 39 percent of GDP in 1933. Roosevelt's New Deal increased both spending and income, but the growth of debt as a percentage of GDP actually slowed, inching up to 45 percent of GDP in 1941, until our all-out participation in World War II caused it to peak at 119 percent of GDP in 1946.[15]

If a disheartened nation, reeling from an economic collapse that brought on the Great Depression of the 1930s, could be rallied around a sensible, but controversial recovery program that entailed deficit spending, why could not our nation today—with eight times the per capita income[16] and twenty-one times the economic output (GDP)[17]—rise to the challenge of opening our economy more fully to those who are currently left on the sidelines, many still living in and others fearing poverty?

The US Response in World War II

Some maintain that the New Deal, with its spending programs, failed to lift us out of the Depression and that it took a war to get us out. That is partly true. The war set in motion unused industrial capacity (an "advantage" no longer as available) that soon employed millions. But it required government intervention with deficit spending on a large scale.

The war aroused the nation to mobilize its resources for a high cause that united us. Measured by inflation-adjusted dollars and as a percentage of our economy, that mobilization required massive borrowing and a far higher deficit (as a percentage of our economy) than that of the Depression-era New Deal or the deficits triggered by the near collapse of the economy in 2008. Yet our part in World War II unleashed industrial and human energies that led to a postwar boom that offset its cost many times over. If, while struggling with an improved but still deeply troubled economy, we could become an even wealthier nation while focusing all efforts on the war, why could we not now, with a vastly stronger economic base, become a more prosperous and healthy nation while addressing the contradiction of hunger and poverty at home, as well as the injustice of hunger and poverty abroad?

European Recovery

Think of our part in the recovery of Western Europe, many of its cities reduced to rubble and much of its industrial capacity in ruins, millions dead, millions hungry, many starving, and millions uprooted. The Marshall Plan had little initial public support; but President Truman reached across party lines to Arthur Vandenberg, chairman of the Senate Foreign Relations Committee, who in turn persuaded Republican colleagues to get behind the plan, which led to its enactment into law in 1948.

The result, as I reported in chapter 6, was an unprecedented peacetime foreign aid program that cost the equivalent of $123 billion in 2015 dollars (or about $300 billion as a comparable percentage of our federal budget). The US economy was far weaker and far more deeply in debt (as a percentage of our economy) than is the case today. But, along with generous private assistance, the Marshall Plan spared countless lives and prevented millions more from untold suffering and hardship. It also paved the way for what eventually became the European Union. Desperate people of Western Europe turned away from communism toward democracy. A cauldron of hatreds and violence became a region of peace, and its countries became trading partners who contributed extensively to postwar US prosperity by keeping our expanded industrial capacity active and growing. The cost of the Marshall Plan pales compared to the economic and social benefits it generated for us and for others.

The GI Bill

The Servicemen's Readjustment Act of 1944, known as the GI Bill, offered 16 million veterans tuition and living expenses for college or vocational training, home loan guarantees, and other benefits. The bill hit stiff opposition in Congress. Opponents argued that paying unemployed veterans $20 a month (about $285 in 2018 dollars) would undermine their incentive to look for work (as SNAP is alleged to do now). For that reason it stalled in a deadlocked House-Senate conference. The bill ultimately passed because a missing Georgia congressman was frantically tracked down by the Georgia state police and, with the help of World War I flying ace Eddie Rickenbacker's Eastern Airlines, was flown to the capital to cast a last-minute tie-breaking vote that prevented the bill from dying. It then passed unanimously in both houses of Congress.[18]

What accounted for the unanimous vote? The American Legion, which helped draft the bill, spearheaded a national campaign for it that included petitions, spot radio announcements, two-minute movies for local theaters, and newspaper editorials. Most of all, people flooded members of Congress with letters, telegrams, and personal visits. Citizens had aroused the nation with a strongly emotional appeal on behalf of the troops. Despite stalling and opposition in Congress, once the bill came to the floor of each chamber for a vote, not a single member of Congress dared to go on record against GIs who had risked their lives for our country.

Half of our 16 million war veterans used the GI bill for college, vocational training, or apprenticeships. Ironically, less than 20 percent of the money set aside for veterans' unemployment was ever used. Thanks to the

GI bill, millions of veterans who would have overloaded the job market and perhaps triggered a recession opted for education, making a better future for themselves and for the nation. To our shame, however, African Americans were denied those benefits. Veterans Affairs followed the Federal Housing Authority's racially discriminatory policies, so entire white suburbs and metropolitan neighborhoods were off-limits to returning black GIs. In addition, the VA denied them mortgage subsidies to which they were entitled. The VA also frequently restricted education and training for African Americans to lower levels than those for which they qualified.[19]

Except for its shameful racism, the GI bill was one of the finest and most rewarding initiatives the country has ever taken. It not only did the decent thing of rewarding service personnel, it also educated future teachers, doctors, scientists, entrepreneurs, academics, and political leaders. By 1956 the education and training part of this government program had cost the nation $14.5 billion—worth hundreds of billions of dollars in educational value today. That does not count the home loan guarantees and other benefits.[20] The GI bill was an investment in human capital that paid an immeasurably huge return to the nation's economic and social well-being. It still does, but the main beneficiaries were, and still are, white Americans. What a huge missed opportunity that was for African Americans and for the entire nation.

The Interstate Highway System

Proposed by and launched under President Dwight D. Eisenhower, the interstate highway system was approved by Congress in 1956. By 1994 its total construction cost was about $500 billion (adjusted for inflation in 2016 dollars). Since then it has been expanded. Until 2008 all of this was done on a pay-as-you-go basis, with revenue from highway user taxes (mostly gasoline taxes) placed in a highway trust fund. An expensive program to be sure, but one that contributed to the nation's prosperity. It created jobs, businesses, shopping centers, industries, and housing complexes. According to one estimate, by 1994 each dollar spent had generated $6 in economic gains, and the interstate had prevented 187,000 fatalities and almost 12 million injuries.[21]

There was also a dark side to the highway system. The project sliced urban neighborhoods in half in city after city. The most vulnerable and politically weakest urban areas were the prime candidates for the new freeway, which uprooted people and left abandoned and depressed sections behind.[22]

In doing so it contributed to economic and racial woes of people who also felt abandoned and depressed. As a child, Anthony Foxx, US transportation secretary in the Obama administration, couldn't ride his bike far from his Charlotte home without being blocked by a freeway. Homes, stores, and churches made way for the highway, and neighborhood friends were walled off from one another. In combination, highway construction and urban renewal displaced families, about two-thirds of whom were poor and mostly African American, according to Foxx. As transportation secretary he made it his mission to see that transportation initiatives would serve the communities through which they pass.[23]

For most Americans the Interstate expanded free enterprise and social mobility, another case of public investment paying large returns for most of us, while exacting costs that can never be fully measured from many of our most disadvantaged citizens.

The interstate highway system now needs to be repaired, modernized, and widened over the next two decades, just one piece of the much larger challenge of repairing the nation's infrastructure, a program that could enhance free enterprise, travel, national parks, schools, human development, and much more. Because opportunities are connected to transportation, that program should give high priority to serving impacted communities and their people and avoiding the mistakes of the past. For that to happen, mayors and governors, states and localities, must also be on board.

What Success Tells—and Does Not Tell—Us

One could add other initiatives, such as the Tennessee Valley Authority and the Rural Electrification Program, but the point is this: when the nation has seized the opportunity to strengthen its economy by facilitating the construction of roads, bridges, canals, railroads, seaports, and airports, laying the groundwork for expansion and growth of agriculture, increasing educational opportunities, furthering research, preserving forests, building parks, and extending rights and opportunities to excluded citizens, rewards have followed. Far from hindering private enterprise, these government initiatives, though seldom without their glaring flaws, enabled enterprise to flourish. As a result, life is immeasurably better for almost everyone who reads these words.

The Marshall Plan foreshadowed gains that have often assisted people in poor countries. By extending a helping hand through poverty-focused foreign aid, our assistance has a way of helping us as well. When we have "cast our bread upon the waters" it has returned to us,[24] not only in good will, but in trade with recipient and former recipient countries. As Bill Gates reminded President Trump, eleven of the country's top fifteen trading partners once received US foreign aid.[25]

Precedents, of course, do not tell us what will happen in the future. I am not suggesting a big payback from any and every idea for a new initiative. Unique circumstances surrounded those I have cited, just as new obstacles and opportunities face us today. But an aggressive, carefully designed economic initiative along the lines that I have been suggesting, one that shifts us clearly toward investing in people by ending hunger and poverty, creating more jobs, and reducing our inequalities, makes sense. Not to pursue such a path would be reckless.

What if bold initiatives prove to be too ambitious for an economy that refuses to grow fast enough to accommodate them? In that case the economic program, designed carefully (and not "a little pork for everyone to get this thing passed"), would fall back on a less ambitious "Plan B" in order to avoid running up excessive deficits. But a Plan B is always Plan B, not called into service when a much better outcome is plausible. Under Plan B we could still end hunger here and help end it abroad; tax reforms could be enacted; and other economic initiatives could be modified. In this way even Plan B could bring about a more equitable economy to which all of us could adjust together, with affluent Americans contributing more and those needing a job, training, or assistance boosted toward self-reliance.

Citing two newly published books, political pundit E. J. Dionne Jr. cautions against the nostalgia of seeking to replicate the New Deal and the exceptional gains in the era that followed; but he also warns against the amnesia of forgetting the kind of initiatives that made the nation prosper.[26] Wise and courageous government leadership stimulated the economy and helped unify the nation. Those precedents show that we need not accept a pinched and fearful future for the nation. We can advance our founding ideals if we are willing to rise above what Dionne's colleague Dan Balz calls "the standoff between the parties as the country weathers transformational changes akin to those of the Industrial Revolution."[27] But the standoff will continue until more members of Congress reject obstructionist tactics, relinquish the illusion that we must cut but never increase taxes, and abandon the reflex that entitlements are always untouchable.

Carefully planned and well executed, programs to end hunger and expand the economy could yield returns that far outweigh their cost. We need to weigh the cost of *not* doing them. Precision eludes us, of course, but imagine what the cost would have been to the nation and the world if we had *not* done the Marshall Plan, or the GI bill, or the interstate highway system, or recovery from the Great Depression, or rescue from the near economic collapse of 2008. Had we saved money by not doing these things, the loss to all of us would have been staggering.

Consider, as well, the costs of allowing hunger and poverty to persist: poor health, ill-fed and ill-educated youth dropping out of school and adding to the growing statistics on drug addiction, delinquency, family breakdown, and social dysfunction. Imagine the cost of additional crime, police, courts, jails and prisons, added healthcare, absenteeism, unemployment; and the loss of never-realized productive workers, civic leaders, teachers, and inventors.

Ending hunger is a noble idea, but, of course, human selfishness and political division stand in the way of many noble ideas. However, a minority of sufficiently determined citizens can often overcome deeply rooted obstacles. Think of the slave trade and slavery, or restrictions on the civil rights of African Americans, women, and same-gender couples. These seemingly permanent fixtures changed legally and to a great extent in practice. As Richard Goodwin has observed, "Our government always lags behind an originating movement."[28]

The time is ripe for a movement to end hunger and make our economy work for everybody.

13

Breaking the Silence

We will have to repent in this generation . . . for the appalling silence of the good people.
—Martin Luther King Jr.[1]

I have argued that we could end most hunger in this country within a few years and help end most of it globally in less than a generation. But that will happen only if, as citizens, we break our silence and persuade our leaders to make it a high national priority. We could also make our economy work for everybody. That too requires us to speak up persistently until it happens.

Perhaps you are not convinced that your speaking up would change anything. Why add this inconvenience to an already-busy life? You may prefer to "wait and see," at least for now. That was the thinking of many well-meaning Germans who privately deplored the rise of the Nazis before World War II and opted for silence. They foolishly trusted a strongman to make Germany great again and overlooked his lies or calculated that they could control his behavior. Or they were driven by fear or fooled by their own complacency to remain silent. But silence can kill. It can diminish and shorten lives. It did so then, and it does so now.

If enough citizens had spoken up and worked earlier to prevent a ruthless, determined man from seizing power in Germany, the outcome would have been different. But soon it was too late. Speaking out became dangerous and invited punishment, sometimes death. Before long war broke out and deaths occurred on a massive scale.

In contrast to Germany during the rise and reign of Adolf Hitler, almost everyone who reads this book can speak up for justice without fear of government retaliation. We have no such excuse for remaining silent and contributing to the shortening and diminishing of lives.

The possibility of ending most hunger and poverty holds true even in the face of political turns in the opposite direction or events such as wars, recessions, and climate-related disasters. Any or all of these setbacks could intervene to limit, halt, or even reverse progress toward a hunger-free nation and a hunger-free world. In that case, too, speaking out against hunger and the inequalities that surround it would not be a wasted effort. Setbacks make it all the more crucial that citizens not surrender to injustice, but be vocal and determined in pushing to limit the diminishment of lives.

The impact of advocacy usually cannot be precisely measured, but it is never wasted. Our Pledge of Allegiance, reflecting our founding documents, commits us individually and corporately to "liberty and justice for all." Everyone who honors that pledge by advocating policies to end hunger and humanize our economy is one more voice that, combined with other voices, helps leverage national decisions that bring hope to others. I have seen this happen year after year through the work of faithful advocates.[2] The effort and money invested in advocacy may generate returns on the scale of 100 to 1 in benefits[3]—big gains for hungry people and for the well-being of all of us.

With much else competing for our attention, it is easy to push aside the hunger of people we do not know. But if we are to "do unto others" as we would have them do unto us, what conclusion can we draw but that advocacy against hunger is a compelling cause when the well-being of so many others is at stake?

Taking Personal Responsibility

If silence kills, and we remain silent, are we not morally responsible? Responsibility means exactly that: response-ability. When we have the ability to respond and fail to do so, we fall short of what it means to be truly human. You don't need to push people into the water to be complicit in their drowning. Not jumping in to save them—or simply observing and not calling for help—will accomplish that.

Yet who is entitled to pass judgment on others? On Germans, say, who wanted the Nazi nightmare to vanish, but faced dangers that would have made cowards of any of us? Or on the mother or father who cannot face the idea of adding advocacy against hunger when they are overwhelmed by work and family concerns? Or on the person already devoting long hours to some other crucial cause or issue? Or on someone who is honestly struggling to figure these things out? No one, including this writer, has a right to judge.

Still, the impact of our individual and collective silence while hunger and poverty are cheating people of life is quite clear.

I suspect that the vast majority of well-meaning people who choose silence over advocacy are simply not aware of what their influence as citizens could accomplish and the difference it can make.

Why did the resolve of the 1974 World Food Conference (chapter 3 above), "that within a decade no child shall go to bed hungry" not bring about the political will to end hunger? It failed to do so because the people who made the resolve were mostly development specialists or government leaders whose commitment hinged on the extent of public support. The media gave it only passing attention, and too few citizens urged political leaders to take steps needed to accomplish that goal—and few even realized such urging was needed. Think of President Roosevelt's comment to good-cause petitioners, "Now go back and make me do it" (chapter 4 above). Still, limited efforts led to progress, and since then the world has made remarkable gains against extreme hunger and poverty. Now, decades later, far fewer but still too many children throughout the world go to bed hungry, so Bread for the World was beating the drums for them yet again in 2019 with a campaign of messages to Congress to rouse our nation and other nations to put an end to child and maternal hunger.

The civil rights movement of the 1950s and 1960s brought about the political will to end some of the most extreme forms of racial discrimination in this country. There was nothing automatic or inevitable about it. It took two and a half centuries of slavery, a Civil War, and another century of lynchings, Jim Crow laws, and the cruelties of segregation before public outcries aroused the Supreme Court, presidents, and the Congress to act.

In April 1963 Dr. Martin Luther King Jr. and scores of others were jailed in Birmingham, Alabama, following peaceful demonstrations against racial segregation on Good Friday and Easter. A group of eight prominent white Alabama clergymen wrote a statement, published in *The Birmingham News*, criticizing King's action as unwise and untimely. They urged patience. King's reply to them (written first on the margins of a newspaper and scraps of paper) became one of the most eloquent documents in American history, and it is instructive for us now.[4]

"You deplore the demonstrations taking place in Birmingham," he wrote, and consider them ill-timed. "But your statement, I am sorry to say, fails to express a similar concern for the conditions that brought about the demonstrations." King said, "I have yet to engage in a direct-action campaign that was 'well timed' in the view of those who have not suffered unduly from the disease of segregation." We are asked to wait, he wrote, but we have waited for 340 years, and "'Wait' has almost always meant 'Never.'"

> I have almost reached the regrettable conclusion that the Negro's great stumbling block in the stride toward freedom is not the White Citizens Councilor or the Ku Klux Klanner but the white moderate who is more devoted to "order" than to justice; who prefers a nega-tive peace which is the absence of tension to a positive peace which is the presence of justice. . . . Shallow understanding from people of good will is more frustrating than absolute misunderstanding from people of ill will.

"I have also been disappointed with the white church and its leadership," King wrote. Some, he said, have been outright opponents of freedom, and "all too many others have been more cautious than courageous and have remained silent behind the anesthetizing security of stained-glass win-dows." King said he had "watched white churchmen stand on the sidelines and merely mouth pious irrelevancies and sanctimonious trivialities." In the middle of a mighty struggle against racial and economic injustice "I have heard many ministers say, 'Those are social issues with which the gospel has no real concern.'" The power structure of the average community, he said, "is consoled by the church's silent—and often even vocal—sanction of things as they are." He added:

> We will have to repent in this generation not merely for the vitriolic words and actions of the bad people but for the appalling silence of the good people. We must come to see that human progress never rolls in on wheels of inevitability. It comes through the tireless efforts and persistent work of men willing to be coworkers with God, and without this hard work time itself becomes an ally of the forces of social stagnation.

It is not hard to see striking similarities between the silence of good people (perhaps our own) in the face of poverty and hunger and the silence that King encountered. The courage that speaking out against racial injustice required was courage in the face of widespread prejudice and fear of change, and for some people courage in the face of death. I witnessed that person-ally in Dr. King at Selma, Alabama, on the Tuesday that followed "Bloody Sunday" in 1965, while marching past block after block of hostile onlookers.

King's physical vulnerability was so stark that the terrible thought flashed in my mind, "This man does not have long to live." The courage required of us in speaking out against the injustice of hunger is small by comparison, but it still jars our comfort and complacency. Yet our silence reinforces a status quo that is morally unacceptable. Advocating against hunger may mean choosing between a negative peace which is the absence of tension and a positive peace which is the presence of justice.

King welcomed personal kindness, but not as a substitute for civil rights. We likewise should welcome and support the kindness of charity for hungry people, but not as a substitute for their right to a nutritionally adequate diet and their opportunity to work at a wage that lifts people out of poverty.

Steps We Can Take

You might think that getting Congress to set a national goal to end hunger would be easy. After all, who wants children to go hungry and live impaired lives? Polls consistently indicate that a large majority of Americans favor the reduction of hunger, both foreign and domestic.[5] Unfortunately this widely held sentiment is soft, too seldom urged upon our leaders as a vital national policy. When other issues arouse more voters to contact members of Congress, support for action against hunger takes a back seat.

Consider that it has been difficult to get even modest gun controls legislated, though a majority of the US public favors them. The National Rifle Association's opposition has been so intense and so effectively targets political figures who favor any steps in that direction that, no matter how many people are killed and maimed by bullets day after day, it has been impossible to get Congress to pass even so basic a step as requiring the registration of guns—fishing licenses and auto licenses and cosmetic licenses, but not guns. The *intensity* of the NRA's lobbying and the politics of fear override the majority favoring sensible control. However, the February 2018 gunning down of seventeen students in Parkland, Florida, aroused their shaken survivors and students elsewhere to descend on their state capitol with a lobbying force that shamed the legislators and governor into enacting at least a few modest but substantive remedial reforms—a surprising setback to the NRA. It showed that students could become a promising new force nationally for putting legislators on the defensive in what could become a turning point against gun violence.

The lesson for us regarding hunger? We need *more* advocates, but we also need more *intensive* advocacy—the intensity of the NRA combined with the wisdom of angels. Our history shows us that when a good cause is backed by growing public insistence, change occurs. Think of the women's suffrage movement that led to ratification of the Nineteenth Amendment and the right of women to vote; or the American Legion's campaign in 1944 that got an avalanche of messages from voters to persuade a reluctant Congress to pass the GI Bill; or the civil rights movement of the 1950s and 1960s that overcame enormous resistance. Justice can win, but it takes political will, driven by determined citizens, students among them, who demand it.

There are many levels and forms of advocacy. Usually people climb up the ladder of intensity one step at a time. It may begin with a click-of-the-mouse to Congress, or a handwritten letter. For many it stays at that level, and millions of people are needed who faithfully do this in a timely fashion. But we also need a growing cadre of people who, like the Parkland students, seize the power of their citizenship and decide to become more active agents of change.

To become an effective advocate at any level against hunger, each of us needs to be part of an organization that keeps us well informed so we can act in a timely manner in concert with others. Some organizations do direct lobbying on both domestic and international hunger and can focus without restrictions on legislation. Other organizations, with varying agendas, also engage citizens in advocacy. Here are some of the main ones:

- Alliance to End Hunger
- Bread for the World
- Bread for the World Institute
- Food Research & Action Center (FRAC)
- Friends Committee on National Legislation (FCNL)
- Global Citizens
- Network
- ONE Campaign
- RESULTS

The list is alphabetical, but in this book I have reflected a natural tilt toward Bread for the World because of my part in it from the time of its founding, having seen up close, year after year, the commitment and effectiveness of those who participate in it—members, donors, and activists, as well as board and staff members. Advocates closely associated with other groups would say much the same about their respective organizations. Though drawing from my own experience in this book, I want to say how important the work with other justice, charity, and advocacy groups has been and how grateful I am for it, for our partnership, and for the mutual respect and collegiality we have.

The web gives detailed information on each of the groups listed, as well as others. The Alliance to End Hunger provides a place for companies, foundations, universities, and other nonprofits to interact and together promote government policies that reduce hunger. Bread for the World, FCNL, Network, ONE Action (an arm of the ONE Campaign), and RESULTS are registered to do unrestricted legislative lobbying. Bread for the World Institute does policy analysis, education, and advocacy rather than lobbying. FRAC focuses on domestic hunger and has strong ties with advocates on state issues. Global Citizens deals with a wide array of global issues. ONE Action focuses mainly on extreme poverty and preventable disease in Africa. The main strength of most of these groups is not that they do your advocacy for you, but that they engage you to act as a citizen advocate. However, advocacy groups also work directly as organizations to influence Congress and the media, engage in research, education, and strategy, as well as help their members take action at the right time and in the right way.

To do these things increasingly well, while expanding their outreach, they need financial support—a tougher hurdle for them than it is for charities engaged in food assistance. Having limited funds for advocacy plays into the hands of the silence that kills, so a contribution for charitable food assistance arguably merits at least a matching contribution for advocacy. In the words of travel expert and hunger advocate Rick Steves, "It's important to balance our charity giving with big-picture advocacy in a way that helps bend government policy to the needs of the hungry."[6]

Along the same line, we should consider giving time and money to support candidates for public office who can provide strong leadership for ending hunger and making our economy work for everybody. Many small contributions can help to offset the otherwise prevailing influence of big-money donors, especially if you tell them *why* you are giving.

Any nonprofit organization, including churches, can advocate without restrictions for or against government *policies*. They can also do a limited amount of lobbying on *specific legislation*.[7] Positions taken by a respected organization are important, but they are no substitute for personal messages from voters. Members of Congress want to know the views of people in the state or district they represent, so a good advocacy organization will give their members timely information on key issues as well as advice on whom to contact and what to write or say.

Ending hunger requires action from the nation's decision-makers. That usually means members of Congress, though state legislators and other state or local officials also have influence that they can be asked to use. Except for people living in the District of Columbia, each of us has two US senators and one US representative. You can contact them:

1. By mail. Personal handwritten or hand-typed letters are highly effective. Addresses for them and for the President:

- US Senate, Washington, DC 20010
- US House of Representatives, Washington, DC 20015
- The White House, Washington, DC 20500

2. By email. Addresses are available from the senator's or representative's website. Emails are often messages prepared by an advocacy group and sent by a simple click of the mouse. However, because clicks are so easy, they usually do not have nearly as much impact as thoughtful letters or personally crafted emails. Still, many advocates start with clicks on prepared online messages, and when the numbers mount, legislators pay attention.

3. By phone. A phone call is important when a committee or floor vote is soon to occur or to reinforce a previous message. On rare occasions you may get to talk to your House or Senate member, but usually you ask for the aide who handles the particular issue in question. If none is available, you can ask for a return call or leave a message. The switchboard numbers for reaching House and Senate members: 202-224-3121 or 800-826-3688 (toll free).

4. A **personal visit** is usually best of all, whether in the nation's capital or in your state or district. A small group may have more influence than a one-on-one visit. And meeting with a staff aide who handles a specific issue may be as valuable as meeting with the senator or congressperson for whom she or he works. Good preparation, courtesy, and respect, with firmness, always help.

Former Congressman Spencer Bachus (R-AL) looks back at the way Bread for the World members cultivated a personal relationship with him and introduced him to the need of poor countries for debt relief. His advice is that, if possible, advocates should not only send letters, but one or more of them should develop a strategy for relating on a personal basis with their member of Congress, meet with him or her, and share their special interest in reducing hunger.[8] A good relationship goes a long way. Chapter 4 has a sketch of how advocates did this effectively with Bachus for the Jubilee Debt Campaign.

You may want to become part of a small team that takes initiatives together. You could write an occasional newspaper article, perhaps a piece for the editorial page (an op-ed) or a letter to the editor, on a key issue. Shortly before initially writing the previous sentence I received via the internet the copy of a letter printed on June 28, 2017, in *The St. Louis Post-Dispatch* from Jane Klopfenstein of Edwardsville, Illinois, urging three area members of Congress by name to oppose cuts to SNAP, pointing out that hungry Americans overwhelmingly rely on SNAP, not charity, for food assistance. Her letter almost certainly got the attention of those congresspersons as well as thousands of voters. You might do that or even arrange for a few people to meet with the editor or editorial staff to present the case for an editorial on a bill before Congress.

You could have an "offering of letters" to Congress in your church or book club. Perhaps you could get some students fired up to work for making the end of hunger a national goal. Your group could host a conference or workshop to attract and train new advocates. You might join with other groups to invite one of your US senators or your US representative to address such a conference. You could take advantage of a "town hall" meeting or other public event featuring a member of Congress by posing questions and urging him or her to take assertive leadership against hunger. These are just a few of the ways to influence leaders. Even when you get a negative response, you may soften opposition and lay the groundwork for subsequent efforts. Surprises do occur. And if you are quite sure your senators or representative are already on your side, thanking them and encouraging them to be champions of the issue with their congressional colleagues can stir further support.

There is plenty of room for imagination. In 2016 Zach and Sarah Schmidt of Crystal Lake, Illinois, and a small group of advocates met with their congressman, Randy Hultgren (R), to urge him to co-sponsor the Global Food Security Act. Hultgren did, so later Zach lined up for a picture with his five smiling kids, each holding one piece of a sign that said, "Thank—you—Congressman—Hultgren—!!!—Proverbs 31:8–9." The picture was posted on Facebook. A delighted Hultgren sent them a note of thanks. You can bet that Zach and Sarah have a friendly ear in Hultgren when other issues come up for consideration. Kids are often the best advocates. And in this case social media amplified their message.

You could enlist staff, volunteers, and food recipients at a food bank, local food pantries, or a soup kitchen to become citizen advocates. Recipients, deeply affected by hunger, often feel powerless as citizens, when in fact their own experience is often the most persuasive of messages to a member of Congress, whether written by letter or told in person. It enables recipients to give to others in an effective way. Like other advocates, but especially so, they deserve to discover the satisfaction of helping to influence decision-makers on legislation affecting hungry people.

You can *vote* to end hunger. Candidates for president or Congress seldom mention hunger or poverty—a consequence of our silence—but we can change that by urging them to make it a priority. All of us can actively support candidates who take a strong stand against hunger. Attending a public meeting where one or more candidates for Congress are speaking can provide an excellent opportunity to ask what they have done or intend to do about hunger and to address the nation's inequalities. That's also a foot-in-the-door for following up on actual performance.

You can talk with friends, neighbors, colleagues at work, and people at your church or social club about hunger and advocacy. Doing so with family members at mealtime or while watching the news may be even more important, so it becomes a deeply felt family value—a gift to your children, often life-changing and a powerful foundation for ending hunger.

Years ago, I asked a prominent World Bank economist, "What is the single most important thing we can do to end hunger?" His response was, "Pray. If we are truly praying for an end to hunger, action follows."[9] If you don't pray, you can establish another way to remind yourself daily of those who are hungry and our need to speak up for them.

A Driving, Unifying Cause

When President John F. Kennedy challenged the nation to put a man on the moon before the end of the 1960s, it soon became a national goal, though throughout the 1960s a majority of Americans did not believe it was worth the cost.[10] In this case presidential leadership preceded public support. We were driven in large part by Cold War competition with the Soviet Union, which had successfully launched the first manned spaceship, so patriotism played a big role. So did media coverage. No doubt scientists, as well as industry, labor, and military leaders, sensed opportunities. Whatever the combination of motives, getting an American to the moon within a decade became a goal toward which laws were passed, money appropriated, and a vast complex of people organized. And it wasn't cheap.[11]

Of course, putting a man on the moon, as a project of science and industry, involved more precision than the complexities of dealing with human behavior. Still, given what we now know about steps to reduce and eliminate hunger, were we to commit the same determination and even a fraction of its cost to it, we could end hunger here and do more to help end it globally. And if we did, or even came close, is there any reason to doubt that the economic and social benefits would be enormous, and that our nation and the world—and we ourselves—would be better for having done it?

We can learn (with appropriate discretion) from the successes and mistakes of earlier national goals. We can use as a model the global debt forgiveness campaign (chapter 4) that showed how citizens could change prevailing political winds to help desperate people abroad. We can build on the outcome of the Millennium Development Goals for 2015 and the challenge of reaching the new Sustainable Development Goals for 2030.

In pushing for an end to hunger we are making a positive contribution toward lifting our nation out of the political quagmire that endangers our democracy and perpetuates the awful inequalities that haunt us. We can point out how the process of ending hunger could bring us together across political lines and help us begin to achieve a more just and inclusive economy.

To build on these things we need people who care enough to push our leaders to take action. Envision a growing array of people and organizations—religious and nonreligious, unions and businesses, food providers and food aid recipients, public policy groups and private assistance agencies, students and senior citizens—becoming part of a grand coalition to end hunger. This coalition would include not only hunger-related charities and advocacy organizations, but a wide range of individuals and groups, civic and religious, working on causes related to hunger and poverty, such as penal reform, housing, child and family development, prevention and treatment of substance abuse, job creation, immigration, racial justice, climate change, education, and healthcare, to mention a few. People committed to such causes are already helping, at least indirectly, to erase hunger and poverty by nudging political consideration of these connected issues.

Anti-hunger advocates can help boost those related causes—and many of them do. In turn, supporters of those causes can speak up for ending hunger—and many of them also do that. In this way we can generate a more powerful movement. What could especially help turn the tide would be adding new advocates from the host of people who now support charitable efforts to reduce hunger but have yet to step forward and speak up for poor and hungry people at the political level. If recipients of food from charities, who number in many millions, were to relay their stories of need to their members of Congress and urge national action to end hunger, they could do a great service to other hungry people and feel empowered as citizens rather than passive recipients of charity. As more of us push for national action, we erect a stronger alliance against both hunger and the poverty that generates it.

I write these lines at the outset of 2019 and all of its political uncertainties. Democrats have regained control of the House, while Republicans have kept their Senate majority. What has not changed is the nation's need of a unifying vision with a moral center. I have been contending throughout this book that the goal of ending hunger could become that moral center and serve as a corrective lens through which we could see more clearly the way toward addressing other inequalities that now confound and divide us.

Rigid political stances, abetted by voter apathy, may prevent us from setting such a goal now. But if enough of us break our political silence regarding hunger and press the need for a more inclusive economy, the "unachievable" will become remarkably attractive and political leaders will begin to see it as a necessity. Public support can persuade members of both political parties not only to affirm the goal but to work seriously across party lines toward achieving it. President Trump or his successor, and this Congress or the next one, could pull us together around policies that would put our nation and the world on track toward ending hunger and dealing with our inequalities. That would be a courageous and historic step forward.

I am not forecasting what *will* happen. I am saying that it *could* happen if enough of us break our silence and speak out. The silence is deafening, because it deafens the nation to the common good and our leaders to the cry of the oppressed. No person acting alone and no group by itself can bring the nation to its senses on this. But a multitude of people and organizations working together could break the deadly silence and put hunger where it belongs: in the dustbin of history. Together we could repeal hunger and follow the trails that lead us to a more inclusive economy.

There is not a moment to lose, because patience is easy only for those who are comfortable and well fed.

*　　　*　　　*

That impatient word may conclude the book for many of you, but I am adding a chapter addressed specifically to religious believers, for reasons that I mention briefly in the Preface and expand on in the first few pages of chapter 14, which you are welcome to read.

Thirteen Things to Consider Doing

1. Join an advocacy organization and become active in calling for an end to hunger. Start small, but start.
2. Learn from the experience of a food-insecure family or person in your own vicinity what problems they face and what might be done to solve them.
3. Write, call, or visit your members of Congress when key hunger and poverty issues surface for congressional action.
4. Contribute time and/or money to a food pantry, soup kitchen, or food bank, and support a private organization working abroad to assist poor people. But give similar support to an anti-hunger advocacy organization.
5. Talk about hunger and poverty with your family members, friends, and associates. Make it a topic of conversation that engages the mind and heart of your children and others.
6. Become better informed. Get reports from an advocacy organization, and a balance of viewpoints from news and commentary of reliable print and electronic media. PBS News Hour and NPR do this well with background information. Read books and journals that deal with aspects of hunger and poverty.
7. Pray daily for an end to hunger and/or express daily your desire for its end in other ways.
8. Join or start a local group, no matter how small, even if it's teaming up with just one other person, to advocate for poor and hungry people. Stay in touch as developments occur, and contact your member of Congress. Your two could become three, then four, then more. Or maybe the two of you could simply be a dynamic duo. Start now as a dynamic uno.
9. Try to arrange an "offering of letters" in your church, synagogue, or service club to alert your US senators or representative to a key hunger issue at least once a year.
10. Visit a poor neighborhood or a poor country and learn about the struggles and hopes of people. See what you have in common and what your respective challenges are.
11. Attend a conference, a "lobby day," or a workshop on hunger and advocacy. View some videos that feature stories of effective advocacy. Bread for the World Institute's *2019 Hunger Report*, available on the web, has such videos, as may others.

12. Be creative. What special gifts and opportunities might you have to impact others? A teacher, for example, might be able to lead students to find a purpose in civic participation by helping to end hunger, for example by writing a letter to your US House member or one of your two US senators, or by interviewing a family member or neighbor about hunger.

13. Persist. Know that you are engaged in a matter of national and global importance that touches the lives and needs of people no less human than you.

14

Faith, Love, and Justice

Two things are now at stake in America. First, the soul of the nation. Second, the integrity of our faith.

—Jim Wallis[1]

Little that I have written so far is explicitly religious. I have made the case for ending hunger and reducing our inequalities based on an appeal to reason and morality that is accessible to all. It could be embraced by anyone who is morally sensitive, secular or religious, purely on the grounds of conscience or enlightened self-interest.

Now, however, I directly engage people of faith for two reasons. First, a vast number of Americans are people of faith. Many of them find their relationship with God, as I do, a powerful motivation for helping others. A disproportionately high number of food pantries and soup kitchens, for example, are church-related;[2] and private relief and development agencies working abroad are either faith-based or often attract substantial support from religious believers. Research indicates that, on average, Americans who regularly attend church give more money and volunteer more time to assist poor people through private charity, and are more active in civic life, than nonmembers or casual adherents to religion.[3] It would be foolish to ignore this motivation.

However, when it comes to addressing the structural causes of poverty through *government*, devoutly religious people—especially religious white people, it turns out—prefer charity. They tend to be less supportive of government programs than their secular counterparts.[4] Black and Hispanic church members are more supportive of government action than white members. Their experience of injustice and of charity's limitations in addressing it may at least partly account for that. One national poll shows that Christians in general, but predominantly white evangelical Christians, are more inclined than non-Christians to blame poverty on individual failings.[5]

The way people relate to God has a bearing on this. The 62 percent who "very often" feel God's love tend to love and trust others. Conversely, the 39 percent who very often feel God's judgment are inclined to judge and distrust others.[6] It is not a stretch to see how the experience of each may lead to different views on social and political engagement. One who has received mercy more easily extends mercy to others. This suggests a positive link between people's trust in God's love and their pursuit of government action for social justice. In David Beckmann's words, "People who experience God as loving are more likely to support food stamps and foreign aid. People who attend church but experience God as remote or as a judge are just as likely to volunteer in a food pantry—but less likely to support food stamps."[7]

That introduces my main reason for focusing now on religion: to convince believers that to engage in charity for hungry people, while remaining silent about it at the political level, not only limits their impact on hunger, but actually works against their faith. It is an inconsistency that results in widespread suffering and death. In order to reduce hunger they may offer God their time and money, but not the influence they have as citizens. Because they bury that treasure,[8] they are drawing a small circle around their stewardship of God's gifts, responding to hunger with a self-inflicted disability instead of a full-strength effort to help end it. Because these believers care about hungry people, they offer the best prospect for a surge in the political will to end hunger—if they can be aroused to do so. Their step into advocacy would be a game changer.

Let me be clear. I do not think of God as a means to a higher end, even such a noble end as ridding the world of hunger and poverty. God, if God there be, is the highest good, in which case to value anyone or anything more highly is idolatry. However, if a sovereign God lives and cares passionately for poor and hungry people and lays it on our hearts to do the same—not simply with casual sentiments, but with actions that matter—then we are not merely considering a good suggestion, but a transcendent imperative.

I focus here on Christian faith because it is the faith that I and a majority of Americans claim—always imperfectly, and often not seriously—as our own. Jews, of course, came first with the Hebrew Scriptures that underlie the faith and ethics of the New Testament; Christians also have common ground with Muslims and many others, including nonbelievers, regarding our response to human need.

Love and Justice

Though few seem to notice, concern for poor and hungry people is pervasive in the Bible: instance upon instance, more than two thousand citations in all.[9] The power of this appeal lies not only in the frequency and intensity of such texts, but in their connection to God's redemptive love. Christians believe it is out of God's self-giving, sacrificial love for us in Christ that love for others is to flow. "We love, because he first loved us."[10] This love prompts us to seek the good of others, recognizing that we are all children of God, created "in the image of God,"[11] each one of us given an unsurpassed dignity and worth, created to reflect God's goodness, trust God completely, and love others as much as we love ourselves. Our failure to do so is emphasized in the Bible at its outset in the story of Cain killing his brother Abel and God's affirmative answer to Cain's question, "Am I my brother's keeper?"[12] The murder gives stark evidence of the need for justice when love falls short, just as the limits of justice expose the need for love.

Justice is only an approximation of love; but as hunger illustrates, justice is also a way of expressing love on a large scale. Our ability to show compassion to others in a direct, person-to-person way is quite limited. If a neighbor is hungry, we can offer food, and maybe even help a family through a prolonged crisis. If that neighbor becomes a thousand or a million neighbors, we may be able to help through an organized charity; but charity is not enough. Charity is limited in both the extent of its reach and its authority. The government, however, has the authority and the responsibility of ensuring public justice and, in our "government of the people," citizens are responsible for holding government leaders accountable for that.

The church and the government have distinctive but interrelated roles with respect to love and justice. The church's core mission is to proclaim and live the good news of God's love for us in Christ, which is not an appropriate work of the government. Christians teach and do things that are most deeply needed but for which the government is not suited, such as offering God's mercy and peace to troubled hearts, instilling in people a sense of purpose and hope, urging one another to grow in love and respect for others as equally cherished by God, caring for God's creation, and inviting others to become part of a community of faith.

But the church's mission also includes God's command that people practice justice as an expression of love. This connects us directly to the government's role of legislating, administrating, and adjudicating public justice. The church, if it engages faithfully in its mission, pursues justice when it helps people understand that because following Christ applies to every aspect of life, it includes our life as citizens. Through our power as citizens we can help shape public policies not for personal advantage, but for the good of others, both here and abroad, paying particular attention to those who are denied justice. In this way justice is an extension of love applied more broadly.

Precisely at this point Christians tend to give a feeble response by retreating into the comfort zone of charity for others without entering the "political" territory of justice. But to avoid justice is a grave sin of omission that, by default, encourages us to turn to our pocketbooks and personal biases rather than biblical guidance in forming our political views and actions. That is a narrow, pinched way of understanding the Christian calling, which embraces all of life.

Consider how deeply justice is anchored in the Bible.

Biblical Roots

Justice may mean retribution (punishment, perhaps prison), restoration (bringing an offender and/or victims to wholeness in society), or social-legal arrangements that are fair and inclusive in enabling people to live and flourish together. The Bible reflects each of these forms of justice and sees them as coming from a God who signals to us a special concern for people who are often ignored and stepped on—widows, orphans, immigrants, refugees, the poor, the hungry. God commands us as individuals and as a nation to treat them well. God condemns not only outright oppression but also neglect, which is oppression's deceptively soft face. At the same time, the biblical writers repeatedly stress, God is eager to extend forgiveness to us oppressors and neglectors—a mercy that, when genuinely received, prompts us to become merciful to others.

In the Hebrew Bible that Christians call the Old Testament, God's justice is seen in the emancipation of slaves and their exodus from Egypt, with Moses as advocate-in-chief. God does not ask the reluctant Moses to take up a collection of food and clothes for the abused Hebrews, but instructs him, "Tell the Pharaoh [the king] to let my people go!"[13]—an audacious and hazardous insistence on justice.

The story of the flight of the Hebrews from Egypt in the biblical book of Exodus reveals something central about the nature of God. Justice for the oppressed turns out to be a treasured form of God's love, because it secures freedom for those who are mistreated. As people who had experienced the brutality of slavery, Israelites were urged to anchor their life in a special covenant-relationship with the God who had set them free. That covenant was their Declaration of Independence. Their constitution was the Torah, the law given to guide them, the essence of which was "Love the Lord your God with all your heart, soul and mind" and "Love your neighbor as yourself."[14] The Ten Commandments were a bill of obligations that also served as a bill of rights to protect people. The Ten Commandments summarized the law and were introduced with the words: "I am the Lord your God, who brought you out of the land of Egypt, out of the house of bondage," followed by an implied "therefore"—*therefore* you shall have no other gods, and *therefore* you shall love your neighbor.[15]

Love for neighbor was guided by legislation that

- established the fair distribution of land;[16]
- gave poor people gleaning rights in the harvest fields;[17]
- gave poor people a share in the 10 percent tax (tithe);[18]
- provided for the cancellation of debts every seventh year;[19]
- gave various legal protections for slaves and servants, orphans, widows, and immigrants, along with the reminder that "you were a slave in the land of Egypt; therefore I command you to do this."[20]

These and other laws create a safety-net, a foundation of minimal justice. But love exceeds the requirements of the law, so Israelites are commanded not to harden their hearts or shut their hands to the poor, but to be generous and give freely.[21] God's desire is that "there will be no one in need among you."[22]

Israel is supposed to be a society with neither extreme wealth nor poverty. When the people beg for a king, they are warned that this will compromise that ideal. "The king shall not multiply to himself horses, wives, or gold," the law instructs.[23] But that is exactly what the kings do, so the gap between rich and poor quickly begins to widen. King David takes Uriah's wife, then Uriah's life.[24] David's son, King Solomon, lives lavishly and builds lavishly by imposing forced labor and a heavy tax burden on the people, which leads to a deeply divided kingdom.[25] King Ahab kills Naboth, his neighbor, in order to seize Naboth's vineyard.[26] Well-connected and privileged families expand their estates and their wealth at the expense of the poor. Extreme inequalities emerge.

Hearing the cries of oppressed people, prophets denounce this injustice. Amos, a charismatic shepherd from rural Judah, begins to preach (without invitation or proper credentials) in the sanctuary of Israel's King Jeroboam in Bethel. "The Lord roars in Zion," he warns, then denounces the men of wealth in Israel who impoverish people to satisfy their own greed.[27] He implicates their wives as well for demanding luxury while the poor are being crushed.[28] "Woe to you," he tells them, saying they will be the first to be captured and sent into exile.[29]

The prophets reject the religious worship of those who turn a blind eye to injustice. "I hate, I despise your feasts, and I take no delight in your solemn assemblies," God announces through Amos. "Take away from me the noise of your hymns; to the melody of your harps I will not listen. But let justice roll down like waters, and righteousness like an ever-flowing stream."[30]

Isaiah is no less outspoken. He accuses the elders and princes of getting rich by crushing others, filling their own houses with what belongs to the poor.[31] Like Amos and other prophets, Isaiah and his successors reject religious ceremony that is blind to oppression. They urge a change of heart:

> Is not this the fast that I choose:
>> to loose the bonds of injustice,
>> to undo the thongs of the yoke,
>> to let the oppressed go free . . . ?
> Is it not to share your bread with the hungry,
>> and bring the homeless poor into your house . . . ?
> Then your light shall break forth like the dawn,
>> and your healing shall spring up quickly.[32]

Even the Psalms (the Hebrew hymnal) praise the God of justice. In singing of creation and redemption, Jewish people (ancient and contemporary) celebrate God's compassion for the poor, God's justice for the oppressed, God's feeding the hungry, setting prisoners free, opening the eyes of the blind, God's lifting up those who are bowed down, watching over foreigners, widows, and orphans—and, yes, God's fearful judgment of those who mistreat such people.[33] Yet for waywardness of the worst sort God holds out the promise of forgiveness, if only people will reverse course, trust God and, as recipients of mercy, become merciful to others.

Jesus

Jesus preached and taught in the tradition of the prophets, honoring especially those who were poor and at the bottom of the social pyramid. This is apparent in each of the four Gospels, but most pronounced in the Gospel recorded by Luke, which has Mary, even before the birth of Jesus, praising God for bringing down the proud and powerful and lifting up the lowly, filling the hungry with good things, and sending the rich away empty.[34]

When Jesus embarks on his public ministry, he takes his statement of mission from the prophet Isaiah:

> The Spirit of the Lord is upon me,
>   because he has anointed me
>   to bring good news to the poor.
> He has sent me to proclaim release to the captives
>   and recovery of sight to the blind,
>   to let the oppressed go free,
>   to proclaim the year of the Lord's favor.[35]

"The year of the Lord's favor" refers to the year of Jubilee, when slaves were to be freed, debts forgiven, and lands restored to the family that originally owned them[36]—a monumental call to social justice that gave impetus to the debt forgiveness campaign reported in chapter 4 of this book.

Jesus challenges religious leaders for their preoccupation with legalistic details—straining gnats, he calls it—while they "neglected the weightier matters of the law, justice and mercy and faith."[37] Jesus reaches out to the poor, the sick, and the disabled,[38] to socially despised tax collectors and prostitutes,[39] and to others who were devalued—women,[40] children,[41] immigrants,[42] and the humble in status and spirit.[43] In his parables the beggar Lazarus is blessed, the rich man condemned.[44] The despised Samaritan "foreigner" is a model of compassion, religious leaders deficient.[45] The prosperous are urged to sell their excess and give to the poor.[46] The poor and the hungry are blessed, the rich warned of God's judgment.[47] Faithful governing is exemplified not by a show of power, but by the manager who sees to it that everyone in the household has enough to eat.[48] Jesus sees an upside-down world turned right-side up.

This good news for the poor sounds like bad news for the rich, but most deeply it is also good news for the rich, because it invites them to give up an addiction that is doing great injury to themselves as well as others. Jesus urges people instead to find genuine life in God. The rich man in one of Jesus's illustrative stories is condemned not because he is rich, but because he fails to recognize the beggar Lazarus as his brother.[49] When inviting people to follow him as disciples, Jesus is not asking them to grit their teeth and accept less of life, but urging them instead to let go of lesser things for a greater joy and destiny.

In his famous portrayal of judgment day Jesus depicts people from every nation gathered before him in two groups: those who fed him when he was hungry, clothed him, and visited him in prison; and those who failed to do so. His verdict startles each group: "Lord, when did we do that?" they ask. His answer: "When you did it, or failed to do it, to the least of my sisters and brothers. As you treated them, you treated me."[50] The scene holds us starkly accountable to God for our response to those in need. Our sins of omission are exposed. Just when Jesus is focused on God's judgment of us after this life and we might expect him to be "otherworldly," he shines a disturbing light on what we are doing with our lives right now.

How could so many of us, who think of ourselves as biblically literate, have missed these things or brushed them aside as optional? Because it is so very difficult to grasp a disturbing truth, when our comfort depends upon not grasping it.

A few years ago, I read about a survey done by a national sampling of churchgoers. It found that, by age thirteen or so, most of us who grow up in the church think we know the main teachings of the Bible. We are unaware of how sketchy that understanding is and how it is mostly shaped by the culture that surrounds us. As a result, from early age our minds tend to filter out teachings such as the whole-life aspect of Jesus's call to follow him and the biblical imperatives to love others and seek justice for those so desperate for it. As a result, when we are asked to help end hunger as citizen advocates we may remain strangely silent, because it seems alien to our view of Christian life. Jesus, however, urges us to see things not through the lens of the prevailing culture and our own self-interest, but through the lens of God's love, a radical love that prompts us to "speak up for the poor and helpless, and see that they get justice."[51]

Two days after depicting the great judgment scene Jesus is arrested, and the next day executed[52] as a threat to the status quo. Key religious authorities are convinced he is leading people astray and fear that he will trigger an uprising against Rome that would surely be crushed and imperil the entire nation. Pontius Pilate, the governor, becomes unnerved at the prospect of a riot over someone claiming a kingship independent of the Roman emperor. As Jesus anticipates, those in power decide to have him crucified, a truly cruel and horrible ending.

Or so it seemed. Then something happens that turns a terrified group of disillusioned followers into champions of a startling announcement. They claim, at great personal risk, that the crucified Jesus has been raised to life and has appeared to them physically on numerous occasions to instruct and even eat with them. If empirical science has the last and only word, the resurrection is beyond belief. But these disciples say that through the death and resurrection of Jesus, the God of the universe has intervened in human history to overthrow sin and death. They now have not only his teaching and his example of what it means to be truly human; they believe they have been rescued by Jesus and empowered to live a new life by his death and resurrection and his ongoing presence with them through the Holy Spirit of God.

Among Christians today the death and resurrection of Jesus are often trivialized as consent to information that gives people a one-way ticket to heaven but has little connection with earthly concerns. Christians through the ages, however, have seen Jesus's death and resurrection as "the power of God for salvation"[53] that sets them free from the grip of sin and death to pursue the love and justice of God on earth before they enjoy it fully in God's New Creation. That promised future gives them courage to do so, whatever the momentary cost. God's self-giving love poured out for the world in Christ empowers believers to follow Jesus in loving and serving others. Because they do so imperfectly, they live by the forgiveness that God extends to us in Christ.

The Church and Social Justice

The early Christians instinctively began following Jesus. The extensive sharing of possessions in Jerusalem[54] and the apostle Paul's collection of funds from gentile churches for the impoverished Jewish Christians in Judea[55] come to mind. Organizing for social justice was not permitted under Roman rule, so the justice espoused by Jesus took the form of radical love and equality before God. When the apostle Paul wrote to Christian converts under threat of persecution, he urged them to "pay, pray, and obey"—obey those in authority, pay taxes, and pray for those who govern so that people might lead peaceful lives.[56] However, the equality of people under God proclaimed by Paul ("There is neither Jew nor Greek, there is neither slave nor free, there is neither male nor female; for you are all one in Christ Jesus"[57]) had powerful implications for justice, as shown in his letter to a convert, Philemon, asking Philemon to welcome his runaway slave, Onesimus, no longer as a slave but as a brother.[58]

As the church grew over the centuries under various forms of autocratic governments, its people wrestled with how to be faithful disciples in a still-fallen world. They struggled with issues such as freedom and authority, wealth and poverty, church and state, slavery and gender equality.

Their thinking not only shaped, but was extensively shaped by, conditions that were restrictive and frequently hostile to the following of Jesus. As a result, their attempts were often seriously flawed. However, along the way countless ordinary believers, as well as thinkers such as Saint Augustine, Thomas Aquinas, and Protestant reformers, made lasting contributions. The impetus of biblical faith, prodded by the Enlightenment, led eventually to democratic forms of government under which more and more people claimed both the right and the opportunity to achieve social justice. In this way the end of the slave trade and slavery itself, along with civil rights in our own country, plus a host of laws to moderate some of the most onerous aspects of the Industrial Revolution came about. In these things the churches and Christians were deeply engaged—often lagging, even opposing change, but frequently leading the way.

Consider two exemplars of living the gospel under complex circumstances, one Protestant, the other Roman Catholic.

Dietrich Bonhoeffer, Lutheran pastor and gifted young theologian, was executed at the age of thirty-nine for his part in plotting the death of Adolf Hitler. Bonhoeffer was one of the first to publicly denounce the Nazi regime as a complete contradiction of Christianity, because of its vicious anti-Semitism and idolatrous nationalism. He helped organize an underground seminary and a Confessing Church body that stood against the co-opted state church.

Bonhoeffer came out of a Lutheran tradition that had largely lost its vitality by treating God's sacrificial forgiveness as a cheap gift. In *The Cost of Discipleship* he wrote, "Cheap grace is the grace we bestow on ourselves . . . grace without discipleship, grace without the cross, grace without Jesus Christ, living and incarnate."[59] Cheapened grace permits us to live as we wish and absolves us of the need to follow Jesus, he said. The true grace of Christ, however, is an undeserved mercy that captures hearts and changes lives. It prompts us to be champions of the love and justice of God.

For Bonhoeffer discipleship meant following Jesus in all of life, not restricting him to a separate religious compartment.

> So long as Christ and the world are conceived as two opposing and mutually repellent spheres, man [sic] will be left in the following dilemma: he abandons reality as a whole, and places himself in one or other of the two spheres. He seeks Christ without the world, or he seeks the world without Christ. In either case he is deceiving himself.[60]

Even the Confessing Church held a narrow understanding of how church and state were related, confining its resistance to ways in which the church itself was directly threatened. So it remained passive in 1935 when Nuremberg Laws stripped Jews of their rights as citizens and human beings. For Bonhoeffer, the church existed not for itself but for the world, so it was obliged to speak out. "Only he who cries out for the Jews may sing Gregorian chants," he is said to have declared.[61] Bonhoeffer chose to follow Christ in the world, refusing to keep silent. Instead he spoke up and acted against injustice, and he was hanged for it a few days before Germany's collapse.

The second exemplar is Pope Francis, elected in March of 2013 to lead the Roman Catholic Church. He has gained widespread affection with his simplicity of life and the authentic way in which he seeks out people who are poor, imprisoned, handicapped, or in other ways marginalized. His open, nonjudgmental emphasis on mercy is disarming. He seems a lot like Jesus.

The first words of his initial Exhortation to the church were: *"The Joy of the Gospel* fills the hearts and lives of all who encounter Jesus. Those who accept his offer of salvation are set free from sin, sorrow, inner emptiness and loneliness. With Christ joy is constantly born anew."[62] He goes on to say that those who have received such love are moved to share it with others in many different ways. In a chapter on "communal commitment" Francis calls for action against economic injustices. In it he issues a resounding "No"

to an economy of exclusion,
to the new idolatry of money,
to a financial system which rules rather than serves,
and to the inequality which spawns violence.[63]

Pope Francis said these things because, he explained, the joy of the gospel leads us to oppose the kind of economics that undermine human dignity. He deplores ideologies that "defend the absolute autonomy of the marketplace" and "reject the right of the states, charged with vigilance for the common good, to exercise any form of control." The result, he says, is a system that "tends to devour everything which stands in the way of increased profits." We have to say "'thou shalt not' to an economy of exclusion and inequality. Such an economy kills." He urges instead the primacy of the human person and an economy that has a truly human purpose. All of this he puts in the context of celebrating the mercy and joy that he sees as the gift of Christ.

Pope Francis was drawing from a strong tradition of Roman Catholic social teaching that in modern times began in 1881 with the Church's first formal statement on economic and social justice, *Rerum Novarum*.[64] In it, Pope Leo XIII alerted the Church to the terrible conditions of industrial workers. Subsequent popes, as well as the Second Vatican Council of the 1960s and the US Conference of Catholic Bishops, have addressed the weaknesses of both socialism and capitalism. They have consistently supported a free market economy, but one in which all could participate and enjoy shared benefits. They have also made a powerful case for rich countries to help poor countries overcome hunger and poverty.

Pope Francis exemplifies this. But the life of an exemplar is not easy. Francis entered the year 2019 facing the scandal of widespread sexual abuse on the part of many trusted priests over a period of decades. The scandal was not new, but exposure of it became so extensive in the media that the public, within and outside of the church, called for immediate reforms. Francis himself speaks vigorously for reform, but his papacy may be judged in large part by the extent of his success in gaining zero tolerance for both abuse and efforts to hide it—an awesome challenge.

Francis has called on people everywhere to pray for the end to hunger, an appeal that diverse faith leaders as well as anti-hunger advocates in this country have taken up by enjoining their own followers to pray for and help to implement hunger's demise.

Why Are Christians Reluctant Advocates?

The Bible presents a great cloud of witnesses, including Jesus himself, followed by centuries of subsequent church teaching regarding hunger, poverty, and justice. And whether you believe it is God's doing or not, history has unfolded in such a way that we now have the opportunity to exercise our influence as American citizens to help bring hunger to a near end and make headway on the poverty and economic imbalances that surround it. Why then are Christians who sincerely want this to happen so reluctant to step up and say so in the political arena, where leadership to bring it about is sorely needed? Among the reasons:

1. Comfort and familiarity with charity. Direct assistance is what the church and its faithful have been doing for centuries. Believers expect it and like doing it. Advocacy, however, is a newcomer, because conditions are not what they were at Jesus's time or in the Middle Ages, or even a few generations ago. How many pastors or ministers encourage their members to think and act faithfully as Christian citizens, at the political level, on matters concerning hunger and poverty or race? "We've never done that" is a common reaction.

2. Advocacy seems complicated. People instinctively "get" the hands-on help. It's simple and something they can see and do. Advocacy requires explaining. And the idea of contacting a member of Congress intimidates many.

3. Advocacy is "too political." People are often wary about bringing up anything political in church. Caution is well advised because a policy position identified as "Christian" may in fact be nothing of the sort. So, "Let's stick to the gospel and stay out of politics" is a convenient default position, though it ignores the fact that silence is also political. The church should avoid partisanship, but assert moral principles deeply embedded in its faith; and justice is deeply embedded in the Bible. The church will not serve its members well unless Christians help one another come to a clear, heartfelt understanding of the key role that justice plays in Christian love. When it comes to race, for example, we may focus on personal good will but avoid structural injustices. The same tends to be true of our response to hunger and poverty. We are afraid to arouse the elephant in the room. We may genuinely want both racial and social reconciliation, because Christ joins us in bonds of equality with others. But the sins of injustice, unconfessed and unaddressed, eat away at the authenticity of our faith.

To justify silence, people frequently invoke the separation of church and state, a principle that is widely misunderstood. Church and state are institutionally separate but can be functionally interactive. When a church building is in flames, the local fire department appropriately rushes to put the fire out. Separation of church and state is too often taken to mean the separation of faith from life. If, as Christians believe, Christ is Lord, then he is Lord of a believer's entire life, not just selected parts of it. One cannot take key aspects of life, such as political and economic matters that affect the well-being of others, and declare them off-limits to faith. That puts faith in a private compartment and turns much of life over to hostile forces. Privatized faith becomes our "tithe"—that small religious part of life that God gets. It allows our finances, our prejudices, and social pressure rather than the common good to shape our politics. In one of the Lincoln-Douglas debates, Abraham Lincoln criticized clergy who said they were personally against slavery but refused to take a public stand against it.[65] Or think of the silence of Christians during Hitler's rise to power—and of our own political silence while hunger destroys and diminishes life. That kind of silence may seem benign, but in fact it is deadly.

4. Fear of controversy. People want to avoid issues that might divide a congregation. Hunger is not usually one of them because responding to it is an obligation highlighted by Christ himself. The Bible makes very clear that it is shameful for a nation as prosperous as ours to allow millions of children to live in hunger and poverty; but it does not specify what legislation or programs should be enacted. That is our responsibility. A wise priest or pastor does not try to impose a politically partisan agenda on others, but offers opportunities for action in ways that respect political differences. Bread for the World's approach allows a church to be clear about biblical principles, while enabling members to respond as individual citizens. Its nonpartisan (or bipartisan) approach provides a way for churches to encourage advocacy. Indifference to public policy regarding hunger is a way of dodging the compassion that Jesus seeks from us.

5. Lack of immediate gratification. When you volunteer in a soup kitchen or contribute to a food pantry or an overseas agency, you can visualize in a concrete way how your effort is helping someone. But when you urge a member of Congress to take action on a bill that may affect millions of people, you may wonder, "Does my effort really make any difference?" Yes, it does, though not because it always clinches support. Working in a timely fashion in concert with others locally and nationwide has an impact that leverages benefits (or prevents harm) for hungry people far out of proportion to the time and effort invested. Whenever a member of Congress is urged to take action against hunger, even if she does not do it, the message nudges her awareness forward and the collective result moves us toward the goal. In any case we are called to be faithful and to seek justice, whether success is apparent or not.

6. Cynicism about the government. Not everything the government does or fails to do is good. But giving up on government merely contributes to its failure and to the persistence of poverty and hunger. The family is not perfect, but we work to make it better. The same is true of school, work, and many of our civic institutions. Government is a flawed instrument of God, as biblical writers knew from experience. If the apostle Paul could speak well of the Roman authorities,[66] we by comparison are blessed. Our government is not an "it" for us to curse, but a "we" for us to participate in, with the common good as our aim.

7. Apathy. There is apathy within each one of us and in every congregation. Apathy closes the heart to the suffering of others. It hinders charitable giving as well as advocacy. To care little about others and much about our own comfort is, for believers, evidence of failure to grasp the depth of

God's love. Apathy holds us back, prevents us from trusting God as a loving presence in our lives. If we think of God as a harsh and remote judge, we are prone to judge and distance ourselves from others, perhaps looking down on poor people as having no one to blame but themselves for their poverty. We may wonder if they are sufficiently worthy of our help—unlike God, who "makes the sun rise on the evil and on the good, and sends rain on the just and on the unjust."[67] Perhaps our contribution to a food pantry or overseas relief gives us a fig leaf of respectability, while we avoid seeking for others the basic justice we ourselves enjoy. Apathy may account for our silence as citizens about an economy that treats us well but leaves many others in the dust. But God's love can rescue us from apathy. That love is extravagant in mercy and forgiveness, and so genuine that it will not let us stay the way we are, but restlessly helps us become more fully formed in Christ so that we reflect toward others the love we have received. We have much to celebrate and every reason not to surrender to apathy.

"Our citizenship is in heaven," the apostle Paul wrote,[68] a treasured gift and a promised inheritance. But earthly citizenship is the arena in which we are asked to carry out our current assignment of reflecting the love of God until that promise is brought to completion.

Jesus taught us to pray, "Thy Kingdom come. Thy will be done on earth, as it is in heaven."[69] Working to repeal hunger and replace it with a more humane economy is a powerful way of aligning our lives with that prayer.

Acknowledgments

I am indebted to those who read my manuscript and steered me well, above all, David Beckmann, president of Bread for the World, whose advice and encouragement have been exceptional. Father William J. Byron, SJ, educator and economist, one of the co-founders of Bread for the World, read my initial draft and offered early guidance. Their part in my journey with the ongoing hunger crisis began decades ago. So did that of Harold Remus, friend and colleague from seminary days and a New Testament theologian of note. Harold used his keen eye for both substance and style to improve the writing of this book, as he did for my previous books. I also credit Alice Croft, his wife, for organizing and formatting our exchanges of copy. Paul Jersild, a former college roommate and a published specialist in Christian ethics gave helpful suggestions on a penultimate draft.

I thank Adlai Amor, Alice Walker Duff, and Nancy Rhodes of Bread for the World's staff for their comments after reading an early draft; and Michele Sumilas, managing director of Bread for the World and Bread for the World Institute, who did the same for a semi-final draft.

Barbara Howell, Bread for the World's domestic policy leader for more than two decades, and Lane Vanderslice, economist, who also served with me on Bread for the World's staff and in retirement edits *Hunger Notes*, gave helpful information. So did Asma Lateef, director of Bread for the World Institute, and Todd Post, who edits the Institute's annual *Hunger Report*, which has been a source for me of valuable perspective on both domestic and global hunger. Christine Matthews, Bread's librarian, loaned me books and articles, and other Bread staff members, Christine Melendez Ashley, Sophie Milam, Ryan Quinn, Derek Schwabe, and Jordan Teague, assisted in tracking down data. So did Michelle Learner, who helped with data and editing suggestions. Jamie Thomas, Beckmann's executive assistant, kept information flowing promptly whenever the need arose.

David Miner, avid anti-hunger advocate in Indiana and a leader both on and off Bread's board of directors, helped me describe (in chapter 5) the Indy Hunger Network's effort to make Indianapolis a hunger-free city. His wife Robin prepared much of the data for IHN.

The late Howard Hjort, who became deputy director-general of the UN Food and Agriculture Organization, helped me on food and agriculture policy for my initial draft. I first met Howard when he was chief economist at the US Department of Agriculture in the Carter administration and helped Bread for the World design legislation for the farmer-held grain reserve of 1977, for which our members and many others lobbied vigorously. Howard became a devoted Bread member and in his retirement years participated actively in our annual "lobby day."

Experts from various policy institutes (left, right, and center), along with writers of books and articles, have extensively informed my understanding. Their contributions, insufficiently acknowledged, are apparent mostly in the endnotes but sometimes in the main text as well.

All of the above deserve my thanks. None of them is responsible for opinions of mine that may be inadequate or simply mistaken.

Throughout my life, mainly in this country but occasionally abroad, people have helped me by sharing their own struggle with poverty, especially friends and parishioners on New York's Lower East Side. Their experience opened my eyes to a human reality that challenged my otherwise cushioned life. Those who shaped my understanding include my parents, as well as teachers, colleagues, and others, especially those I have worked with over the years at Bread for the World, including its members, its staff members, and its boards of directors, as well as colleagues from other agencies. Let me add outstanding examples of public service, including my brother Paul, a newspaper editor who served in the Illinois state legislature for many years, then in the US House and Senate. From Paul and others I learned how much a political leader can do, sometimes on a large scale, for people who are normally bypassed by the rest of us. I miss him.

On a more personal note, David Mitchell, my neighbor, helped me get a computer, then got it up and running more than once, no small contribution. My daughter, Leah Dowling, helped me again and again through operational glitches that confronted my lagging computer skills. I thank both of them for their generosity of time and talent.

In "the best for last" category is my wife Shirley, to whom I have dedicated the book. The project took much longer than expected. The 2016 presidential campaigns and their outcome prompted me to refocus the book in response to the political crisis that is shaking our nation. The various drafts took time, but Shirley held on, offering useful suggestions, endless patience, and encouragement all the way. For her part in bringing this book to fruition I am grateful beyond words.

Notes

1. Prinz was a young rabbi and Jewish leader in Berlin who spoke out forcefully against National Socialism long before Hitler took power. He urged Jews to leave Germany, was frequently arrested, and was then expelled in 1937. He and his family came to the United States, where he became one of the leading figures of Judaism. At the 1963 March on Washington he spoke immediately before Martin Luther King Jr. delivered his riveting "I Have a Dream" speech. Prinz's speech, text and audio, can be found at http://www.joachimprinz.com/biog raphy.htm.

2. Six million is a conservative estimate that includes deaths from infections and illnesses not resisted due in significant part to malnutrition. The statistical starting point is the evidence-based conclusion that 3.1 million children under age five die each year from hunger or causes connected to it (45 percent of annual under-age-five deaths) according to the UN World Food Program, "Hunger Statistics," July 9, 2015, https:www.wfp.org/hunger/stats, which cites the British medical journal *The Lancet* and its 2013 "Series on Maternal and Child Nutrition." If birth-related maternal deaths are added, the total is 3.5 million, according to an executive summary of that series.

3. UN Food and Agriculture Organization, *The State of Food Security and Nutrition in the World 2018*, p. 2, http://www.fao.org/state-of-food-security-nutrition/en/.

4. *Transforming Our World: The 2030 Agenda for Sustainable Development* (New York: United Nations, 2015), https://sustainabledevelopment.un.org/post2015/transformingour world. The SDGs are qualified by an introduction, which states that targets for each goal are "aspirational global targets, with each government setting its own national targets."

5. In all likelihood the decline in hunger coincided closely with the decline in poverty in the 1960s and 1970s, as I explain in chapter 2.

1. Michael Gerson, "A Week of Hunger," *The Washington Post*, July 9, 2008, A15.

2. Michael Harrington, *The Other America* (Baltimore: Penguin 1964 edition of Macmillan's 1963 first edition), acknowledgments page.

3. Arthur Simon, *Faces of Poverty* (St. Louis: Concordia, 1966; and New York: Macmillan, 1968).

4. Alisha Coleman-Jensen et al., *Household Food Security in the United States in 2017*, US Department of Agriculture, Economic Research Service, ERR-256, September 2018, p. 7. People have *very low* food security if adults report six or more food-insecure conditions, and eight or more for households with children. Their food intake was reduced at times and their eating pattern disrupted because the households lacked money and other resources for food.

5. Kayla Fontenot et al., *Income and Poverty in the United States 2017*, US Census Bureau, Current Population Reports, P60-263, 11–12.

6. SNAP expects a family to spend 30 percent of its income on food. The full benefit in 2018 for a family of three with no net monthly income is $504, so $192 of Angela's salary is subtracted from $504. SNAP's Electronic Benefit Transfer (EBT) card functions like a bank debit card but can be used only for SNAP-qualified grocery products. For details of fiscal year 2018 eligibility for SNAP benefits based on income and assets, https://www.fns.usda.gov/snap/eligibility. See also the Center on Budget and Policy Priorities, "A Quick Guide to SNAP Eligibility and Benefits," September 14, 2017, https://www.cbpp.org/research/a-quick-guide-to-SNAP-eligibility-and-benefits.

7. US Department of Agriculture, Food and Nutrition Service for 2018, note 6 above.

8. Kathryn J. Edin and H. Luke Shaefer, *$2.00 a Day: Living on Almost Nothing in America* (Boston: Houghton Mifflin Harcourt, 2015).

9. Victor Oliveira, "The Food Assistance Landscape: FY 2017 Annual Report," US Department of Agriculture, March 2017, www.ers.usda.gov/publications/pub-details/?pubid=88073. Electronic debit cards reduce the stigma and increase the security and efficiency of the program.

10. Feeding America, *Hunger in America 2014: A Report on Charitable Food Distribution in the United States in 2013*, prepared for Feeding America by Westat and the Urban Institute, August 2014, written by Nancy S. Weinfield et al., pp. 160, 162, http://help.feedingamerica.org/HungerInAmerica/hunger-in-america-2014-full-report.pdf.

11. Center on Budget and Policy Priorities, "Policy Basics: Introduction to the Supplemental Nutrition Assistance Program Household: Fiscal Year," March 24, 2016, p. 2, http://www.cbpp.org/research/policy-basics-introduction-to-the-supplemental-nutrition-assistance-program.

12. US Department of Agriculture, Food & Nutrition Service, "Characteristics of USDA Supplemental Nutrition Assistance Program Households: Fiscal Year 2016 (Summary)," November 2017.

13. Bernadette D. Proctor et al., *Income and Poverty in the United States 2016*, US Census Bureau, Current Population Reports, P60-259, September 2017, p. 3.

14. Hilary W. Hoynes et al., *Long Run Impacts of Childhood Access to the Safety-net*, November 2012, http://www.nber.org/papers/w18535.

15. Jim Tankersley, "How Ben Carson Beat the Odds: His Escape from Poverty Was Fueled

by His Drive, His Faith, His Mother—and a Leg Up from His Government," *The Washington Post*, October 31, 2015, A1.

16. See Gerson, "A Week of Hunger." Gerson was an advisor and speechwriter for President George W. Bush.

17. David R. Obey, *Raising Hell for Justice* (Madison: University of Wisconsin Press, 2007), 24-25.

18. $149 billion in US food exports in 2014, with Netherlands next at $93 billion. World Atlas, http://www.worldatlas.com/articles/the-american-food-giant-the-largest-exporter-of -food-in-the-world.html.

19. "Report of the Special Rapporteur [Philip Alston] on Extreme Poverty and Human Rights on His Mission to the United States of America" to the UN Human Rights Council, June 22, 2018, pp. 3-7.

20. "Americans' Views on Hunger," October 2014, conducted jointly by Democrat and Republican consultants on behalf of Tyson Foods and the Food Research and Action Center, p. 7, http://frac.org/wp-content/uploads/frac_tyson_oct_2014_public_view_hunger_poll.pdf.

21. Food insecurity was 11.9 percent in 1995. US Department of Agriculture, Economic Research Service, "Key Statistics & Graphics," 2016, pp. 2 and 7, https://www.ers.usda.gov /topics/food-nutrition-assistance/food-security-in-the-us/key-statistics-graphics.aspx.

22. *Income and Poverty*, note 5 above, 11-12.

23. Although the federal government failed to do a nationwide documentation of hunger before 1995, Bread for the World, Second Harvest (now Feeding America), and Food Research and Action Center (among others) did local surveys in various parts of the country. These showed results consistent with those of the more extensive Census Bureau surveys that began in 1995. There were also specialized professional studies, such as a ten-state study on the nutritional status of the poor ordered by Congress and partly completed by the Department of Health, Education and Welfare but cut short (to avoid political embarrassment, some charged); also a study by the Centers for Disease Control, and another by the National Center for Health Statistics. There was documented evidence concerning hunger, but no single study comprehensive enough to be accepted as valid for the nation as a whole.

24. Executive Order 10914 begins, "Whereas one of the most important and urgent problems confronting the nation today is the development of a positive food and nutrition program for all Americans," and ends with an order "to expand and improve the program of food distribution throughout the United States" to make available "to all needy families a greater variety and quantity of food out of our agricultural abundance." The American Project, http://www.presidency.ucsb.edu/ws/?pid=58853. The original Food Stamp Plan of 1939 had the dual purpose of (1) enabling depression-poor people to buy surplus farm products at reduced prices with the government reimbursing the grocer, and (2) indirectly helping farmers. It ended in 1943 when food surpluses became a wartime scarcity, even though higher prices made the program more necessary. When postwar surpluses returned, John F. Kennedy, as a US Senator in 1959, sponsored legislation allowing the USDA to resume the program, which provided the basis for Kennedy's executive order when he was president. Gus Schumacher et

al., "Food Stamps: Once We Had It Right," in *A Place at the Table*, ed. Peter Pringle (New York: Public Affairs, 2013), 80–82.

25. Community action programs were especially controversial. An idea that initially appealed to liberals and conservatives alike, community action funded communities to plan their own initiatives. It offered no clear path toward poverty reduction, however, and spawned organizing that often challenged elected political leaders, who felt bypassed and threatened. Restrictions were soon imposed and community action began morphing into less contentious community development projects.

26. George McGovern, Bob Dole, and Donald E. Messer, *Ending Hunger Now* (Minneapolis: Augsburg Fortress Press, 2005), 65. I heard McGovern recount this experience on several occasions.

27. Working to End Hunger in America, www.frac.org.

28. Nixon threatened to withhold, and sometimes did withhold, appropriations for programs that were inconsistent with his policies, a process known as impoundment. This prompted legislation in 1974 that reasserted Congress's constitutional control over the budget. The legislation included establishing of House and Senate budget committees and—to provide impartial information about budgetary and economic issues—the nonpartisan Congressional Budget Office, https://www.cbo.gov/about/founding.

29. Nick Kotz, *Hunger in America: The Federal Response* (New York: Field Foundation, 1979), 9.

30. The SPM was developed as an experimental alternative to the official poverty measure. It sets the poverty line at the thirty-third percentile of expenditures on food, clothing, shelter, and utilities.

31. Center on Budget and Policy Priorities, https://www.cbpp.org/poverty-rate-has-fallen -significantly-since-1960s-under-anchored-supplemental-poverty-measure-0. As the years go back toward the 1960s, the graph shows that an SPM *anchored* to a specific year and *adjusted for inflation* has increasingly higher rates of poverty than would a plain SPM (though a plain SPM also shows higher rates than do the official rates). For applying a plain SPM to earlier years, the threshold for poverty has to be refigured for each year, which means it is relative to other factors for each of those years. To make the SPM more nearly absolute (rather than relative) Columbia University researchers *anchored* it to the year 2012 as a fixed point of reference, from which (going backward or forward) it can be adjusted for inflation. An anchored SPM adjusted for inflation is considered more nearly accurate in studies by both the right-leaning American Enterprise Institute (AEI) and the left-leaning Center on Budget and Policy Priorities (CBPP).

32. The prime example is Social Security, which by the SPM lifted 26 million people above the poverty line in 2016. The SPM poverty rate shows more people in poverty than the official rate. Liana Fox, *The Supplemental Poverty Measure: 2016*, US Census Bureau, P60-261 (RV), September 2017, pp. 1, 4–5, and 10, https://www.census.gov/library/publications/2017 /demo/p60-261.html.

33. Martin Luther King Jr., "Beyond Vietnam," an address at Riverside Church, New York, April 4, 1967, http://mlk-kpp01.stanford.edu/index.php/encyclopedia/documentsentry /doc_beyond_vietnam.

34. Nicholas Lemann, "The Unfinished War," part 2, *The Atlantic Monthly*, January 1989, 53–68. The two Lemann articles (for part 1 see note 35 below) were billed as "the first full journalistic account of the War on Poverty—the first one based primarily on interviews with the living principals." They are embodied also in Lemann's book, *The Promised Land: The Great Black Migration and How It Changed America* (New York: Knopf, 1991).

35. Nicholas Lemann, "The Unfinished War," part 1, *The Atlantic Monthly*, December 1988, 37–59. That poor people did not receive more money is not entirely accurate, because the number of welfare (AFDC) recipients increased from 4.3 million in 1965, Johnson's first year in office, to 6.7 million in 1969, with the cost tripling from roughly $5 billion to $15 billion (in real 1996 dollars). However, most of the costs (and benefits) came later through Medicare, expansion of Social Security, and other programs. The number of AFDC recipients climbed to 14 million by 1993 when President Clinton took office but dropped to 12.6 million in 1996, the year a welfare reform bill was enacted.

36. Steven V. Roberts, "Food Stamps Program: How It Grew and How Reagan Wants to Cut It Back," *The New York Times*, April 4, 1981.

37. Michael Harrington, *The New American Poverty* (New York: Penguin, 1984), 7–10. Cited by Janet Poppendieck, *Sweet Charity* (New York: Viking, 1998), 84.

38. Reagan's February 15, 1986, radio address to the nation on Welfare Reform. https://www.reaganlibrary.gov/research/speeches/21586a. It became a popular quip.

39. Alice M. Rivlin, *Systematic Thinking for Social Action* (Washington, DC: Brookings Institution Press, 1971 and reissued in 2015), 72–73. *Could* is italicized by Rivlin.

40. Cited by Jeff Stein and Tracy Jan, "Declaring Success in War on Poverty," *The Washington Post*, July 14, 2018, A1.

41. The Council of Economic Advisers, "Expanding Work Requirements in Non-Cash Welfare Programs," July 2018, 24–29.

42. The 5 percent that has to "reduce food at any point during the year" is not necessarily at odds with the official 12.3 percent for food insecurity, which covers *households* that reduce food during the year in which, for example, adults may skip meals in order to feed children. It is also true that "at any point" reduced food will capture an overlapping but changing population.

43. Nicholas Eberstadt, *The Great Society at Fifty: The Triumph and the Tragedy* (American Enterprise Institute, 2014), 15–19. The "tangle of pathologies" is a phrase he takes from a report by Daniel Patrick Moynihan, which I take up in chapter 9.

44. Poverty is not *only* relative. Michael Harrington, who explains why poverty is relative, also offers this nonrelative definition: "Poverty should be defined in terms of those who are denied the minimal levels of health, housing, food, and education that our present stage of scientific knowledge specifies as necessary for life as it is now lived in the United States." Harrington, *The Other America*, 191.

45. According to the Bureau of Economic Analysis, cited by Eberstadt, *The Great Society at Fifty*, 15–16.

46. Nicholas Eberstadt, *A Nation of Takers* (West Conshohocken, PA: Templeton Press, 2012), 19.

47. "The Distribution of Household Income and Federal Taxes, 2011," Congressional Budget Office, publication 49440, November 2014, p. 8, https://www.cbo.gov/publication/49440.

48. William A. Galston, "Have We Become a 'Nation of Takers'?," a response to Nicholas Eberstadt in Eberstadt's book *The Great Society at Fifty*, 96.

49. Neeraj Mehta, "Raise Your Hand If You Live in Subsidized Housing," *Sojourners*, June 2017, 22–25. The Joint Committee on Taxation estimated that the home interest mortgage deduction (HIMD) cost the US Treasury $69.7 billion in 2013.

50. For federal subsidized rental housing, Center on Budget and Policy Priorities, Will Fischer, and Barbara Sard, "Chart Book: Federal Housing Spending Is Poorly Matched to Need," March 8, 2017. For Home Interest Mortgage Deduction, Pew Research Center, Drew DeSilver, "The Biggest U.S. Tax Breaks," April 6, 2016.

51. *The War on Poverty 50 Years Later: A Progress Report* by the President's Council of Economic Advisers, January 2014, 3.

52. There were outstanding exceptions in Congress, and President Carter, who appointed a bipartisan commission on hunger, seemed intent on using its recommendations to make domestic and world hunger reduction a major initiative during a second term, which never materialized after he lost the 1980 election to Ronald Reagan.

53. Christopher Ingraham, "Child Poverty in the U.S. Is among the Worst in the Developed World," *The Washington Post*, October 29, 2014. For its 2014 report UNICEF used 2008 pre-recession data, then applied the standard of 60 percent of median household incomes for measuring household poverty, a rough way of including the impact of the recession in its estimates. That placed one-third (32.2 percent) of US children in poverty households. Norway, by contrast, had only 5.3 percent of its children in poverty. The US measurement for poverty, stricter than UNICEF's, shows 18 percent of children in poverty.

54. Congressional Budget Office, "An Overview of the Supplemental Nutrition Assistance Program," April 19, 2012, https://www.cbo.gov/publication/43175.

55. "Feeding America, Donor Impact Report," Summer 2014, p. 7, reports that on average each person in a food-insecure household would need an additional food budget of $15.82 per week ($823 a year) to purchase enough food. That cost, multiplied by the 41 million individuals in those households (in 2016), would be $33.7 billion. However, many cannot be reached or decline to receive food assistance (which would reduce the cost). And systems to improve nutrition and outreach, e.g., school meals, would also benefit many who are food-secure (which would increase the cost). So the estimate of a maximum $40 billion additional cost in an economy tilted toward extreme inequalities, but much less in a more inclusive economy, seems plausible. For the $99 billion in 2017, see the USDA report, note 9 above.

56. The estimate comes from the third of the three studies (anchored respectively at Harvard, Brandeis, and Boston universities), this one by John T. Cook and Ana Paula Poblacion, "Estimating the Health-Related Costs of Food Insecurity and Hunger," published in *Hunger Report 2016: The Nourishing Effect: Ending Hunger, Improving Health, Reducing Inequality*, ed. Todd Post (Washington, DC: Bread for the World Institute, 2016), 183–200. The $160 billion omits costs not related to health.

57. Donald S. Shepard et al., *Hunger in America: Suffering We All Pay For*, Center for

American Progress (Washington, DC, 2011), 17, https://www.americanprogress.org/wp-content/uploads/issues/2011/10/pdf/hunger_paper.pdf. The Health Impact Project, sponsored by the Pew Charitable Trusts and the Robert Wood Johnson Foundation, assessed the health impact of SNAP and came to similar findings. See www.healthimpactproject.org.

58. Shepard et al., *Hunger in America*, 5. By 2010 the recession had increased the number of food-insecure households by 30 percent. So both the cost of *permitting* hunger was unusually high, as was the cost of expanded food assistance to *reduce* hunger.

59. *Kaiser Health News*, May 24, 2011, cited in *Hunger Report 2013: Within Reach: Global Development Goals*, ed. Todd Post (Washington, DC: Bread for the World Institute, 2013), 147.

60. Medicare, Medicaid, Children's Health Insurance Program, veterans' medical care, and subsidies for ACA health insurance exchanges accounted for $980 billion, more than 25 percent of total federal spending in 2015. That does not include tax expenditures of almost $260 billion, mostly by excluding from taxation employers' contributions for medical insurance and care. The Tax Policy Center's estimate is based on CBO, OMB, and Joint Committee on Taxation data, https://www.taxpolicycenter.org/briefing-book/how-much-does-federal-government-spend-on-health-care.

61. *Hunger Report 2016*, 32–33.

62. Center on Budget and Policy Priorities, note 6 above.

63. *Hunger Report 2016*, 144–47. Also *ProMedica: Community Advocacy and Government Relations*, 1–19; and *Addressing Hunger Essential to Improving Health*, 1–7, both from ProMedica (Toledo, 2013). ProMedica (www.promedica.org/advocacy) is the region's largest employer, operating eleven hospitals and more than 300 other healthcare facilities, employing 1,700 physicians, 14,000 other staff, plus 1,600 volunteers. ProMedica became the first healthcare system in the nation to join the Alliance to End Hunger and is actively engaging businesses, nonprofits, faith groups, and elected officials to help make its twenty-seven counties a hunger-free region.

64. *Hunger Report 2016*, viii–69, especially 3, 25, 52–56.

65. Cook and Poblacion study published in *Hunger Report 2016*, 70–71, 183–200, especially 185.

66. *Household Food Security*, note 4 above, 7–8.

67. Caitlin Dewey, "The Hidden Crisis on College Campuses: Going Hungry," *The Washington Post*, April 4, 2018, A11.

FEEDING AMERICA

1. Feeding America, *Hunger in America 2014* (note 10 of chapter 2, above), 44. "60,000 food programs" is a September 19, 2017, email update from Diana Aviv, then CEO of Feeding America. The $8.5 billion is from Feeding America's 2016–17 IRS Form 990, Schedules M and O. Disclosure: I served on the Feeding America board of directors for six years during the 1990s, when its name was Second Harvest.

2. *The War on Poverty 50 Years Later: A Progress Report*, by the President's Council of Economic Advisers, January 2014, p. 7.

3. Feeding America, *Hunger in America 2014*, p. 8.

4. The 55 percent participation rate in SNAP reported by Feeding America in *Hunger in America 2014*, note 10 above, p. 139, probably understates participation, because 72 percent of Feeding America's households that do *not* receive SNAP may be eligible for it, according to the same report, p. 19. Some clients may prefer to hide their participation in SNAP.

5. Feeding America, *Hunger in America 2014*, p. 134.

6. Feeding America, *Hunger in America 2014*, pp. 120, 121, 126, 131, and 169.

CHAPTER 3

1. Robert Gates, Secretary of Defense under presidents George W. Bush and Barack Obama, video and transcript, "Roundtable on the Administration's New Global Development Policy," September 28, 2010, US Global Leadership Coalition, https://www.usglc.org/blog/the -administrations-new-global-development-policy-a-roundtable-discussion/.

2. Reported by the British medical journal *The Lancet*, in "Maternal and Child Nutrition: Executive Summary of *The Lancet* Maternal and Child Nutrition Series," 2013, http://thousand days.org/resource/the-2013-lancet-series-on-maternal-and-child-nutrition/.

3. Roger Thurow and Scott Kilman, *Enough: Why the World's Poorest Starve in an Age of Plenty* (New York: Public Affairs, 2009), x–xi, 278–83.

4. Todd Post, ed., *Hunger Report 2013: Within Reach: Global Development Goals* (Washington, DC: Bread for the World Institute, 2013), 47–48.

5. *The Lancet*, note 2 above. Also Roger Thurow, *The First 1,000 Days* (New York: Public Affairs, 2016), 13–16, 73–80. It is also a period during which irreversible stunting occurs.

6. UN agencies (Food and Agriculture Organization, International Fund for Agricultural Development, and World Food Program) measure chronic hunger by two different indicators: the prevalence of undernourishment and the prevalence of underweight children under five years of age. FAO, IFAD, and WFP, *The State of Food Insecurity in the World 2015* (Rome, FAO), 19 and 53.

7. Angus Deaton, *The Great Escape* (Princeton: Princeton University Press, 2013), 167.

8. I saw, carefully noted, and saved that estimate on October 17, 1996, from an old Food and Agriculture Organization poster (probably from its pre-UN days) in a USDA exhibit on President Franklin D. Roosevelt. Robert Kates of Brown University, in a review of David Grigg's *The World Food Problem 1950–1980*, in *Economic Geography* 63, no. 2 (1987): 183–84, refers to an "oft-quoted claim" of the first director-general of the FAO, Sir John Boyd-Orr, "that a lifetime of malnutrition and actual hunger is the lot of at least two-thirds of mankind." Eleanor Roosevelt reported the same estimate multiple times in her syndicated "My Day" column, according to the FDR Memorial Library, and did so also in a speech published in *The New York Times*, December 8, 1959: "We cannot exist as a little island of well-being in a world where two-thirds of the people go to bed hungry every night." But "two-thirds" was an estimate not sufficiently defined or verified by empirical data.

238

9. Franklin D. Roosevelt, Second Inaugural Address, January 20, 1937.

10. John F. Kennedy, an address to the World Food Congress, Washington, DC, June 4, 1963. The American Presidency Project, http://www.presidency.ucsb.edu.

11. UN Food and Agriculture Organization, *The State of Food Security and Nutrition in the World 2018*, pp. 2–3 from a forty-three-page version of the full report. Prevalence of undernourishment in 2017 was 10.9 percent, http://www.fao.org/state-of-food-security-nutrition/en/.

12. In the United States and Germany only 8 percent, and in the United Kingdom only 12 percent of those surveyed knew that extreme poverty had declined worldwide, according to a survey commissioned by Oxfam and others, cited by Max Roser and Esteban Ortiz-Ospina, "World Poverty," p. 12, from the Oxford-based Our World in Data, https://ourworldindata.org/world-poverty/, accessed January 23, 2017.

13. David Beckmann, *Exodus from Hunger* (Louisville: Westminster John Knox Press, 2010). Beckmann is president of Bread for the World, Bread for the World Institute, and the Alliance to End Hunger.

14. It had dropped by 44.4 percent (short of the goal of 50 percent). *State of Food Insecurity*, note 6 above, 17.

15. UN Millennium Development Goals, MDG 1 Infographic, "Goal 1: Eradicate extreme poverty & hunger," http://www.un.org/millenniumgoals/poverty.shtml. Accessed February 22, 2017.

16. *A New Global Partnership: The Report of the High-Level Panel of Eminent Persons on the Post-2015 Development Agenda* (New York: United Nations, 2013), executive summary.

17. The SDGs set the bar high. Goal #1 is: "End poverty in all its forms everywhere." But the goal's targets modify that to mean "eradicate *extreme* poverty" and reduce at least by *half* "poverty in all its dimensions" by 2030 (italics added). The World Bank defines the goal for ending extreme poverty as "no more than 3 percent" of the world's population. Goal #2 is: "End hunger." Its targets include not only chronic hunger but "ending all forms of malnutrition." However, the SDG *targets* for all seventeen goals are called "aspirational global targets, with each government setting its own national targets guided by the global level of ambition, but taking into account national circumstances." This realism modifies the goals on a country-by-country basis.

18. Based on reports from several international agencies. See Homi Kharas, Kristofer Hamel, and Martin Hofer, "The Start of a New Poverty Narrative," Brookings Institution, June 19, 2018, https://www.brookings.edu/blog/future-development/2018/06/19/the-start-of-a-new-poverty-narrative.

19. UN Food and Agriculture Organization, note 11 above, 2–3, 24–33.

20. The World Bank defines the end of absolute poverty as allowing 3 percent for "frictional" poverty, caused by such things as unexpected economic change, political conflict, and war. *Prosperity for All / Ending Extreme Poverty: A Note for the World Bank Group Spring Meetings 2014* (Washington, DC: World Bank), introduction, http://siteresources.worldbank.org/INTPROSPECTS/Resources/334934-1327948020811/8401693-1397074077765/Prosperity_for_All_Final_2014.pdf.

21. The poverty line was adjusted from $1.25 to $1.90 by including a new measurement that reflects more accurately the variation in purchasing power within each country. "The

international poverty line has just been raised to $1.90 a day, but global poverty is basically unchanged. How is that even possible?" World Bank blog, October 4, 2015. The article explains how the adjustment leaves previous reports on poverty levels largely unchanged, http://blogs .worldbank.org/developmenttalk/international-poverty-line-has-just-been-raised-190-day -global-poverty-basically-unchanged-how-even.

22. "Rapid, Climate-Informed Development Needed to Keep Climate Change from Pushing More Than 100 Million People into Poverty by 2030," World Bank, November 8, 2015, http://www.worldbank.org/en/news/feature/2015/11/08/rapid-climate-informed-development -needed-to-keep-climate-change-from-pushing-more-than-100-million-people-into-poverty -by-2030.

23. With a complexity of factors to consider, it is not possible to determine with precision the effect of the MDGs, but accelerated progress on a number of goals, especially in sub-Saharan Africa since 2000, suggests a substantial impact. John W. McArthur and Krista Rasmussen, *Change of Pace: Accelerations and Advances during the Millennium Development Goal Era*, Brookings Institution, January 11, 2017, https://www.brookings.edu/research/change-of -pace-accelerations-and-advances-during-the-millennium-development-goal-era/.

24. The USDA measurement is demand-oriented in capturing food insecurity variations within deciles, rather than putting everyone within a decile at the same level. It more accurately projects food consumption of people as they respond to prices and income. Stacey Rosen et al., *International Food Security Assessment, 2016–2026*, GFA-27, US Department of Agriculture, Economic Research Service, June 2016, Abstract, Summary, and pp. iv, 1, 9–11, 13–15.

25. "Hopeless Africa," *The Economist* (May 11, 2000), cited by *Hunger Report 2013*, 59.

26. John McArthur, "What Does the Past Tell Us about the Future? Possibilities for Child Survival in 2030," Brookings, May 7, 2015.

27. UN Development Program, *Africa Human Development Report 2012*, cited by *Hunger Report 2013*, 58. The human development index is based on life expectancy, educational expectancy, and per capita income.

28. Indermit Gill and Kenan Karakulah, "Africa's 3 Deadly Deficits: Education, Electricity, and Taxes," Brookings Institution, June 8, 2018, https://www.brookings.edu/blog/future -development/2018/06/08/africas-3-deadly-deficits.

29. *Our Big Bet for the Future*, the annual letter of the Bill and Melinda Gates Foundation, January 2015, pp. 19–30. It cites the World Bank as the source for the $50 billion figure. See http://www.gatesnotes.com/2015-Annual-Letter?page=0&lang=en.

30. Gina Bergh and Claire Melamed (May 2012), "Inclusive Growth and a Post-2015 Framework," Overseas Development Institute. Cited by *Hunger Report 2013*, 35.

31. Save the Children (2010), *A Fair Chance at Life: Why Equity Matters for Child Mortality*. Cited by *Hunger Report 2013*, 12. Bangladesh also made much faster gains than India in moving toward the MDG goal of cutting hunger in half by 2015 (though neither country achieved it). *The State of Food Insecurity 2015*, note 6 above, Annex 1, p. 46.

32. Oxfam, "Behind Brazil's Amazing Success against Hunger and Poverty, Questions Remain," June 2012, https://www.oxfam.org/sites/www.oxfam.org/files/oxfam-rioplus20 -case-study-brazil-jun2012.pdf. A question Oxfam raises is the viability of a highly aggres-

sive and environmentally costly agribusiness sector that exists in tension alongside of Zero Hunger.

33. Dom Phillips, "'People Are Getting Poorer': Hunger and Homelessness as Brazil Crisis Deepens," *The Guardian*, July 19, 2017, https://www.theguardian.com/global-development/2017/jul/19/people-getting-poorer-hunger-homelessness-brazil-crisis. For a more detailed description of Zero Hunger, Inter-réseaux, "Brazil's 'Zero Hunger' Strategy," September 2012, http://www.inter-reseaux.org/IMG/pdf/Note_FaimZe_ro_Sept2012_EN_vp.pdf. Also Sarah Illingworth, *Huffington Post* blog, "The Success and Future of Brazil's Biggest Benefit, Bolsa Família," December 6, 2017, https://www.huffingtonpost.com/sarah-illingworth/the-success-and-future-of_b_12913176.html.

34. Jose Carlos Ferreyra, "Striving to Invest in People: Peru's Success in Overcoming Its Stunting Crisis," The World Bank, accessed January 26, 2018, listed by author and title at https://medium.com/world-of-opportunity/archive.

35. Homi Kharas, Kristofer Hamei, and Martin Hofer, "Rethinking Global Poverty Reduction in 2019," Brookings Institution, December 13, 3018, https://www.brookings.edu/blog/future-development/2018/12/13/rethinking-global-poverty.

36. Kennedy, address to the World Food Congress, Washington, DC, June 4, 1963.

37. "World Food Conference Meets at Rome: Addresses by Secretary Kissinger and Secretary of Agriculture Butz and Texts of Resolutions," *The Department of State Bulletin* 71, no. 1851 (December 1974): 821, 829, 832.

38. National Academy of Sciences, *World Food and Nutrition Study* (Washington, DC: National Academy of Sciences, 1977), 5 and 54. In submitting the report to President Carter, Philip Handler, President of the NAS, reiterated its conclusion about political will, p. iv.

39. Kennedy, address to the World Food Congress, Washington, DC, June 4, 1963.

40. *World Food and Nutrition Study*, 5 and 52.

41. Jeffrey D. Sachs, *The End of Poverty* (New York: Penguin, 2005), 69–70.

42. All donor nations combined gave 0.34 percent of their national income in 1990, a rate that dropped to 0.23 percent in 2002. UN Millennium Project 2005, *Investing in Development: A Practical Plan to Achieve the Millennium Development Goals*, p. 59, http://web.worldbank.org/archive/website01021/WEB/IMAGES/TF1MAINR.PDF.

43. From 2008 to 2015 funding for PEPFAR ranged between $6 billion and $7 billion a year for prevention, treatment, and care of HIV/AIDS. By 2013 it had supported antiretroviral treatment for almost 7 million, care for 17 million (including 5 million orphans and vulnerable children), and antiretroviral treatment for pregnant women that enabled 240,000 babies to be born HIV-free. In 2009 the Obama administration made it the centerpiece of the US Global Health Initiative that continues to include malaria and TB as targets. "The U.S. President's Emergency Plan for AIDS Relief (PEPFAR)," by the Henry J. Kaiser Family Foundation, June 4, 2014. Also "Evaluation of PEPFAR" by the Institute of Medicine of the National Academy of Sciences, February 20, 2013, http://www.nationalacademies.org/hmd/Reports/2013/Evaluation-of-PEPFAR.aspx.

44. The fear of long-term food shortages and high prices was based not only on population growth but also on rising standards of living in developing countries, which enable

people to eat more meat and dairy products, which requires more livestock consuming more grain.

45. The period from conception to age two is the most crucial time for securing good health and preventing mental and physical disabilities. Timely interventions for mother and child can have a greater long-term impact than later interventions. See Thurow, *The First 1000 Days*, note 5 above. USAID calls its program "Feed the Future." Many developing countries are focusing more heavily on this first thousand-day period under the theme of "Scaling Up Nutrition."

46. Bread for the World's estimate. It refers to assistance within the larger foreign aid account that specifically addresses "issues of human needs among the world's poorest populations: issues like agricultural development and nutrition, emergency humanitarian assistance, global health, education, gender equality, and water and sanitation." David Beckmann, testimony to the House Appropriations Subcommittee on State, Foreign Operations, and Related Programs, March 25, 2015. By 2016 the estimate had reached $26.6 billion according to a Bread for the World infographic.

47. *MDG Report*, 7. During the same period US aid to Africa tripled from $2.8 billion to $9.3 billion. OECD, "Official Development Assistance (ODA) 2000-2015," https://data.oecd .org/oda/net-oda.htm.

48. *Hunger Report 2013*, 58. However, there was a regrettable lag in fulfilling the pledges.

49. Yun Sun, "China's Aid to Africa: Monster or Messiah?," Brookings East Asia Commentary, Number 75, February 2014. China began serious engagement with Africa in 1963 and announced that by 2015 it will have provided Africa with $1 trillion in financing, in the form of direct investment, commercial loans, and low-interest loans. China is among a growing number of nontraditional donor nations now helping to finance development, especially infrastructure, with loans and investments. Traditional donors are part of the Western-led Organization for Economic Cooperation and Development.

50. *The State of Food Security and Nutrition in the World 2017* (Rome: UN Food and Agriculture Organization), FAO, IFAD, UNICEF, WFP, and WHO, 31-39, 52, 60, 71-73.

51. The UN Millennium Project, an independent advisory body commissioned by the UN Secretary-General and directed by Jeffrey Sachs, in 2005 proposed strategies for meeting the Millennium Development Goals by 2015. The strategies included increasing annual official development assistance (ODA) from donor nations to $195 billion by 2015. Donor nations did double their aid, but only to the level of $137 billion by 2014. Partly because of the increase and in spite of the shortfall, some of the key MDG targets were exceeded and others fell short. My proposal that traditional donor nations increase their ODA by $90 billion, building on the $137 for a total ODA of $227 billion, seems consistent with the proposal of the UN project's detailed and nuanced analysis. The dollar increase I have proposed is $30 billion more than the $195 billion proposed by the project for the "mid-station" MDGs. However, we are starting from a higher base of aid and building on the gains and momentum of the MDGs and previous increases in ODA. But because so much is at stake, and bringing an end to most remaining hunger and extreme poverty (along with the other related aims of the new Sustainable Development Goals) is such an immense challenge, the $237 billion estimate is warranted. See the UN Millennium Project, *Investing in Development: A Practical Plan to Achieve the Millennium*

Development Goals, 60–64, http://web.worldbank.org/archive/website01021/WEB/IMAGES/TF1MAINR.PDF. Also Sachs, *The End of Poverty*, 288–308.

52. "Final Official Development Assistance Figures in 2014," Organization for Economic Cooperation and Development, http://www.oecd.org/dac/stats/final-oda-2014.htm. (Twenty-eight donor nations make up the Development Assistance Committee of the OECD.)

53. The goal was formally approved in October 1970 by the UN General Assembly. The United States supported the general aims of the UN resolution, but did not subscribe to specific targets or timetables. OECD, "History of the 0.7% ODA Target," June 2010, https://www.oecd.org/dac/stats/45539274.pdf.

54. A $30 billion increase would bring US official development assistance to about $63 billion, 1.5 percent of our federal budget, and about 0.35 percent of our national income, half of the international donor standard of 0.7 percent of national income. The increase, relatively small given the size of our economy, would nevertheless give a huge boost to ending hunger and poverty, while helping countries deal with the impact of climate change.

55. The numbers assume an annual 2 percent growth in the US economy and budget projections (outlays) by the Office of Management and Budget in fiscal year 2017.

56. Jon Meacham, "Free to Be Happy," *Time* magazine, July 8–15, 2013, 38–46.

57. Gates, "Roundtable on the Administration's New Global Development Policy," note 1 above.

ONE LITTLE CHILD

1. Anne Barnard and Karam Shoumali, "Image of Drowned Syrian, Aylan Kurdi, 3, Brings Migrant Crisis into Focus," *The New York Times*, September 3, 2015, https://www.nytimes.com/2015/09/04/world/europe/syria-boy-drowning.html.

CHAPTER 4

1. Elie Wiesel, Holocaust witness, in accepting the Nobel Peace Prize in Oslo, Norway, December 10, 1986. Cited by Dan Rather and Elliot Kirschner, *What Unites Us: Reflections on Patriotism* (Chapel Hill, NC: Algonquin Books, 2017), 269.

2. The backing came most prominently in the form of Pope Paul's encyclical, *The Development of Peoples*, March 26, 1967, published in the United States by the US Catholic Conference, Washington, DC. His encyclical urged rich countries to assist poor countries to overcome the injustices of hunger and poverty.

3. Both editorials were titled "The Right to Food," *The Wall Street Journal*, April 8, 1976, and *The New York Times*, September 24, 1976.

4. Janis Johnson, "3 Back Right-to-Food Plan," *The Washington Post*, June 25, 1976, B16, cites the State Department and USDA statements in opposition to, as well as the testimony of religious leaders and others in support of the resolution at a congressional hearing on the

resolution. It also reports Bread for the World's role. The three religious leaders featured with photos were Eugene Carson Blake, former head of the World Council of Churches and chair of Bread for the World's board of directors, Rabbi Marc Tanenbaum, head of the American Jewish Committee, and Bishop James Rausch, general secretary of the US Catholic Conference.

5. For a more detailed account of the campaign see my book, *The Rising of Bread for the World: An Outcry of Citizens against Hunger* (Mahwah, NJ: Paulist Press, 2009), 95–100.

6. Use of growth charts to spot nutrition problems, oral rehydration (using the right combination of salt and sugar with pure water when diarrhea occurs), promotion of breastfeeding, and immunization. The four were sometimes called by the acronym GOBI.

7. *UNICEF Annual Report 1985*, p. 3. Web access by that title.

8. "Remarks by Administrator Rajiv Shah at the Acting on the Call Conference," June 25, 2014. A USAID press release for that date said the US had invested more than $13 billion in child and maternal survival since 2009 and would "realign $2.9 billion of the Agency's resources to save up to 500,000 children from preventable deaths" by the end of 2015, https://geneva.usmission.gov/2014/06/25/usaid-and-partners-unveil-new-efforts-to-save-millions-of-women-and-children-from-preventable-deaths/.

9. John C. Quinley and Timothy D. Baker, "Lobbying for International Health: Bread for the World and the Agency for International Development," *American Journal of Public Health* 76, no. 7 (July 1986): 797–99.

10. UN World Health Organization fact sheet, "Children: Reducing Mortality," January 2016, http://www.who.int/mediacentre/factsheets/fs178/en/.

11. Bill and Melinda Gates, *gatesnotes* (annual letter), February 14, 2017, https://www.gatesnotes.com/2017-Annual-Letter.

12. Bill Gates, *G20 Report* to G20 leaders, Cannes Summit, November 2011, p. 15, http://www.gatesfoundation.org/What-We-Do/Global-Policy/G20-Report.

13. For example, the fertility rate per woman of childbearing age in Bangladesh dropped from 6.2 percent in 1981 to 2.2 percent in 2015; and for India from 4.8 percent to 2.4 percent. On the other hand, the fertility rates for most African countries remained at high levels. World Bank, Data, "Fertility Rate, Total (Births per Woman)," http://data.worldbank.org/indicator/SP.DYN.TFRT.IN.

14. Victor Oliveira, "The Food Assistance Landscape: FY 2017 Annual Report," US Department of Agriculture, March 2017, www.ers.usda.gov/publications/pub-details/?pubid=88073.

15. Food and Nutrition Service, US Department of Agriculture, www.fns.usda.gov/wic, accessed October 4, 2018.

16. Barbara Howell in conversation with the author in October 2018.

17. The Organization of the Petroleum Exporting Countries (OPEC) cut back production, causing a sudden surge in oil prices. This triggered lineups for gasoline and an economic jolt in the United States, but more than a jolt in many poor countries. It also gave OPEC countries a huge cash inflow, some of which they needed to deposit in rich-country banks. The banks in turn needed borrowers for that money. So economically strapped poor countries were urged to borrow to build their economies. The result was reckless lending and foolish borrowing.

18. Deuteronomy 15 and Leviticus 25.

19. Jeffrey D. Sachs, *The End of Poverty* (New York: Penguin, 2005), 342.

20. David Beckmann, *Exodus from Hunger* (Louisville: Westminster John Knox Press, 2010), 95.

21. Michael Grunwald, "GOP's Bachus Makes Debt Relief His Mission," *The Washington Post*, October 9, 1999, A3.

22. Beckmann tells how Rep. John Kasich, who chaired the House Budget Committee, and several other key members of Congress from both parties, along with five religious leaders (including Beckmann), met in the cabinet room of the White House with President Clinton. They sought ways to win final passage for debt relief. The meeting convinced Pat Robertson to speak in favor of it on his *700 Club* broadcast. He told viewers in Texas to contact Senator Gramm. Beckmann, *Exodus from Hunger*, 98-99.

23. World Bank Group Macroeconomics and Fiscal Management, http://pubdocs.world bank.org/en/702021492519096192/Debt-relief-facts-April-2017.pdf. See also Sachs, *The End of Poverty*, and Beckmann, *Exodus from Hunger*, 94-100.

24. SNAP had 26.3 million recipients in 2007 and 47.6 million in 2013, an 81 percent increase. US Department of Agriculture, Food and Nutrition Service data as of October 5, 2018.

25. "Circle of Protection: A Statement on Why We Need to Protect Programs for the Poor."

26. For more detail, see Beckmann, *Exodus from Hunger*, chapters 6 and 7. Also Simon, *The Rising of Bread for the World: An Outcry of Citizens against Hunger*.

27. Peter Dreier, "Go Out and Make Me Do It," *Huffington Post* blog, November 9, 2009, updated May 25, 2011, huffpost.com. Dreier also relayed this account in an interview on Bill Moyers Journal, PBS, "A New Generation of Activists," October 25, 2013.

28. Its original full name: Senator Paul Simon Water for the Poor Act of 2005. With enhanced monitoring and evaluation, it was reenacted as the Senator Paul Simon Water for the World Act of 2015. Both bills passed with strong bipartisan support.

29. *The Miami Herald*, March 17, 1992.

30. I know Sharon through her participation in Bread for the World's board of directors, but material here is also taken from her chapter on the Oregon Food Bank in *A Place at the Table*, ed. Peter Pringle (New York: Public Affairs, 2013), 153-58.

31. Nicholas Kristof, "Polluted Political Games," *The New York Times*, May 28, 2015, A25.

32. Willy Brandt, in the introduction to *North-South: A Program for Survival*, the report of the Independent Commission on International Development Issues, Willy Brandt, chairman (Cambridge, MA: MIT Press, 1980), 16. Brandt, the Chancellor of West Germany from 1969 to 1974, received the Nobel Peace Prize in 1971.

33. Leviticus 19:16, New American Bible Translation. (Hebrew: "stand against the blood," that is, the life.)

CHAPTER 5

1. Gunnar Myrdal, *An American Dilemma* (New York: McGraw-Hill, 1964; Harper & Row edition, 1944, volume 1), 11. His two volumes were the Nobel Prize economist's magisterial

documentation of racial oppression in America as a contradiction of its ideals of liberty and equality.

2. The figures here and on *Visual 3* represent food value and omit most operating costs. The $14 billion estimate for charities is based on the $8.5 billion value of total food distribution by the Feeding America national network for fiscal year 2016–2017 (IRS Form 990, Schedule O) plus an estimated $3.6 billion of food obtained from other sources by local Feeding America-related food outlets (based on Feeding America's *Hunger in America 2014*, executive summary, table on p. 59), and an estimated $3.4 billion of food distributed by food banks, organizations, and outlets not related to Feeding America, for a total of $15.5 billion. From that I subtracted $1.5 billion for government grants to regional food banks and other distributing agencies, and allowed for some overlapping and duplication of reporting, and for enhanced tax deductions claimed by food manufacturers and retailers for an IRS-specified part of their food contributions, including $2.4 billion of such contributions to Feeding America in 2016–17 (Form 990, Schedule O, above), tax deductions for which I have credited to the government. The net total is $14 billion (13 percent) for charity's part of the nation's food assistance. The $91 billion (87 percent) for federal food benefits for fiscal year 2017 includes all federal food assistance programs, which, with operating costs (of 7.3 percent), totaled $98.2 billion. SNAP alone accounted for $63.7 billion of federal food assistance benefits (70 percent of the federal total). US Department of Agriculture, "Annual Summary of Food and Nutrition Service Programs," March 9, 2018, www.fns.usda.gov/pd.

3. The Feeding America network accounts for 46 million individuals, no double counting. Perhaps 10 million or more outside of its network also received charitable food assistance. See note 2 above.

4. Nicholas Kristof, "A Little Respect for Dr. Foster," *The New York Times*, March 29, 2015, A25.

5. Feeding America reports that 62 percent of the 46,000 local agencies that its food banks serve identify as faith-based. *Hunger in America 2014*, executive summary, 4–5. Robert D. Putnam reports that "half of all personal philanthropy is religious in character" and that "religious adherents are also more likely to contribute time and money to activities beyond their own congregation." Putnam, *Bowling Alone* (New York: Simon & Schuster, 2000), 66–67.

6. Acts 16:35–40; 22:22–29; 25:10–12.

7. 2 Corinthians 8 and 9.

8. Richard Stearns, *The Hole in Our Gospel* (Nashville: Thomas Nelson, 2009), 126.

9. Ken Stern, *With Charity for All: Why Charities Are Failing and a Better Way to Give* (New York: Doubleday, 2013), 53–65.

10. Stern, *With Charity for All*, 2–4 and 53–65. The "more than $1.5 million" figure is from the National Center for Charitable Statistics, http://nccs.urban.org/data-statistics/quick-facts-about-nonprofits.

11. *Giving USA 2017: The Annual Report on Philanthropy for the Year 2016* (Chicago: Giving USA Foundation, 2017), 21 for dollar figures; but the reference to "ten human service areas" comes from *Giving USA 2014*, 16–17.

12. Carol Adelman, Bryan Schwartz, and Elias Riskin, *The Index of Global Philanthropy and Remittances 2016* (Washington, DC: Hudson Institute Center for Global Prosperity, 2017),

9, https://www.hudson.org/research/13314-index-of-global-philanthropy-and-remittances -2016.

13. Philanthropy of US corporations, religious groups, foundations, and universities has distinctive purposes, though aspects of each may qualify as antipoverty aid. Therefore the question of what constitutes private charitable giving for hunger and poverty abroad is complex. Personal remittances of money to home countries, which totaled $109 billion from the United States in 2014, are not included. Each remittance gives a boost to a family or person, say, in Central America or India, but that is not charitable US aid. When an American works in Mexico and sends money home, we consider that personal or family support, not Mexican aid to the United States.

14. *Giving USA 2017*, 309–30.

15. Italics added. "Rotary International's Global Update on Polio Eradication," October 27, 2014, http://www.polioeradication.org/mediaroom/newsstories/Rotary-International -s-Global-Upddate.

16. The Alliance to End Hunger, a secular affiliate of Bread for the World, sponsors an annual Hunger Free Communities Summit in Washington, www.hungerfreecommunities.org.

17. Todd Post, ed., *Hunger Report 2014: Ending Hunger in America* (Washington, DC: Bread for the World Institute, 2014), 121–25. Also personal correspondence from David Miner, IHN chair, which included a short "Early History" of IHN, plus a twenty-eight-page "Indy Hunger Network Overview," February 21, 2017.

18. Arthur C. Brooks, *The Conservative Heart* (New York: HarperCollins, 2015), 140.

19. Matt Knott, "Feeding America in Times of Change," in *A Place at the Table*, ed. Peter Pringle (New York: Public Affairs, 2013), 137–42.

20. Data on the Greater Chicago Food Depository comes from its report on IRS Form 990 for 2016 (July 2016 through June 2017) available on the web, and from its 2017 Annual Report. Volunteer hours are not included in income, though recruitment and supervision of volunteers is a cost. Management and fundraising cost $9.3 million (less than 9 percent of expenses), with the rest of operational costs attributed to program services.

21. Data on Cook County are based on its SNAP report for July 2017, part of the US Department of Agriculture's Food & Nutrition Services report of January 16, 2018, on SNAP project areas nationwide, which I received from SNAP headquarters on February 26. I multiplied Cook County's July 2017 report by twelve for the year's estimate. I also credited private charity with 75 percent of the food bank's total, because the government accounts for the other 25 percent of the food it distributes. Because SNAP accounts for about 70 percent of total federal food assistance (note 2, above), the government's combined total for Cook County comes to about $2 billion, twenty times that of the Chicago food bank's distribution or about twenty-seven times the amount of that food bank's *private charitable* distribution.

22. "In FY 2017, Feeding America's legislative focus was on protecting funding for federal nutrition programs in the federal budget and appropriations process. . . . We continue to build advocacy capacity and engagement across our network by developing advocacy training programs for food bank staff and providing grants to our network for advocacy." Feeding America's IRS Form 990 report for fiscal year 2016–2017, Schedule O.

23. The statistics on Bowie are based on US Census data updates, and for the Bowie food pantry on IRS Form 990 report for 2016–2017 plus extensive data on the pantry's website, including detailed bi-monthly reports from January through December 2017. Conversations with Debora Langdon, its director, and Bridget Kopetzky, treasurer, as well as an on-site visit were especially helpful.

24. In August 2013 the US Department of Agriculture reported that from 2009 to 2011 the rate of trafficking was 1.3 percent of total SNAP benefits, http://www.fns.usda.gov/extent-trafficking-supplemental-nutrition-assistance-program-2009-2011-august-2013.

25. Fran Quigley, "For Goodness' Sake: A Two-Part Proposal for Remedying the U.S. Charity/Justice Imbalance," *Virginia Journal of Social Policy and the Law* 23, no. 1 (2016): 55. Web access: Virginia Journal of Social Policy and Law, Volume 23.1, 2016.

26. Reinhold Niebuhr, *Moral Man and Immoral Society* (New York: Scribner's, 1932), 127.

27. Martin McLaughlin in an undated note to the author, probably in 1985.

28. *Giving USA*, note 11 above, 47, shown in dollars adjusted for inflation.

29. Feeding America's IRS Form 990 (Schedule O) reports for 2008 and 2016 show its total network's contribution of food growing from 2.6 billion pounds in 2008 to 4.9 billion pounds in 2016. Contributions and grants received by Feeding America grew from $588 million to $2.7 billion during those years.

30. An average of $66 million a year for fiscal year 2015–2016 and fiscal year 2016–2017 according to Feeding America's annual reports on IRS Form 990, Schedule O.

31. Feeding America's fiscal year 2016–2017 report on IRS Form 990, Schedule M.

32. Andrew Fisher, *Big Hunger: The Unholy Alliance between Corporate America and Anti-Hunger Groups* (Cambridge, MA: MIT Press, 2017).

33. Fisher, *Big Hunger*, 77–78, 89–96.

34. Bob Aiken, "Severe Cuts to Food Programs in House Farm Bill Would Increase Need, Overwhelm Charities," press release from Feeding America, May 17, 2013.

35. The automatic cut of $4.5 billion came from a temporary increase for SNAP as part of the economic stimulus to counteract the recession. But the number of households facing food insecurity (food shortages) remained far above the prerecession level.

36. Robert Samuels, "Food Stamp Cuts to Hit Washington Area Hard," *The Washington Post*, November 1, 2013, B1.

37. Diana Aviv and Jim Weill, "President, Congress Must Protect Programs That Keep Hunger at Bay," *The Hill*, March 3, 2017, http://thehill.com/blogs/congress-blog/politics/322178-president-congress-must-protect-programs-that-keep-hunger-at-bay.

38. "The Future of Hunger Relief," a mailing from Feeding America, received in the spring of 2018.

39. J. Larry Brown, Donald Shepard, and others, *The Economic Cost of Domestic Hunger: Estimated Annual Burden to the United States*, June 5, 2007 (commissioned by the Sodexho Foundation with the Public Welfare Foundation and Spunk Fund), 13, http://us.stop-hunger.org/files/live/sites/stophunger-us/files/HungerPdf/Cost%20of%20Domestic%20Hunger%20Report%20_tcm150-155150.pdf.

40. Janet Poppendieck, *Sweet Charity* (New York: Viking, 1998), 4–12 and throughout.

She contends that hunger charities relieve pressure for addressing the underlying structural problem of poverty and argues that people (including public officials) are led to believe that charity is or could be a more adequate solution to hunger, a view that invites neglect of government and gives officials a pretext for cutting hunger and poverty programs.

41. EITC and CTC benefited almost 32 million people, including 13 million children in 2013. "Chart Book: The Earned Income Tax Credit and Child Tax Credit," Center on Budget and Policy Priorities, Jan. 16, 2015, http://www.cbpp.org/research/federal-tax/chart-book-the -earned-income-tax-credit-and-child-tax-credit.

42. Medicaid and CHIP had a combined enrollment of 70 million in January 2015 according to the Kaiser Family Foundation, http://kff.org/report-section/recent-trends-in-medicaid -and-chip-enrollment-as-of-january-2015-issue-brief/.

43. In 2016 TANF assisted 2.7 million recipients, most of them children, https://www .acf.hhs.gov/ofa/resource/tanf-caseload-data-2016. TANF benefits leave family incomes below half of the poverty line in every state, reports the Center on Budget and Policy Priorities, http://www.cbpp.org/research/family-income-support/tanf-cash-benefits-have-fallen-by -more-than-20-percent-in-most-states.

44. HUD reports that 1.2 million households benefit, http://portal.hud.gov/hudportal /HUD/src=/topics/rental_assistance/phprog.

45. Social Security Disability Insurance benefits were paid to 10.2 million people in 2013, http://www.ssa.gov/policy/docs/statcomps/di_asr/2013/di_asr13.pdf.

46. Scott Pelley, CBS, *60 Minutes*, segments web accessible as published November 27, 2011, and May 7, 2013.

47. William Sloane Coffin Jr., *The Collected Sermons of William Sloane Coffin: The Riverside Years* (Louisville: Westminster John Knox, 2008), vol. 2, 91. Cited by Quigley, "For Goodness' Sake," 9.

CHAPTER 6

1. Bill Moyers in 2011, cited by Elaine Mejia, "Getting beyond the 'Charity versus Government' Paradigm," *Public Works*, February 22, 2015.

2. Landrum Bolling, *Private Foreign Aid: U.S. Philanthropy in Relief and Development* (Boulder, CO: Westview Press, 1982), 2.

3. Bolling, *Private Foreign Aid*, 2.

4. Christine Kinealy, "International Relief Efforts During the Famine," *Irish America*, August/September 2009, https://irishamerica.com/2009/08/international-relief-efforts-during -the-famine/.

5. Timothy J. Sarbaugh, "'Charity Begins at Home': The United States Government and Irish Famine Relief 1845–1849," https://www.historyireland.com/18th-19th-century-history /charity-begins-at-home-the-united-states-government-irish-famine-relief-1845-1849/. Although bigotry surfaced in the debates, Sarbaugh concludes that it was "constitutional limitations and laissez-faire economics that killed the Irish relief bill." The objection contradicted the

precedent set in 1812 under President James Madison when he and the Congress approved the sending of aid worth 50,000 British pounds to Caracas, Venezuela, after a severe earthquake.

6. George H. Nash, "An American Epic: Herbert Hoover and Belgium Relief in World War I," *Prologue* (National Archives) 21, no. 1 (Spring 1989).

7. Ronald Radosh, "The Politics of Food: How America Kept Russia from Starving," *Humanities* (NIH) 32, no. 2 (March/April 2011). Hoover hoped the aid would encourage people to seek an alternative to the Bolsheviks—and Lenin feared outside assistance for the same reason. So assistance encountered many obstacles.

8. "Between 1941 and 1945 a total of $50.1 billion of supplies (equivalent to about $760 billion in current dollars) were shipped to various allies all over the world," 14 percent of it in food products, according to the US Department of State, "Lend-Lease: Facts and Numbers," April 2, 2010, http://iipdigital.usembassy.gov/st/english/article/2010/05/20100518114619z jsredna0.3529736.

9. "In Praise of . . . Lend-Lease," *The Guardian*, May 4, 2006, http://www.theguardian .com/commentisfree/2006/may/05/secondworldwar.comment. Also "Lend-Lease Act (1941)," Encyclopedia.com, http://www.encyclopedia.com/topic/lend-lease.aspx. Historian James MacGregor Burns considered Lend-Lease "a milestone in the organizing of world resistance to Hitler." *Roosevelt: The Lion and the Fox* (New York: Harcourt, Brace, 1956), 457.

10. Bolling, *Private Foreign Aid*, 17.

11. Based on the US Bureau of Economic Analysis, "Current-Dollar and 'Real' Gross Domestic Product," https://www.bea.gov/national/xls/gdplev.xls. Or $3 billion according to the Consumer Price Index Inflation Calculator of the Bureau of Labor Statistics, http://www.bls .gov/data/inflation_calculator.htm.

12. Bolling, *Private Foreign Aid*, 17.

13. Rachel M. McCleary, *Global Compassion: Private Voluntary Organizations and U.S. Foreign Policy since 1939* (New York: Oxford University Press, 2009), 67-68.

14. CARE was formed in 1946 to obtain US Army food packed for soldiers who were expected to invade Japan. CARE then sent the packages to people in Europe who faced famine. CARE packages saved lives and generated good will toward our country, as did relief efforts of other agencies.

15. James Reston, "The Marshall Plan," *The New York Times*, May 24, 1987.

16. Theodore A. Wilson, *The Marshall Plan: 1947-1951* (New York: Foreign Policy Association, June 1977), 32-37.

17. Lend-Lease, much larger, was wartime military aid. Tony Judt, "Introduction," in *The Marshall Plan: Fifty Years After*, ed. Martin A. Schain (New York: Palgrave, 2001), 2.

18. $12.6 billion would be worth $123 billion in 2015 dollars; 7.4 percent of federal budget spending in 2016 would be about $288 billion; and 1.05 percent of national income about $193 billion in 2016. The estimates are based on the four years of the Marshall Plan (April 1948 to December 31, 1951). Data are from *Fiscal Year 2014 Historical Tables: Budget of the U.S. Government*, Office of Management and Budget. Also Roy Gardner, "The Marshall Plan Fifty Years Later: Three What-Ifs and a When," in *The Marshall Plan: Fifty Years After*, note 17, p. 120, http://eh.net/book_reviews /the-marshall-plan-fifty-years-after/. Also the CPI Inflation Calculator, Bureau of Labor Statistics, US Department of Labor, http://www.bls.gov/data/inflation_calculator.htm.

19. Luther G. Tweeten, *Foundations of Farm Policy* (Lincoln: University of Nebraska Press, 1979), 438.

20. Wilson, *The Marshall Plan: 1947–1951*, 47–48.

21. Henry Cabot Lodge, "Foreword," in Wilson, *The Marshall Plan: 1947–1951*, 4.

22. Wilson, *The Marshall Plan: 1947–1951*, 27.

23. McCleary, *Global Compassion*, 77.

24. Bolling, *Private Foreign Aid*, 23–24.

25. William Easterly, *The Tyranny of Experts: Economists, Dictators, and the Forgotten Rights of the Poor* (New York: Basic Books, 2013), 43–127.

26. Lester B. Pearson, *Partners in Development: Report of the Commission on International Development* (New York: Praeger, 1969), 18. Pearson submitted the report to Robert S. McNamara, President of the World Bank, who asked him to form the commission.

27. John F. Kennedy, address to the Protestant Council of Churches, New York City, November 8, 1963. Congress, he noted, had rejected a recommended $600 million addition for helping struggling people abroad, "an amount less than this country's annual outlay for lipstick, face cream, and chewing gum." He added, "I do not want it said of us what T. S. Eliot said of others some years ago: 'These were a decent people. Their only monument: the asphalt road and a thousand lost golf balls.'" http://www.jfklibrary.org/Research/Research-Aids/JFK-Speeches/Protestant-Council-NYC.

28. In 2016 the 0.18 percent for US development assistance compared with the average of 0.40 percent for all twenty-nine donor countries, but in total dollars the US assistance of $33.6 billion was highest, as all donor countries combined reached a new peak of $142.6 billion. Organization for Economic Cooperation and Development, *Development Co-operation Report 2017: Data for Development* (Paris: OECD Publishing, 2017), 141.

29. Bread for the World estimated that US poverty-focused development assistance had quadrupled since 2000. See note 47 of chapter 3 above and David Beckmann's March 25, 2015, testimony to the House Appropriations Subcommittee on State, Foreign Operations, and Related Programs.

30. Two of the most prominent critics of official development assistance (though not of all aid) are William Easterly, *The Tyranny of Experts*; and Angus Deaton, *The Great Escape* (Princeton: Princeton University Press, 2013). Easterly's criticism is based on the World Bank (and often other donors) remaining politically neutral, therefore uncritical of authoritarian governments and their violations of human rights. Easterly would focus only on human rights and let development occur spontaneously. His emphasis on human rights has merit, but letting development occur spontaneously oversimplifies.

31. Twenty-one percent according to a 2011 survey of the University of Maryland Program for Public Consultation, reported by Talea Miller, "Foreign Aid Facing Proposed Cuts and a Public Perception Problem," PBS NewsHour, March 10, 2011, http://www.pbs.org/newshour/rundown/foreign-aid-facing-proposed-cuts-public-perception-problem. Twenty-eight percent according to a 2013 Kaiser Family Foundation poll, reported by Ezra Klein, "The Budget Myth That Just Won't Die: Americans Still Think 28 Percent of the Budget Goes to Foreign Aid," *The Washington Post*, November 7, 2013.

32. Fifty-nine percent according to a January 2011 USA Today/Gallup poll, reported by Talea Miller for PBS NewsHour, note 31 above. And from 1971 to 1996 "fully 70 percent of the public persistently say that we are spending 'too much' on foreign aid," while less than 10 percent said we are spending too little, wrote Columbia University political scientist and public opinion specialist Robert Shapiro. "The Legacy of the Marshall Plan: American Public Support for Foreign Aid," in *The Marshall Plan: Fifty Years Later*, 273–74. However, a Pew Research Center February 2013 poll found that 48 percent favored decreasing "aid to world's needy" (not quite the same as foreign aid) with 28 percent in favor of "keep spending the same" and 21 percent for "increasing it." (Web access: Pew Poll on foreign aid cut, February 26, 2013.) However, if the 28 percent who wanted to "keep spending the same" had to choose between decreasing or increasing aid and split evenly, the percentage for decreasing would closely match the 70 percent that prevailed from 1971 to 1996. If instead of asking whether they favor more or less foreign aid, people are asked if they believe that improving health or reducing hunger should be a high priority of aid, high percentages say they should be, according to polls reported by Bread for the World, "Fact Sheet: International Food Aid Reform," October 2013. Much depends on the framing of questions.

33. University of Maryland Program for Public Consultation, note 31 above. Also Kaiser Family Foundation poll, note 31 above.

34. McCleary, *Global Compassion*, 103, 123–24.

35. OECD, "Aid to Developing Countries Rebounds in 2013 to Reach an All-Time High," April 8, 2014, http://www.oecd.org/newsroom/aid-to-developing-countries-rebounds-in-2013 -to-reach-an-all-time-high.htm.

36. *The Index of Global Philanthropy and Remittances* (Washington, DC: Hudson Institute, 2013), 9, https://www.hudson.org/research/13314-index-of-global-philanthropy-and -remittances-2016.

37. "The Evolution of Foreign Aid Research: Measuring the Strengths and Weaknesses of Donors," a July 11, 2014, news release from the Brookings Institution on a report by Homi Kharas and Nancy Birdsall on 2012 aid disbursements. The OECD reports and assesses official development assistance of most donor nations, http://www.brookings.edu/blogs/brookings -now/posts/2014/07/evolution-foreign-aid-research.

38. "MDGs Still in Reach, but 2015 Deadline Will Be Missed, Bill Gates Says," news release, April 7, 2011, by Medical News from Kaiserhealthnews.org and accessed September 13, 2014.

39. Some agencies acknowledge the government subsidy. Appeals that I received by mail in 2015 included several from World Vision's CEO who wrote, "Thanks to government grants, we're able to offer you this incredible opportunity to make four times the impact and help save severely malnourished children in countries like South Sudan, Ethiopia, and Somalia." I received similar letters from the CEO of CARE, who wrote, "CARE has access to an additional $4 worth of donated supplies and government grants for every dollar we raise." These two agencies, along with Catholic Relief Services, Save the Children, and Church World Service (among others), received about one-third of their combined income from the US government in 2014, indicating the extent of this partnership with a number of agencies.

40. McCleary, *Global Compassion*, describes that relationship up to 2005 as it pertains

to US foreign policy. The government sees the work of the PVOs as an extension of its policy, especially in times and places of armed conflict. This can put PVOs in a difficult position if they don't want to be seen as an arm of the government.

41. OECD, note 28 above.

42. Between 2000 and 2015 average life expectancy increased 9.4 years in Africa, driven by improvements in child survival, malaria control, and expanded treatment for HIV/AIDS. World Health Organization, *World Health Statistics 2016*, 7 and 50. Data also from Michael Gerson, interviewed by Johnny Cruz, "Reasons to Hope in the Fight Against Poverty," *World Vision* magazine, August 2017, 11–13.

43. Rajiv Shah, "Remarks by Administrator Rajiv Shah at the New Alliance Event," USAID news release, September 28, 2012.

44. Sources: (1) White House fact sheet, "Power Africa," June 30, 2013. (2) World Bank news release, "World Bank Group Commits US $5 Billion to Boost Electricity Generation in Six African Countries," Aug. 5, 2014. (3) Andrew Herscowitz, USAID coordinator of Power Africa, "Scaling a New Model of Development," Brookings Institution, August 8, 2014.

45. George Ingram, "The U.S.-Africa Leaders Summit: Africa's Dramatic Development Story," Brookings Institution, July 28, 2014, 5–6.

46. An infographic from Bread for the World shows $26.6 billion in poverty-focused development assistance for 2016, half of the total international affairs budget.

47. Juliet Eilperin and Katie Zezima, "Billions of Dollars in Aid Pledged for Africa," *The Washington Post*, August 6, 2014, A4, reported that USAID funds are being taken from programs supporting democracy and governance in Africa in order to support Power Africa.

48. The Foreign Aid and Transparency Accountability Act.

49. USAID, "Feed the Future," September 28, 2018, https://www.usaid.gov/what-we-do/agriculture-and-food-security/increasing-food-security-through-feed-future.

CONSIDER THIS CONTRAST

1. The sources for data in this paragraph: the World Bank and the OECD. For national income, http://data.worldbank.org/region/EUU. For comparative official assistance, http://www.oecd.org/dac/stats/50yearsofofficialdevelopmentassistance.htm. For private assistance, https://data.oecd.org/drf/grants-by-private-agencies-and-ngos.htm. Private agencies in this OECD document include corporate and other for-profit donors as well as foundations and private voluntary organizations (PVOs). I have otherwise restricted the use of private charity to the PVOs.

2. Cited by Jeffrey D. Sachs, *The End of Poverty* (New York: Penguin, 2005), 329–31.

CHAPTER 7

1. Ronald Reagan, inaugural address, January 20, 1981, https://www.presidency.ucsb.edu/documents/inaugural-address-11.

2. Allison Collis Greene, "The Real Depression," *The Christian Century*, March 2, 2016, 26–31. Historian Greene notes that the situation was the worst in the rural south and in southern cities where municipal and state welfare agencies did very little and churches and religious agencies offered most of the assistance, but performed poorly and desperately. "Even before the Depression, religious charities could not meet the demand for aid."

3. Fran Quigley, "For Goodness' Sake: A Two-Part Proposal for Remedying the U.S. Charity/Justice Imbalance," *Virginia Journal of Social Policy and the Law* 23, no. 1 (2016): 40–41. For many it was even worse. Nationwide 10,000 people died in 2016 while waiting in a backlog of judges' disability cases; one still waiting after 597 days was Joe Stewart of Webster County, Mississippi, according to Terrence McCoy, "597 Days. And Still Waiting," *The Washington Post*, November 21, 2017, A1.

4. One of the six purposes of our government named in the opening sentence (preamble) of the Constitution. Two of those purposes were cited by the US Supreme Court in *Goldberg v. Kelly* (1970) when affirming the value of justice over charity: "Welfare . . . can help bring within reach of the poor the same opportunities that are available to others to participate meaningfully in the life of the community. . . . Public assistance, then, is not mere charity, but a means to 'promote the general Welfare, and secure the Blessings of Liberty to ourselves and our Posterity.'" Quoted by Quigley, "For Goodness' Sake," 67.

5. Yuval Levin, "A Conservative Governing Vision," in *Conservative Reforms for a Limited Government and a Thriving Middle Class*, essays by Peter Wehner, Yuval Levin, and others (Washington, DC: YG Network, 2014), 16.

6. Romans 13:4.

7. Cited by Martin E. Marty, the Hastings Lecture, National Cathedral in Washington, DC, November 17, 2000.

8. Those who say, "All politicians are crooked," are implicitly saying, "If I were a politician, I would be crooked."

9. Thomas E. Mann and Norman J. Ornstein, *It's Even Worse Than It Looks* (New York: Basic Books, 2012), 31–43, call Gingrich "the singular political figure who set the tone that followed." The McConnell quote is on p. 190. The authors also mention that when a veteran GOP congressional staffer resigned in protest, he cited an observation by historian Hannah Arendt that a disciplined minority of totalitarians can use the instruments of democratic government to undermine democracy itself (p. 55).

10. George F. Will, "Another Casualty of Vietnam: Trust," *The Washington Post*, August 3, 2017, A13.

11. A 2016 report, "No U.S. History?," by the American Council of Trustees and Alumni, indicates that only five of the top twenty-five colleges and two of the top twenty-five national universities surveyed required any US history in their history curricula and that large percentages of history majors and college graduates scored poorly on basic multiple-choice questions about US history and government. Cited by Martin E. Marty, "History-less Judgments," *Sightings*, August 8, 2016. See also Colbert King, "We're Not Teaching the A-B-C's of Civics. That's a Problem," *The Washington Post*, April 22, 2017, A17.

12. Robert B. Reich, *Saving Capitalism* (New York: Vintage, 2015), 183–219.

13. In 2016 the United States ranked nineteenth among thirty-four industrialized nations in happiness, according to a report that cites the US top-heavy focus on economic growth while neglecting inequality, corruption in business and government, isolation and social distrust. John Helliwell, Richard Layard, and Jeffrey Sachs, eds., *World Happiness Report 2017* (New York: Sustainable Development Solutions Network, 2017), 78–84.

14. William Julius Wilson, *When Work Disappears* (New York: Alfred A. Knopf, 1996), 149, 158, and 215.

15. Reich, *Saving Capitalism*, 153–57

16. Jeffrey D. Sachs, *The Price of Civilization* (New York: Random House, 2011), 9.

17. Cited by Jefferson Cowie, *The Great Exception* (Princeton: Princeton University Press, 2016), 220.

18. Daniel Bell, *The Cultural Contradictions of Capitalism* (New York: Basic Books, 1976), 220–82. Also Malcolm Waters, *Daniel Bell* (London: Routledge, 1996), 81–88.

19. US Department of Agriculture, "U.S. Agricultural Trade and Trade Balance Forecast FY 2018," www.fas.usda.gov/data/us-agricultural-trade-and-trade-balance-forecast.

20. The American Farm Bureau Federation, 2016, https://www.fb.org/newsroom/fast-facts.

21. Eliza Barclay, National Public Radio, "Your Grandparents Spent More of Their Money on Food Than You Do," March 2, 2015, http://www.npr.org/sections/thesalt/2015/03/02/389578089/your-grandparents-spent-more-of-their-money-on-food-than-you-do. Source: USDA Economic Research Service.

22. Clara Simon Stuewer, *Lorchen* (1979), a self-published book about my grandmother, Eleanor Elbert Simon, by one of her daughters, my aunt Clara, now deceased.

23. Juergen Voegele, "Farm and Food Policy Innovations for the Digital Age," Brookings Institution, October 11, 2018.

24. Renée Johnson, "Fruits, Vegetables, and Other Specialty Crops: Selected Farm Bill and Federal Programs," Congressional Research Service, July 11, 2014. *National Geographic* reports that since the early 1980s the real cost of fruits and vegetables has increased by 24 percent, while sodas have dropped by 27 percent, but it is the latter that we heavily, if indirectly, subsidize. Tracie McMillan, "The New Face of Hunger," *National Geographic*, August 2014, 84.

25. Mark Bittman, Michael Pollan, Ricardo Salvador, and Olivier De Schutter, "The Nine Ingredients for a Healthier America," *The Washington Post*, November 9, 2014, B1.

26. *The Washington Post*'s lead editorial, "Junk Food Lobby," September 14, 2015, A16, describes relentless efforts of the food industry to circumvent rules that promote less starchy food and more fruits and vegetables in the nation's school lunch program. The *American Journal of Preventive Medicine* found that 80 percent of food television ads in 2013 promoted foods that should be eaten infrequently, and rarely pitched healthful foods to children, despite an agreement in 2007 by leading food companies to adopt higher standards, for which they promised self-regulation. Reported by Robert A. Ferdman, "Food Industry Still Aiming TV Ads for Unhealthy Fare at Kids, Study Finds," *The Washington Post*, May 12, 2015, A9.

27. A study commissioned by the USDA reports that 20 percent of SNAP benefits pur-

chase junk food and drink. US Department of Agriculture, Food and Nutrition Service, November 14, 2016. https://www.fns.usda.gov/snap/supplemental-nutrition-assistance-program-snap/reports-all. Also Charles Lane, "How Liberals Undermine Food Stamps," *The Washington Post*, February 16, 2017, A19.

28. Randy Schnepf, "U.S. International Food Aid Programs: Background and Issues," Congressional Research Service, September 14, 2016, pp. 9–10, 44, https://fas.org/sgp/crs/misc/R41072.pdf.

29. Maura R. O'Connor, "Subsidizing Starvation: How America's Tax Dollars Are Keeping Arkansas Rice Growers Fat on the Farm and Starving Millions of Haitians," FP [Foreign Policy] Group, January 11, 2013, http://www.foreignpolicy.com/articles/2013/01/11/subsidizing-starvation/.

30. Responding to extraordinary emergencies, US food assistance helped 64 million people in 2016 and 69 million in 2017. USAID, "Fiscal Year 2017 Fact Sheet," https://www.usaid.gov/documents/1866/food-peace-fy-2017-fact-sheet.

31. For a good summary of US food assistance programs and some of the key policy issues, see Randy Schnepf, "U.S. International Food Aid Programs: Background and Issues," note 28 above.

32. Suresh Persaud, "Calculating the Jobs Associated with U.S. Agricultural Exports," USDA Economic Research Service, May 2015, https://ageconsearch.umn.edu/record/209729/files/http---www_ers_usda_gov-amber-waves-2015-may-calculating-the-jobs-associated-with-us-agricultural-exports_aspx_VgKxQJx17h1_pdfmyurl.pdf.

33. Isabel Sawhill, "What the Forgotten Americans Really Want—and How to Give It to Them," a preview of her new book, *The Forgotten Americans: An Economic Agenda for a Divided Nation*, Brookings Institution, October 2018.

34. Mike DeBonis, "The Bulk of GOP Field, If Not the Top of It, Turns Its Attention to Poverty," *The Washington Post*, January 10, 2016, A4.

LET CHARITY DO IT?

1. Data on Cook County are based on its SNAP report for July 2017, part of the US Department of Agriculture's Food & Nutrition Services report of January 16, 2018, on SNAP project areas nationwide, which I received from SNAP headquarters on February 26. I multiplied Cook County's July 2017 report by twelve for the year's estimate. I credited private charity with 75 percent of the food bank's total, because the government accounts for 25 percent of the food it distributes. Because SNAP accounts for about 70 percent of total federal food assistance, the government's combined total for Cook County comes to about $2 billion, twenty times that of the Chicago food bank's distribution or about twenty-seven times the amount of its *private charitable* distribution.

2. *Greater Chicago Food Depository 2015 Annual Report.*

3. The Association of Religion Data Archives, http://www.thearda.com/rcms2010/selectcounty.asp.

Notes

CHAPTER 8

1. John F. Kennedy, Inaugural Address, January 20, 1961.

2. Lincoln began his Gettysburg Address by asserting that the nation was "dedicated to the proposition that all men are created equal," thus invoking the Declaration of Independence as the nation's founding document and equality as its central ideal. Garry Wills, *Lincoln at Gettysburg: The Words That Remade America* (New York: Touchstone/Simon & Schuster, 1992), 38–42, 85–87, 147. Regarding Jefferson, Gunnar Myrdal writes: "In the Declaration of Independence—as in the earlier Virginia Bill of Rights—equality was given the supreme rank and the rights to liberty are posited as derived from equality. This logic was even more clearly expressed in Jefferson's original formulation of the first of the 'self-evident truths': 'All men are created equal *and from that equal creation* they derive rights inherent and unalienable [sic], among which are the preservation of life and liberty and the pursuit of happiness.'" Myrdal's italics. Myrdal, *An American Dilemma* (New York: McGraw-Hill, 1964; Harper & Row edition, 1944, volume 1), 8–9.

3. Robert Reich writes that 1928 and 2007 were the two years in the last hundred when the richest 1 percent received the highest percent (23.5) of total income. *Aftershock: The Next Economy and America's Future* (New York: Vintage Books, 2011), 5.

4. John Kenneth Galbraith, *The Great Crash 1929* (1954; New York: Houghton Mifflin, 2009 with a 1997 introduction), 168–94.

5. "Growing Unequal? Income Distribution and Poverty in OECD Countries: Country Note: United States," Organization for Economic Cooperation and Development, 2008. "Since 2000, income inequality has increased rapidly, continuing a long-term trend that goes back to the 1970s." http://www.oecd.org/els/soc/growingunequalincomedistributionandpoverty inoecdcountries.htm.

6. Economic Policy Institute, based on data from the Bureau of Labor Statistics. https://www.epi.org/productivity-pay-gap/.

7. Peter G. Peterson Foundation chart based on data from the Congressional Budget Office. https://www.pgpf.org/chart-archive/0059_income-growth-disparity.

8. Congressional Budget Office, *The Distribution of Household Income and Federal Taxes, 2013*, June 2015, 5–8, http://www.cbo.gov/sites/default/files/114th-congress-2015-2016/reports /51361-HouseholdIncomeFedTaxes.pdf.

9. Federal Reserve data reported by Tracy Jan, "1 in 7 White Families in U.S. Are Millionaires, Data Shows," *The Washington Post*, October 4, 2017, A20, www.cbo.gov/publication /54646.

10. Congressional Budget Office, "Distribution of Household Income, 2015," November 8, 2018.

11. US Census Bureau, "The Supplemental Poverty Measure: 2015," September 2016, https://www.census.gov/library/publications/2016/demo/p60-258.html.

12. Ben S. Bernanke, "When Growth Is Not Enough," prepared for delivery on June 26, 2017, at a European Central Bank Forum, https://www.brookings.edu/blog/ben-bernanke /2017/06/26/when-growth-is-not-enough/.

13. Chris Isidore, "U.S. Millionaires Control Far More of Nation's Wealth Than Those Elsewhere," CNN Money, June 10, 2016, http://money.cnn.com/2016/06/07/news/economy/millionaires-control-wealth/. On billionaires, Forbes, "The Billionaires 2018," March 6, 2018, www.Forbes.com/billionaires.

14. "Few trends could so thoroughly undermine the very foundations of our free society as the acceptance by corporate officials of a social responsibility other than to make as much money for their stockholders as possible." Milton Friedman, *Capitalism and Freedom* (Chicago: University of Chicago Press, 1962), 133.

15. Harold Meyerson, "Owner-take-all," *The Washington Post*, August 28, 2014, A17. A more detailed analysis is William Lazonick's "Profits without Prosperity," in the *Harvard Business Review*, September 2014, https://hbr.org/2014/09/profits-without-prosperity.

16. Lawrence H. Summers in the Foreword to Arthur M. Okun, *Equality and Efficiency: The Big Tradeoff* (Washington, DC: Brookings Institution Press, 2015), ix.

17. Lawrence Mishel and Jessica Schieder, "CEO Compensation Surged in 2017," August 16, 2018, Economic Policy Institute. The compensation includes salary, bonuses, stock options, and other benefits as an average for CEOs among the 350 largest US companies.

18. Thomas Piketty, *Capital in the Twenty-First Century* (Cambridge, MA: Harvard University Press, 2014), 294–303. Piketty's analysis here does not include government income assistance, but he and colleagues have since found that "even after taxes and transfers, there has been close to zero growth for working-age adults in the bottom 50 percent." Patricia Cohen, "A Bigger Economic Pie, but a Smaller Slice for Half of the U.S.," *The New York Times*, December 7, 2016, B1.

19. National Bureau of Economic Research, *The Measure and Behavior of Unemployment*, 215, http://www.nber.org/chapters/c2644.pdf.

20. Galbraith, *The Great Crash 1929*, 183.

21. Todd Post, ed., *Hunger Report 2018: The Jobs Challenge: Working to End Hunger by 2030* (Washington, DC: Bread for the World Institute, 2018), 19.

22. Chris Isidore, "U.S. Millionaires." The Forbes 2016 ranking of "The World's Billionaires" listed eight of the world's top ten billionaires from the United States. Bill Gates ranked highest with $75 billion, and the Charles and David Koch brothers tied for ninth and tenth place with $39.5 billion each, http://www.forbes.com/billionaires/list/. *U.S. News* reported the Forbes total of 536 billionaires in 2015: Andrew Soergel, "Behind the Numbers in Forbes' Billionaires List," March 2, 2015, https://www.usnews.com/news/blogs/data-mine/2015/03/02/behind-the-numbers-in-forbes-billionaires-list.

23. "Trends in Family Wealth, 1989 to 2013: Holdings of Family Wealth," Congressional Budget Office, August 18, 2016, Trends in Family Wealth, www.cbo.gov/publications/51846. Based on the Census data reported every ten years.

24. Michael Gerson, "Selling a Lie to the Poor," *The Washington Post*, July 10, 2015, A19. Also Gerson, Stephanie Summers, and Katie Thompson, *Unleashing Opportunity: Why Escaping Poverty Requires a Shared Vision of Justice* (Beaver Falls, PA: Falls City Press, 2015), 60–61.

25. Michael De Groote, "Getting Unstuck: Why Some People Get Out of Poverty and Others Don't," *Deseret News*, November 10, 2013. The Pew study said that what helped people move up

the income ladder were getting a college education, coming from a dual-earner family, and not going through a period of unemployment—indicators that produced or used financial assets.

26. Piketty, *Capital in the Twenty-First Century*, 419–20, 484. Piketty says that the best available research shows that when education and earned incomes are measured across generations for narrowing or expanding inequalities in key Western industrial countries, Nordic countries did best; France, Germany, and Britain occupy a middle ground; and the United States showed the least social mobility across class lines. Since World War I "the available data suggest that social mobility has been and remains lower in the United States than in Europe."

27. Eduardo Porter, "Education Gap Between Rich and Poor Is Growing Wider," *The New York Times*, September 22, 2015, https://www.nytimes.com/2015/09/23/business/economy/education-gap-between-rich-and-poor-is-growing-wider.html.

28. Emma Brown, "Pa. Tackles Chasm in School Funding Equality," *The Washington Post*, April 23, 2015, A1.

29. Angus Deaton, *The Great Escape* (Princeton: Princeton University Press, 2013), 207.

30. Robert B. Reich, *Saving Capitalism* (New York: Vintage Books, 2015), 141.

31. US Census Bureau, *Income and Poverty in the United States: 2017*, September 2018, Table 3, www.census.gov/library/publications/2018/demo/p60-263.html.

32. The Kids Count Data Center of the Annie E. Casey Foundation, "Children in Poverty by Race and Ethnicity," 2017 data, http://datacenter.kidscount.org/data/tables/44-children-in-poverty-by-race-and-ethnicity.

33. For the fourth quarter of 2017 the unemployment rate was 3.4 percent for whites, 7.0 percent for African Americans, and 4.7 percent for Hispanics. Bureau of Labor Statistics, "Labor Force Statistics from the Current Population Survey," January 2018.

34. *America's Youngest Outcasts: A Report Card on Child Homelessness* (Waltham, MA: The National Center on Family Homelessness at American Institutes for Research, 2014), 14–15. Based on the US Department of Education count of homeless children in public schools and US Census Bureau data, http://www.air.org/resource/americas-youngest-outcasts-report-card-child-homelessness.

35. *America's Youngest Outcasts*, 77.

36. Federal Reserve 2016 update cited by Camille Busette, "Our Day of Reckoning," Brookings Institution, January 12, 2018, https://www.brookings.edu/blog/social-mobility-memos/2018/01/12/our-day-of-reckoning/.

37. In 2010, 33.9 percent of black households and 35.8 percent of Hispanic households had no net wealth, according to the Economic Policy Institute, "Wealth: The State of Working America," http://www.stateofworkingamerica.org/fact-sheets/wealth/.

38. Amanda Erickson, "In Deed," *Commonweal*, June 1, 2015, 31.

39. Jim Tankersley, "How Ben Carson Beat the Odds: His Escape from Poverty Was Fueled by His Drive, His Faith, His Mother—and a Leg Up from His Government," *The Washington Post*, October 31, 2015, A1.

40. Lyndon B. Johnson, "To Fulfill These Rights," Commencement address at Howard University, June 4, 1965, http://www.lbjlibrary.net/collections/selected-speeches/1965/06-04-1965.html.

41. Michelle Singletary, "One of the Enduring Costs of Racism in America," *The Washington Post*, August 16, 2017, A13.

42. Documentation, for this sentence only, comes from Nick Kotz's review in *The New York Times*, August 28, 2005, of Ira Katznelson's book *When Affirmative Action Was White*. Cited by Jim Wallis, *America's Original Sin* (Grand Rapids: Brazos, 2016), 89. The rest of this and the subsequent paragraph on housing comes from Rothstein's *The Color of Law* (note 43 below).

43. Richard Rothstein, *The Color of Law: A Forgotten History of How Our Government Segregated America* (New York: Liveright, 2017). Levittown, New York, the prototypical American suburb, built 1947–1951, excluded African Americans until required by law to integrate. Yet a half-century after passage of the Fair Housing Act of 1968 its population of 52,000 was less than 1 percent black. In contrast, a Levitt suburb of comparable size built during the 1960s in Bowie, Maryland (where I live), which had a population of 1,000 in 1960, then 35,000 in 1970 and 58,000 in 2016, is 48 percent black and 40 percent white. For the current practice of discrimination in housing, see also the following editorials in *The New York Times*: "Housing Apartheid, American Style," May 16, 2015; "Affordable Housing, Racial Isolation," June 29, 2015; "The Architecture of Segregation," September 6, 2015; and "How Segregation Destroys Black Wealth," September 15, 2015.

44. Ta-Nehisi Coates, "The Case for Reparations," *The Atlantic*, June 2014, 55–71. Housing theft and discrimination included contract sellers who bought cheap and sold high, with contracts in which the seller retained ownership until a house was fully paid, and if a buyer missed a single payment, he lost the house together with all previous payments. Sellers would then attract the next black victim who typically would be turned down for standard mortgages. The Federal Housing Administration insured private mortgages, but redlined maps for areas where blacks lived and were not eligible for FHA backing. Black homebuyers are still more likely than white buyers to be steered to predatory subprime loans that often result in foreclosure. The Fair Housing Act of 1968 prohibits discrimination in the sale, rental, or financing of housing, and requires states and localities that receive federal money to overcome patterns of racial separation, but these requirements are widely ignored, according to an editorial in *The New York Times*, "Ending the Cycle of Racial Isolation," October 18, 2015. Today housing accounts for two-thirds of the equity of typical (median) US households, but African Americans were largely prevented in the past from accumulating that kind of asset. Janelle Jones, "The Racial Wealth Gap: How African-Americans Have Been Shortchanged Out of the Materials to Build Wealth," Economic Policy Institute, February 13, 2017, http://www.epi.org/blog/the-racial-wealth-gap-how-african-americans-have-been-shortchanged-out-of-the-materials-to-build-wealth/. My book, *Stuyvesant Town USA: Pattern for Two Americas* (New York: New York University Press, 1970), describes how the nation's first urban redevelopment project, privately owned but publicly subsidized, excluded African Americans until citizen advocates, city housing laws, court action, and public opinion forced a reluctant change. Stuyvesant Town is the largest residential housing development in Manhattan.

45. Coates, "The Case for Reparations," writes passionately and persuasively about racial injustice, and cites German reparations paid to the State of Israel after World War II despite public resistance in both countries.

46. Rothstein, *The Color of Law*, 284 (for his note, p. 177).

47. Coates, "The Case for Reparations," 68.

48. William Julius Wilson, *The Truly Disadvantaged* (Chicago: University of Chicago Press, 1987), viii–ix, 117.

49. Almost 7 million adult Americans were either incarcerated, on parole, or on probation by the end of 2013, about one in every thirty-five adults. More than 1.5 million were in state or federal prisons, and another 731,000 in local jails, according to the Bureau of Justice Statistics. Reid Wilson, "Fewer Adults under Watch of State Correctional Systems," *The Washington Post*, January 2, 2015, A14.

50. *A Nation in Chains: A Report of the Samuel DeWitt Proctor Conference* (Chicago, 2014), 47. The report presents findings and recommendations from nine statewide justice commission hearings on mass incarceration.

51. Robert D. Putnam, *Our Kids* (New York: Simon & Schuster, 2015), 76–77.

52. Gunnar Myrdal, *An American Dilemma* (New York: McGraw-Hill, 1964, Harper & Row edition, 1944, volume 1), 101. Myrdal quotes Shaw's *Man and Superman* in the footnote.

53. Wilson, *The Truly Disadvantaged*, 14–15.

54. Jim Wallis, *America's Original Sin* (Grand Rapids: Brazos, 2016), 79.

55. "We hold these Truths to be self-evident, that all Men are created equal, that they are endowed by their Creator with certain unalienable Rights, that among these are Life, Liberty, and the Pursuit of Happiness."

56. Curt Rice, "How Blind Auditions Help Orchestras to Eliminate Gender Bias," *The Guardian*, October 14, 2013, http://www.theguardian.com/women-in-leadership/2013/oct/14/blind-auditions-orchestras-gender-bias.

57. Marlysa D. Gamblyn, "Job Segregation Fuels Hunger," in *Hunger Report 2018: The Jobs Challenge*, ed. Todd Post (Washington, DC: Bread for the World Institute, 2018), 90–91.

58. On the spot in Eugene where many were taken away on short notice with only what they could carry, a memorial to those citizens includes a stone with my father's name and the inscription, "Martin P. Simon. He spoke in protest. His courage inspired others." My brother Paul and I were among the "others."

HOW TO SAVE MONEY AND LIVES

1. "Education and Vocational Training in Prisons Reduces Recidivism, Improves Job Outlook," Rand Corporation analysis, August 22, 2013, http://www.rand.org/news/press/2013/08/22.html.

2. Elizabeth Hinton, "Turn Prisons into Colleges," *The New York Times*, March 7, 2018, A27.

3. Vincent Schiraldi, "What Mass Incarceration Looks Like for Juveniles," *The New York Times*, November 10, 2015, https://www.nytimes.com/2015/11/11/opinion/what-mass-incarceration-looks-like-for-juveniles.html.

4. Gerson et al., *Unleashing Opportunity*, 61.

CHAPTER 9

1. R. R. Reno, "The Public Square: Marriage Equality," *First Things*, June/July 2014, 4.

2. See Rachel Anderson, contributing editor, "Families Valued," essays in *Public Justice Review* 4 (2017), Center for Public Justice (Washington, DC).

3. Jeanne Bishop, "Thanksgiving 2013: 'So Far from Want,'" *Sightings*, the Martin Marty Center, University of Chicago Divinity School, November 28, 2013.

4. James MacGregor Burns, *The Crosswinds of Freedom: From Roosevelt to Reagan—America in the Last Half Century* (New York: Vintage Books, 1990), 568–70.

5. Daniel Patrick Moynihan, introduction in *The Negro Family: The Case for National Action*, US Department of Labor, March 1965.

6. Sara McLanahan and Christopher Jencks, "Was Moynihan Right?," *Education Next* 15, no. 2 (Spring 2015), Woodrow Wilson School of Public & International Affairs, Princeton University, http://educationnext.org/was-moynihan-right. The statistical differences reflect some post-birth marriages and parenting by cohabitation.

7. Isabel V. Sawhill, *Generation Unbound* (Washington, DC: Brookings Institution Press, 2014), 56.

8. Robert J. Samuelson, "The Family Deficit," *The Washington Post*, October 27, 2014.

9. Isabel V. Sawhill and Joanna Venator, "Families Adrift: Is Unwed Childbearing the New Norm?," Brookings Institution, October 13, 2014, 4. Web access: Families Adrift, Brookings, October 13, 2014.

10. Sawhill and Venator, "Families Adrift," 3.

11. Sawhill, *Generation Unbound*, 74.

12. *America's Youngest Outcasts: A Report Card on Child Homelessness* (Waltham, MA: The National Center on Family Homelessness at American Institutes for Research, 2014), 78, http://www.homelesschildrenamerica.org/mediadocs/280.pdf.

13. Robert I. Lerman and W. Bradford Wilcox, *For Richer, For Poorer: How Family Structures Economic Success in America* (Washington, DC: American Enterprise Institute and the Institute for Family Studies, 2014), 31.

14. Barack Obama, Father's Day 2008, at the Apostolic Church of God in Chicago, cited by Colbert I. King, "Young, Fatherless—and Fathers Themselves," *The Washington Post*, December 22, 2012, A15.

15. William Julius Wilson, *The Truly Disadvantaged* (Chicago: University of Chicago Press, 1987), 4, 6, 8, 15, 20–21, 149.

16. Cited by Taylor Branch, *At Canaan's Edge: America in the King Years 1965–68* (New York: Simon & Schuster, 2006), 371.

17. Moynihan, *The Negro Family*, 19–22.

18. Moynihan, *The Negro Family*, 21.

19. Moynihan, *The Negro Family*, 6. The evidence is from E. Franklin Frazier, *Black Bourgeoisie* (New York: Collier Books, 1962).

20. Moynihan, *The Negro Family*, 21–25.

21. "Report of the Special Rapporteur on Extreme Poverty and Human Rights on His Mission to the United States of America" to the UN Human Rights Council, June 22, 2018.

22. Wilson notes that Roosevelt saw cash assistance as a temporary means of support for unemployable families with dependent children and gave much greater emphasis to public works projects as a way of preventing the formation of a permanent welfare class. Social Security and unemployment insurance were job-related forms of security not tied to the dole. By contrast, Wilson says, "nearly all of the Great Society programs *were* tied to the dole." *The Truly Disadvantaged*, 118–19.

23. Ronald Reagan, radio address to the nation on welfare reform, February 15, 1986, https://www.reaganlibrary.gov/research/speeches/21586a.

24. "Jobs for the Young in Poor Neighborhoods," *The New York Times*, March 14, 2016, A22.

25. Cited by Taylor Branch, *Pillar of Fire: America in the King Years 1963-65* (New York: Simon & Schuster, 1998), 488.

26. A few months before his assassination King announced a "Poor People's Campaign" that did focus on jobs and income. Crippled by his death, however, the campaign failed to gain traction.

27. Kathryn J. Eden and H. Luke Shaefer, *$2 a Day: Living on Almost Nothing in America* (Boston: Houghton Mifflin Harcourt, 2012), 21.

28. TANF was authorized by the Personal Responsibility and Work Opportunity Reconciliation Act of 1996.

29. Peter Germanis, "TANF Is Broken! It's Time to Reform 'Welfare Reform,'" July 25, 2015 (an unpublished draft inviting comments), 2, 7, 9, 10, and 81. Used with permission, http://mlwiseman.com/wp-content/uploads/2013/09/TANF-is-Broken.072515.pdf. According to the Congressional Budget Office, TANF has reduced overall spending by about $5 billion, mainly by reducing cash assistance, while increasing spending on work support and other services. But its graph shows fewer families "engaged in work" by 2011 than in 1998. CBO, "Temporary Assistance for Needy Families: Spending and Policy Options," January 21, 2015.

30. Wilson, *When Work Disappears*, 11, 18, 30–33, and 142–46.

31. Wilson, *When Work Disappears*, 22.

32. Cited by E. J. Dionne Jr., "Baltimore's Downfall," *The Washington Post*, April 30, 2015, A21.

33. Charles Murray, *Coming Apart: The State of White America, 1960–2010* (New York: Crown Forum, 2012).

34. Murray, *Coming Apart*, 144–231. Belmont and Fishtown (real and fictional) are introduced on pp. 144–48 and serve as the basis for analysis of America's coming apart on pp. 149–231.

35. Murray, *Coming Apart*, 283.

36. Murray, *Coming Apart*, 74–75. Maytag was bought by Whirlpool in 2006.

37. Robert D. Putnam, *Bowling Alone* (New York: Simon & Schuster, 2000).

38. Cited by Robert J. Samuelson, "Trump Is Not Destiny. Here's What Is," *The Washington Post*, June 12, 2017, A17.

39. Robert D. Putnam, *Our Kids* (New York: Simon & Schuster, 2015), 1–45.

40. High poverty as 30 percent or more of households in poverty: Jonathan Grabinsky and Stuart M. Butler, "The Anti-Poverty Case for 'Smart' Gentrification, Part 1," Brookings Institution, February 10, 2015, https://www.brookings.edu/blog/social-mobility-memos/2015/02/10/the-anti-poverty-case-for-smart-gentrification-part-1/.

41. Elizabeth Kneebone, "The Growth and Spread of Concentrated Poverty, 2000 to 2008–12," Brookings Institution, July 31, 2014. Kneebone defines "high poverty" as between 20 percent and 40 percent of families in poverty, not 30 percent or more as in note 40 above. Kneebone reports that 23 percent of poor people in the city lived in "distressed" neighborhoods with poverty rates that exceeded 40 percent, compared to 6 percent of poor people in suburban distressed neighborhoods. But since 2000 the rate of growth of distressed neighborhoods in the suburbs has been almost three times that of such growth in cities.

42. Tanvi Misra, "The Growth of Concentrated Poverty Since the Recession," Brookings Institution, March 31, 2016, www.brookings.edu/research/u-s-concentrated-poverty.

43. Sawhill and Venator, "Families Adrift," 3.

44. Camille Busette, "Our Day of Reckoning," Brookings Institution, January 12, 2018, https://www.brookings.edu/blog/social-mobility-memos/2018/01/12/our-day-of-reckoning/, and William H. Frey, "The US Will Become 'Minority White' in 2045, Census Projects," Brookings Institution, March 14, 2018, https://brookings.edu/blog/the-avenue/2018/03/14/the-us-will-become-minority-white.

45. Putnam, *Our Kids*, 182 and 231.

46. Emily Baxter, with Katie Hamm, "Real Family Values: Child Care and Early Childhood Education," Center for American Progress, April 17, 2014, http://americanprogress.org/issues/religion/report/2014/04/17/88099/child-care-and-early-childhood-education.

47. Emily Badger, "For Poor Kids, Words Can Mean Everything," *The Washington Post*, November 4, 2015, A14.

48. Putnam, *Our Kids*, 130.

49. Baxter and Hamm, "Real Family Values."

50. James S. Coleman et al., *Equality of Educational Opportunity*, US Department of Health, Education and Welfare, Office of Education (Washington, DC: US Government Printing Office, July 2, 1966), 325. See also George F. Will, "Decades of Sobering Evidence," *The Washington Post*, July 7, 2016, A17.

51. Isabel V. Sawhill, "Democrats Have the House, Now They Need an Economic Agenda That Gives Americans Better-Paying Jobs," Brookings Institution, November 29, 2018, https://www.brookings.edu/blog/up-front/2018/11/29/democrats-have-the-house.

52. Wilson, *When Work Disappears*, xix, xiii, 65, and 64.

53. Wilson, *When Work Disappears*, 14.

54. Ron Haskins and Isabel Sawhill, *Creating an Opportunity Society* (Washington, DC: Brookings Institution, 2009), cited by Lerman and Wilcox, *For Richer, For Poorer*, 54. Also Sawhill, *Generation Unbound*, 14 and 92.

55. Sawhill, *Generation Unbound*, 92. It cites Haskins and Sawhill, *Creating an Opportunity Society*, 230.

56. Bruce Stokes, director, Global Economic Attitudes, Pew Research Center, "Public Attitudes Toward the Next Social Contract," January 2013, 6 and 8. The New America Foundation, https://www.newamerica.org/.

DRIFTING INTO PARENTHOOD

1. Sawhill, *Generation Unbound*, 80, 105-7.

2. Pew Research Center, *The Decline of Marriage and the Rise of New Families*, November 18, 2010. Cited by Bread for the World Institute, *Hunger Report 2014: Ending Hunger in America*, ed. Todd Post (Washington, DC: Bread for the World Institute, 2014), 31.

TANF'S FAILURE

1. Germanis, "TANF Is Broken!," 45-47.

2. Germanis, "TANF Is Broken!," 48.

3. "Child Recipients of Welfare (AFDC/TANF)," Child Trends Data Bank. Three-fourths of TANF recipients are children, http://www.childtrends.org/?indicators=child-recipients-of-welfareafdctanf.

4. Bernadette D. Proctor, Jessica L. Semega, and Melissa A. Kollar, *Income and Poverty in the United States: 2015*, US Census Bureau, Current Population reports, P60-256 (RV) (Washington, DC: US Government Printing Office, September 2016), 12 and 17. Also "Key Statistics & Graphics" on food security in 2014, USDA, Economic Research Service, p. 7, http:www.ers.usda.gov/topics/food-nutrition-assistance/food-security-in-the-us/key-statistics-graphics.aspx. The rate as well as the numbers of those who are poor and food-insecure also rose during those years, with 40 percent of the food-insecure facing "very low" food security, and 45 percent of those in poverty dropping below half of the poverty line.

5. Germanis, "TANF Is Broken!," 8. His sources on Wisconsin include the Center on Budget and Policy Priorities and the Government Accountability Office.

DEATHS OF DESPAIR?

1. Data in this paragraph are taken from the following articles in *The Washington Post*: "Americans' Declining Health" (editorial), December 30, 2016, A18; Joel Achenbach, "Once 'So Mayberry,' a Town Struggles with Opioid Epidemic," December 30, 2016, A10; Christopher Ingraham, "Heroin Deaths Surpass Gun Homicides for the First Time," December 9, 2016, A21; Dan Keating and Lenny Bernstein, "U.S. Suicide Rate Has Grown since 2000,

Research Shows," April 22, 2016, A8; Tara Bahrampour, "In a Third of U.S., More Whites Are Dying Than Being Born," December 1, 2016, A8.

2. Lenny Bernstein and Christopher Ingraham, "Drug Crisis Fuels Drop in At-Birth Life Expectancy," *The Washington Post*, December 21, 2017, A1; and Lenny Bernstein, "Life Expectancy in the U.S. Continues to Fall, CDC Reports," *The Washington Post*, November 29, 2018, A1. Both articles are based on reports by the Centers for Disease Control and Prevention.

3. Greg Jaffe and Juliet Eilperin, "Vilsack's Lonely Battle for Rural America," *The Washington Post*, September 27, 2016, A1.

CHAPTER 10

1. Sister Joan Chittister, OSB, interview on *NOW* with Bill Moyers, PBS, November 12, 2004.

2. Not much has changed. In 2016 the State of Illinois faced a massive debt and deficit crisis. Polling showed strong public opposition to additional taxes, although the favored source of revenue was the graduated income tax. A majority or near-majority of the public clung to the illusion "that cutting waste and fraud would be a simple and painless way to deal with the problem." The state was "frozen in a governmental and political gridlock that has . . . created chaos in governmental and non-profit agencies that normally deliver state services." John A. Jackson, Charles W. Leonard, and Shiloh Deitz, "The Climate of Opinion in Illinois 2008–2016: Roots of Gridlock," Paul Simon Public Policy Institute, Southern Illinois University, June 2016, pp. 1, 48, 62–63, 68–69.

3. Larry Blom, "Overview of the Federal Budget," Congressional Budget Office, April 17, 2015, 7, https://www.cbo.gov/publication/45230.

4. Congressional Budget Office, "The Budget and Economic Outlook: 2017 to 2027," January 24, 2017, https://www.cbo.gov/publication/52370.

5. Congressional Budget Office, "CBO's Projections of Deficits and Debt for the 2018–2028 Period," April 19, 2018. Also Keith Hall, CBO Director, "An Overview of the Budget and Economic Outlook 2018 to 2028," April 9, 2018. CBO projects the nation's public debt, excluding internal government obligations.

6. Office of Management and Budget, Interactive Budget, estimate for 2016, February 2, 2015, https://www.whitehouse.gov/interactive-budget.

7. Tax Policy Center, cited by the Economic Policy Institute, "Ten Actions That Hurt Workers during Trump's First Year," January 12, 2018, http://www.epi.org/publication/ten -actions-that-hurt-workers-during-trumps-first-year/1/8/2018.

8. Thomas E. Mann and Norman J. Ornstein, *It's Even Worse Than It Looks* (New York: Basic Books, 2012), ix–x.

9. Michael Gerson, "Politicking Past Each Other," *The Washington Post*, January 13, 2015, A15.

10. Richard Kogan and Isaac Shapiro, "House GOP Budget Gets 62 Percent of Budget Cuts from Low- and Moderate-Income Programs," Center on Budget and Policy Priorities, March 28, 2016. The low-income programs account for 24 percent of program spending but were tar-

geted in 2016 for 62 percent of the proposed cuts. http://www.cbpp.org/research/federal-budget/house-gop-gets-62-percent-of-budget-cuts-from-low-and-moderate-income-programs.

11. Joe Davidson, "GAO Report Says Overlap, Duplication and Fragmentation Still Abound," *The Washington Post*, April 17, 2016, A21.

12. Dwight D. Eisenhower, "The Chance for Peace," an address to the American Society of Newspaper Editors, April 16, 1953. Context: "Every gun that is made, every warship launched, every rocket fired signifies, in the final sense, a theft from those who hunger and are not fed, those who are cold and are not clothed. This world in arms is not spending money alone. It is spending the sweat of its laborers, the genius of its scientists, the hopes of its children."

13. Aaron Gregg, "First Full Audit of Pentagon Notes Compliance Issues," *The Washington Post*, November 26, 2018, A14.

14. Chad Stone and Sharon Parrott, "Examining the Congressional Budget Office Cost Estimate of the Senate Immigration Bill," Center on Budget and Policy Priorities, July 15, 2013, 2–3, http://www.cbpp.org/research/examining-the-congressional-budget-office-cost-estimate-of-the-senate-immigration-bill.

15. George F. Will, "Fixing the 'Rotting Carcass' Tax Code," *The Washington Post*, July 13, 2017, A17.

16. Forbes estimates $63 billion lost in unreported income and says outside estimates on offshore tax evasion add another $40–70 billion (Ashlea Abeling, "How Much Tax Cheating Is Going On?," September 16, 2013). The Committee for a Responsible Federal Budget estimates an average annual loss of $406 billion during 2008–2010, half of it from underreporting ("IRS Loses $400 Billion Per Year in Unpaid Taxes," May 16, 2016). A Brookings report estimates $500 billion to $650 billion annually (Benjamin H. Harris and Adam Looney, "The Tax Cuts and Jobs Act Was a Missed Opportunity to Establish a Sustainable Tax Code," May 24, 2018).

17. Todd Post, ed., *Hunger Report 2016: The Nourishing Effect: Ending Hunger, Improving Health, Reducing Inequality* (Washington, DC: Bread for the World Institute, 2016).

18. The savings would reduce private cost for individuals and families, but a substantial amount would reduce government cost for Medicaid, Medicare, and other subsidized healthcare insurance.

19. Robert E. Rubin, "Why Hurting the Poor Will Hurt the Economy," *The Washington Post*, March 12, 2017, A23.

20. Three points: (1) Presidents spend their first year in office with budgets passed by the previous Congress. The years listed below take that into account. Though presidents exert considerable influence on budgets, Congress legislates the spending, so the graph is only a rough gauge of responsibility. For example, the Great Recession that began in 2007 led to a near financial collapse in 2008 toward the end of the George W. Bush administration. Emergency action to rescue the economy began in the Bush years but continued during the Obama administration. The combination of reduced tax revenue and emergency spending produced huge deficits during the early Obama years. The inability of the president and the Congress subsequently to agree on a satisfactory path forward on spending and taxes resulted in reduced but still sizable deficits during Obama's second term. It is reasonable to attribute most of the

Obama deficits to the impact of the Great Recession, the tax cuts during the Bush years, and subsequent political gridlock.

(2) The national debt figures linked to the presidents come from the Treasury department, which includes both *public* and *internal* debts. Public debts are owed to creditors, both domestic and foreign, outside the US government. Internal debts are money borrowed from the government's own trust funds (mostly Social Security). The difference is similar to that of people borrowing from a bank and borrowing from their own retirement savings. Usually, however, reports about the federal debt and annual deficits exclude internal debts and count only public debts, as does the Congressional Budget Office. The CBO public-debts-only figures are reflected on the graph of annual deficits or surpluses measured as a percentage of Gross Domestic Product (*Visual 7*).

(3) The CBO measure of deficits (or surpluses) from 1965 to 2017 (and projected to 2028) shows *ABOVE AVERAGE DEFICITS* during

- none of the Johnson years (1965–1969)—one a surplus year that reduced the national debt;
- two of the Nixon-Ford years (1970–1977);
- none of the Carter years (1978–1981);
- seven of the Reagan years (1982–1989);
- four of the Bush I years (1990–1993);
- none of the Clinton years 1994–2001—four of them reduced the national debt;
- four of the Bush II years (2002–2009);
- six of the Obama years (2010–2017); plus
- one actual and three projected Trump years (2018–2021).

Of 32 years under Republican presidents: 32 deficit years, 20 of them with deficits above average.

Of 24 years under Democratic presidents, 19 deficit years, 5 of them with deficits above average (4 of which responded to the Great Recession), and 5 years with budget surpluses.

21. Graph: Congressional Budget Office: "The Budget and Economic Outlook: 2018 to 2028," https://www.cbo.gov/publication/53651, p. 81, Table 4-1.

22. Ronald Reagan, "Address to the Nation on the Program for Economic Recovery," September 24, 1981, https://www.reaganlibrary.gov/research/speeches/92481d.

23. Robert B. Reich, *Saving Capitalism: For the Many, Not the Few* (New York: Vintage Books, 2016). Reich explains how this works largely in ways not noticed by the public.

24. Arthur M. Okun, *Equality and Efficiency* (Washington, DC: Brookings Institution Press, 2015), 103.

25. Words engraved on the exterior of the IRS building in the nation's capital, taken from Supreme Court Justice Oliver Wendell Holmes Jr., who wrote, "Taxes are what we pay for civilized society" in a 1927 dissenting opinion on *Compania General de Tabacos de Filipinas v. Collector of Internal Revenue.*

26. Wrong not only by making inequalities more extreme, but also because the economic boost is likely to be temporary. The Congressional Budget Office says longer-term growth in output will be held down "by the reduction in private investment that is projected to result from rising federal deficits." *The 2018 Long-Term Budget Outlook*, summary, June 26, 2018, www.cbo.gov/publication/53919.

27. The Public Religion Research Institute, cited by *The Christian Century*, May 10, 2017, 9.

28. "U.S. Federal Individual Income Tax Rates History, 1862–2013," The Tax Foundation, https://taxfoundation.org/us-federal-individual-income-tax-rates-history-1913-2013-nominal -and-inflation-adjusted-brackets/.

29. Thomas Piketty, *Capital in the Twenty-First Century* (Cambridge, MA, and London: Belknap Press of Harvard University Press, 2014), 513.

30. Robert B. Reich, *Aftershock: The Next Economy and America's Future* (New York: Vintage Books, 2011), 129–32.

31. Joseph E. Stiglitz, *Reforming Taxation to Promote Growth and Equity* (New York: The Roosevelt Institute, May 28, 2014), 1–28. A value-added tax (VAT) is a consumption tax similar to a sales tax with a percentage built into a product at each stage of its development. Almost all western industrialized nations, including thirty-four OECD countries, except the United States, have a VAT. It has many advantages, if combined with other taxes to make the tax system progressive.

32. Chris Isidore, "Buffett Says He's Still Paying Lower Tax Rate Than His Secretary," CNN-Money, March 4, 2013, https://money.cnn.com/2013/03/04/news/economy/buffett-secretary -taxes/index.html.

33. Warren E. Buffett, "Stop Coddling the Super-Rich," *The New York Times*, August 14, 2011, http://www.nytimes.com/2011/08/15/opinion/stop-coddling-the-super-rich.html. He also said, "I have worked with investors for 60 years and I have yet to see anyone . . . shy away from a sensible investment because of the tax rate on the potential gain. People invest to make money, and potential taxes have never scared them off." Cited by Chye-Ching Huang, the Center on Budget and Policy Priorities, "The Reality of Raising Taxes at the Top, Part 3: Would Tax Increases Affect Savings and Investment?," April 27, 2012.

34. Forbes, "The Definitive Net Worth of Donald Trump, 2017," accessed February 10, 2017, http://www.forbes.com/donald-trump/. More than $10 billion by Trump's own estimate in a disclosure form filed with the federal government. Jonathan O'Connell, "President Falls 208 Places in Forbes's Ranking of Billionaires," *The Washington Post*, March 21, 2017, A14.

35. Charles Lane, "Inequality Close to Home," *The Washington Post*, March 27, 2014, A17, citing a 2013 Congressional Budget Office Report.

36. US Department of Housing and Urban Development, cited by Tracy Jan, "Millions of Poor Families That Qualify for Housing Assistance Don't Receive It," *The Washington Post*, August 11, 2017, A12.

37. Keith Ellison, "It's Time to Address the Shortage of Affordable Rental Housing," *The Washington Post*, December 3, 2015, A16.

38. Forbes report, "Final Tax Bill Includes Huge Estate Tax Win for the Rich: The $22.4 Million Exemption," by Ashlea Ebeling, December 21, 2017, https://www.forbes.com/sites /ashleaebeling/2017/12/21/final-tax-bill-includes-huge-estate-tax-win-for-the-rich-the-22 -4-million-exemption/#4b09d10b1d54. "This Isn't Tax Reform," editorial in *The Washington Post*, June 25, 2017, A20. Also Chuck Marr et al., "Eliminating Estate Tax on Inherited Wealth Would Increase Deficits and Inequality," Center on Budget and Policy Priorities, updated April

13, 2015, https://www.cbpp.org/research/federal-tax/eliminating-estate-tax-on-inherited -wealth-would-increase-deficits-and.

39. "This Isn't Tax Reform," note 38 above, A20. Also Marr et al., "Eliminating Estate Tax on Inherited Wealth," note 38 above.

40. Citizens for Tax Justice, "Fortune 500 Companies Hold a Record $2.4 Trillion Offshore," March 4, 2016. CTJ reported that 303 Fortune 500 corporations collectively held $2.4 trillion offshore. Most do not disclose the US tax rate they would pay if their offshore profits were repatriated. Based on twenty-seven who did disclose the numbers, CTJ estimated the total amount owed by the 303 companies could result in $695 billion in one-time additional US tax revenue, https://www.ctj.org/fortune-500-companies-hold-a-record-2-4-trillion-off shore/. However, "parked" or "offshore" are not geographic terms, but a set of rules defining when corporations have to pay taxes on their earnings. See Adam Looney, "Repatriated Earnings Won't Help American Workers—but Taxing Those Earnings Can," Brookings Institution, October 25, 2017, https://www.brookings.edu/blog/up-front/2017/10/25/repatriated-earnings -wont-help-american-workers.

41. Kent Conrad, "Our Nation Needs More Revenue," *The Washington Post*, October 25, 2013, A17.

42. Homi Kharas, "Can Capitalism Be Saved from Itself?," Brookings Institution, January 16, 2018, https://www.brookings.edu/blog/future-development/2018/01/16/can-capitalism-be -saved-from-itself/.

43. *The Budget and Economic Outlook: 2018 to 2028*, Congressional Budget Office, April 2018, p. 134, www.cbo.gov/publication/53651.

44. Lawrence Summers, "A Turn to the Middle Class," *The Washington Post*, January 19, 2015, A15.

CHAPTER 11

1. Comment to Jim Wallis, *America's Original Sin* (Grand Rapids: Brazos, 2016), xxvi.

2. Yuval Levin, "A Conservative Governing Vision," in *Conservative Reforms for a Limited Government and a Thriving Middle Class*, essays by Peter Wehner et al. (Washington, DC: YG Network, 2014), 16. Cited more extensively in chapter 7.

3. Jefferson, *Notes on the State of Virginia*, Query XVIII, https://www.monticello.org/site /jefferson/quotations-jefferson-memorial.

4. In 2013 the US spent almost half-again more on health care as a share of GDP than did each of the next largest health-care spending countries (Netherlands, Switzerland, Sweden, Germany, France). Life expectancy in the US is lower than in most other OECD countries. OECD, "Health at a Glance 2015: How Does the United States Compare?" Organization for Economic Cooperation and Development, https://www.oecd.org/unitedstates/health-at-a -glance-2015-key-findings-united-states.pdf.

5. Walter I. Trattner, *From Poor Law to Welfare State* (New York: Free Press, 1974), 241.

6. Clarke Cochran, "How Individualism Undermines Our Health Care," *Public Justice Re-*

view 3 (2017), Center for Public Justice. Cochran cites, among other things, infectious diseases, clean water and air, addictions, social determinants of health such as poverty and substandard housing, the requirement that hospital emergency departments treat all persons regardless of their ability to pay, and the rationale for health insurance.

7. An OECD survey showed the United States as one of only three out of thirty-four advanced nations whose schools serving higher-income children were allocated more funding per pupil and had lower student-teacher ratios than did schools serving poor students. Cited by Robert B. Reich, *Saving Capitalism* (New York: Vintage Books, 2016), 141.

8. Robert B. Reich blog, cited by Robert David Sullivan, "Defining Neediness," *America*, November 9, 2015, 19.

9. Charles Murray, *Coming Apart: The State of White America, 1960–2010* (New York: Crown Forum, 2012), 131. Murray quotes Henry Adams, who wrote that the abundant opportunity "reached the lowest and most ignorant class, dragging and whirling them upward as in the blast of a furnace."

10. Nicholas Lemann, *The Promised Land* (New York: Vintage Books, 1992), 202.

11. Klaus Schwab, founder and executive chairman, World Economic Forum, in opening address, "The Fourth Industrial Revolution: What It Means, How to Respond," January 14, 2016, https://www.weforum.org/agenda/2016/01/the-fourth-industrial-revolution-what-it-means-and-how-to-respond/.

12. Aaron Smith and Janna Anderson, "AI, Robotics, and the Future of Jobs," Pew Research Center, August 6, 2014, http://www.pewinternet.org/2014/08/06/future-of-jobs/.

13. Mark Muro et al., "Digitalization and the American Workforce," Brookings Institution, November 2017, https://www.brookings.edu/research/digitalization-and-the-american-workforce/.

14. Cited by Robert Shapiro, "The New Economics of Jobs Is Bad News for Working-Class Americans—and Maybe for Trump," Brookings Institution, January 16, 2018, https://www.brookings.edu/blog/fixgov/2018/01/16/the-new-economics-of-jobs-is-bad-news-for-working-class-americans-and-maybe-for-trump/.

15. William Galston, transcript of "Conversations with Bill Kristol," November 14, 2016, p. 19. https://conversationswithbillkristol.org/transcript/bill-galston-transcript/.

16. Jay Shambaugh and Ryan Nunn, "Why Wages Aren't Growing in America," *Harvard Business Review*, October 24, 2017, reprinted by Brookings Institution, November 14, 2017.

17. Fareed Zakaria, "In Defense of Globalization," *The Washington Post*, January 20, 2017, A25.

18. Thor Berger and Carl Benedikt Frey, "Industrial Renewal in the 21st Century: Evidence from US Cities," cited by James Pethokoukis, "What If the Digital Economy Creates Lots of Wealth but Few Jobs?," American Enterprise Institute, December 3, 2015, http://www.aei.org/publication/what-if-the-digital-economy-creates-lots-of-wealth-but-few-jobs/.

19. Pethokoukis, "What If the Digital Economy Creates Lots of Wealth but Few Jobs?"

20. Charles Murray, "A Guaranteed Income for Every American," *The Wall Street Journal*, June 3, 2016, via the American Enterprise Institute, http://www.aei.org/publication/a-guaranteed-income-for-every-american. Murray would let people make up to $30,000 in earned

income without losing a penny of the grant. Above that amount a graduated tax reimburses part of the grant up to $60,000 or more of earned income, at which point the grant drops to $6,500 and remains in place.

21. Murray, "A Guaranteed Income for Every American."

22. Pethokoukis, "What If the Digital Economy Creates Lots of Wealth but Few Jobs?"

23. Ted Nunez, "Life Without Work," *America*, February 22, 2016, 14–18.

24. US Bureau of Labor Statistics report of August 4, 2017.

25. Michael R. Strain, "Employment Policies to Get Americans Working Again," *Conservative Reforms for a Limited Government and a Thriving Middle Class*, essays by Peter Wehner, Strain, and others (Washington, DC: YG Network, 2014), 65–67. Also Michael R. Strain, "Conservatives, Wake Up: The Tax Code Is Not Your Biggest Problem," *The Washington Post*, June 19, 2014.

26. "Youth and the Labour Market," Organization for Economic Cooperation and Development, 2013. https://data.oecd.org/youthinac/youth-not-in-employment-education-or-training-neet.htm. Also Robert J. Samuelson, "The Plight of the NEETs," *The Washington Post*, June 8, 2015, A15. The problem of disengaged NEETs is not limited to the United States. Of the thirty-four advanced countries listed by the OECD, the US is the twenty-first from the top, doing just slightly below the average.

27. Danielle Paquette, "Many of Nation's Child-Care Workers Living in Poverty," *The Washington Post*, July 12, 2016, A14.

28. Nicholas Eberstadt, "Why Is the American Government Ignoring 23 Million of Its Citizens?," *The Washington Post*, April 1, 2016, accessed from the American Enterprise Institute, http://www.aei.org/publication/why-is-the-american-government-ignoring-23-million-of-its-citizens/.

29. The Sentencing Reform and Corrections Act of 2017, S.1917, reported by Prison Fellowship.

30. Steven Watts, *The People's Tycoon: Henry Ford and the American Century* (New York: Vintage Books, 2005), 185–86.

31. Watts, *The People's Tycoon*, 178–98. Unions had fought for an eight-hour day since the late nineteenth century and, because Ford's initiative was voluntary, continued to do so until the Fair Labor Standards Act was passed in 1938.

32. Todd Post, ed., *Hunger Report 2018: The Jobs Challenge: Working to End Hunger by 2030* (Washington, DC: Bread for the World Institute, 2018), 75–78.

33. *Hunger Report 2018*, 77.

34. Measured by the Bureau of Labor Statistics' Consumer Price Index Inflation Calculator.

35. Chuck Marr, "Reagan's Actions Made Him a True EITC Champion," Center on Budget and Policy Priorities blog, August 1, 2014, http://www.cbpp.org/blog/reagans-actions-made-him-a-true-eitc-champion.

36. The Center on Budget and Policy Priorities, "Policy Basics: The Earned Income Tax Credit," updated April 19, 2018, https://www.cbpp.org/research/federal-tax/policy-basics-the-earned-income-tax-credit.

37. William Galston, "The New Challenge to Market Democracies," October 2014, the Brookings Institution, 13, https://www.brookings.edu/research/the-new-challenge-to-market -democracies-the-political-and-social-costs-of-economic-stagnation/.

38. Ladonna Pavetti, "New Evidence That Subsidized Jobs Programs Work," Center on Budget and Policy Priorities, September 9, 2013, https://www.cbpp.org/blog/new-evidence -that-subsidized-jobs-programs-work. Also Pavetti et al., "The Legacy of the TANF Emergency Fund," February 16, 2011, http://www.cbpp.org/research/creating-subsidized-em ployment-opportunities-for-low-income-parents. The TANF Emergency Fund (not TANF itself) was called a "promising approach to creating jobs" by the AEI/Brookings consensus plan. AEI/Brookings Working Group on Poverty and Opportunity, *Opportunity, Responsibility, and Security: A Consensus Plan for Reducing Poverty and Restoring the American Dream* (Washington, DC: American Enterprise Institute and Brookings Institution, 2015), 52.

39. Fernanda Santos, "Albuquerque, Revising Approach Toward the Homeless, Offers Them Jobs," *The New York Times*, December 8, 2015, A20.

40. William Julius Wilson, *When Work Disappears* (New York: Alfred A. Knopf, 1996), 232–35.

41. Rasmussen Reports, July 18, 2012, and February 21, 2013, reported in "Welfare Opinion: Public Opinion Polls on Welfare and Poverty," a synopsis of Gallup, Pew, Rasmussen, and NBC/Wall Street Journal polls from 2012 to 2015. Posted by Federal Safety-net, undated, but accessed March 1, 2016, http://federalsafetynet.com/welfare-opinion.html.

42. Robert J. Samuelson, "Bernie's Big Boondoggle," *The Washington Post*, May 7, 2018, A17.

43. William J. Byron, SJ, has sketched such a program, along with a persuasive rationale for it, in "A Rite of Passage," *America*, March 2, 2015, 16–18. The Aspen Institute's Franklin Project, with prominent backing, envisions one million Americans each year volunteering civilian or military service, according to David Ignatius, in "The Healing Power of Service," *The New York Times*, November 28, 2014, A21.

44. Isabel V. Sawhill, "It's Time to Make National Service a Universal Commitment," Brookings Institution, November 30, 2017.

45. "Literacy for Everyday Life," US Department of Education, 2003, cited by Joseph J. Dunn, "Left Behind," *America*, December 2, 2013, 20. Dunn reported that 54 percent of adults with "below basic" literacy lived in households with annual incomes below $20,000 in 2013.

46. Jared Bernstein and Dean Baker, "The Unemployment Rate at Full Employment: How Low Can You Go?," *The New York Times*, November 20, 2013, https://economix.blogs. nytimes.com/2013/11/20/the-unemployment-rate-at-full-employment-how-low-can-you-go/.

47. The Civil Rights Act of 1964, which outlawed segregation in public facilities and racial discrimination in employment and education; the Voting Rights Act of 1965; and the Fair Housing Act of 1968.

48. Arthur C. Brooks, "Rebuilding Our Moral Consensus," American Enterprise Institute, March 2, 2016, http://aei.org/publication/rebuilding-our-moral-consensus. Also *The Conservative Heart* (New York: Broadside, 2015), 16, 23, 172.

CHAPTER 12

1. From "My Day," her syndicated newspaper column, January 6, 1941. That afternoon her husband presented his famous "four freedoms" (speech, worship, want, and fear) in his annual State of the Union address. Katrina Vanden Heuvel, "The 'Four Freedoms' Are under Assault," *The Washington Post*, January 6, 2016, A17.

2. Both polls reported by Max Stier, "Candidates: It's Time to Prepare," *The Washington Post*, January 18, 2016, A1.

3. David Brooks, "Inside Student Radicalism," *The New York Times*, May 27, 2016, A21.

4. Jesus, Mark 2:27.

5. Jonathan Kozol, *Amazing Grace* (New York: HarperPerennial, 2000), 70.

6. Hannah Fingerhut, "Most Americans Say U.S. Economic System Is Unfair, but High-Income Republicans Disagree," Pew Research Center, February 10, 2016, http://www .pewresearch.org/fact-tank/2016/02/10/most-americans-say-u-s-economic-system-is-unfair -but-high-income-republicans-disagree/.

7. Five of the nine commission members were appointed by Republican Senate and House leaders, and four by Democrat Senate and House leaders. All nine were from the private sector. *Freedom from Hunger: An Achievable Goal for the United States of America*, recommendations of the National Commission on Hunger to Congress and the Secretary of the Department of Agriculture, 2015, 1–2, http://hungercommission.rti.org.

8. *Freedom from Hunger*, 24.

9. Heather Garretson, "Beyond Punishment for the Crime: Collateral Consequences of a Conviction," *Capital Commentary*, Center for Public Justice, January 25, 2016.

10. Commission members set aside differences to craft a report that had their unanimous support. That may account for caution about increased spending. But four proposed pilot programs ask for congressional funding (presumably very little). The first of these would "investigate the effect on hunger of changing the SNAP benefit calculation from the Thrifty Food Plan to the Low Cost Food Plan." Such a change has long been endorsed by health and nutrition experts, so the investigation would predictably show the need for it; but implementing such a change would require further legislation to increase the SNAP budget. See *Freedom from Hunger*, 57.

11. AEI/Brookings Working Group on Poverty and Opportunity, *Opportunity, Responsibility, and Security: A Consensus Plan for Reducing Poverty and Restoring the American Dream* (Washington, DC: American Enterprise Institute and Brookings Institution, 2015), 5–14, 45–48, 72.

12. George Ingram, "Congress Finds Bipartisan Support for Foreign Aid and Aid Reform," Brookings Institution, July 11, 2016, https://www.brookings.edu/blog/future-development /2016/07/11/congress-finds-bipartisan-support-for-foreign-aid-and-aid-reform/.

13. "Feeding America, Donor Impact Report," Summer 2014, 7.

14. Irving Bernstein, *Americans in Depression and War*, chapter 5, US Department of Labor, http://www.dol.gov/dol/aboutdol/history/chapter5.htm. Also http://www.u-s-history .com/pages/h1528.html.

15. Includes public and internal debts, https://www.thebalance.com/national-debt-by
-year-compared-to-gdp.

16. $5,133 in 1933, and $39,791 in 2008, both figures adjusted for inflation. Sources: US
Bureau of Economic Analysis, US Bureau of Census, and GDP Deflator. Web access: USA
Personal Income per Capita 1929-2008—Demographia.

17. $0.78 trillion in 1933 and $16.44 trillion in 2015 (in 2009 dollars adjusted for inflation). Source: US Bureau of Economic Analysis, http://www.multpl.com/us-gdp-inflation
-adjusted/table

18. Meredith Hindley, "How the GI Bill Became Law in Spite of Some Veterans' Groups,"
Humanities, July/August 2014. Some veterans' groups opposed the bill because they feared its
passage would make it harder for *disabled* veterans to get assistance from Congress.

19. Richard Rothstein, *The Color of Law: A Forgotten History of How Our Government
Segregated America* (New York: Liveright, 2017), 70-71, 84, 167.

20. "Servicemen's Readjustment Act of 1944," http://www.ourdocuments.gov/doc.php
?flash=true&doc=76. R. B. Pitkin, "How the First GI Bill Was Written," *The American Legion
Magazine*, January 1969, 24-53, and February 1969, 22-59, http://www.legion.org/education
/history. GI Bill "History and Timeline," US Department of Veterans Affairs, https://www.benefits
.va.gov/gibill/history.asp. "Born of Controversy: The GI Bill of Rights," US Department of
Veterans Affairs, http://www.va.gov/opa/publications/celebrate/gi-bill.pdf.

21. Wendell Cox and Jean Love, "40 Years of the U.S. Interstate Highway System," the
American Highway Users Alliance, June 1996, http://www.publicpurpose.com/freeway1.htm.
Their cost estimate to 1994 was $329 billion, which by the US Department of Labor's Inflation
Calculator was worth $497 billion in 2016. They estimate that each dollar spent returned
$6 in economic gains. They also estimate that the Interstate saved 187,000 lives by 1994 and
prevented 11.8 million injuries.

22. "The Interstate Highway System," http://www.history.com/topics/interstate-highway
-system.

23. Ashley Halsey III, "On a Mission to Redirect Nation's Highway Legacy," *The Washington Post*, March 29, 2016, A2.

24. Ecclesiastes 11:1.

25. Joe McCarthy, "The 2 Things Bill Gates Told Trump During Their Meeting," Global
Citizen, March 16, 2018, https://www.globalcitizen.org/en/content/bill-gates-meeting-with
-donald-trump-foreign-aid/.

26. E. J. Dionne Jr., "Fighting Nostalgia and Amnesia," *The Washington Post*, July 7, 2016,
A17. He cites two books: Jefferson Cowie, *The Great Exception: The New Deal and the Limits of
American Politics* (Princeton: Princeton University Press, 2016), and Jacob S. Hacker and Paul
Pierson, *American Amnesia: How the War on Government Led Us to Forget What Made America
Prosper* (New York: Simon & Schuster, 2016).

27. Dan Balz, "More Than Demography as Destiny in a Divided Era," *The Washington
Post*, November 29, 2015, A2.

28. Richard N. Goodwin, "How Selma Unified a Nation," *The Washington Post*, January
31, 2015, A15.

CHAPTER 13

1. Letter from Birmingham Jail, April 16, 1963. First published in *The Christian Century*, June 12, 1963, 767–73. Quotation is on page 770.

2. Arthur Simon, *The Rising of Bread for the World: An Outcry of Citizens against Hunger* (Mahwah, NJ: Paulist Press, 2009).

3. The estimate is that of David Beckmann and Bread for the World. Such an estimate defies precision, but I think it is defensible when measuring advocacy efforts against likely impact on outcomes over a period of more than forty years.

4. Letter from Birmingham Jail, see note 1, above.

5. Program on International Policy Attitudes, "Americans on Foreign Aid and World Hunger," executive summary, February 2, 2001, http://worldpublicopinion.net/americans-on -foreign-aid-and-world-hunger/. Food Research & Action Center and Tyson Foods, sponsors of a national survey, "Americans' Views on [US] Hunger," October 2014, http://frac.org/wp -content/uploads/frac_tyson_oct_2014_public_view_hunger_poll.pdf.

6. Rick Steves, in a Christmas 2018 letter to his network of travelers, offering matching contributions to Bread for the World.

7. Only registered 501(c)(4) lobbying groups can do unlimited lobbying on specific legislation, but other nonprofit groups can do *limited* lobbying on specific legislation and *unlimited* advocacy on policies that relate to legislation (such as favoring an increase in child nutrition or seeking reforms in US foreign aid, as distinct from promoting or opposing a specific bill, which is lobbying). Lobbying includes messages to a group's members or the public to urge Congress to vote a certain way on a specific bill. However, the restrictions do not prevent a nonprofit organization from doing *some* lobbying or from advocating policies that relate to but are a step removed from supporting or opposing a specific bill. In addition, the law prevents a donor from deducting taxes from donations to a lobbying organization, but a donor can give tax-deductible gifts to nonprofit charities, including advocacy groups. For example, Bread for the World, as a registered lobby, cannot receive tax-deductible contributions, but its affiliate, Bread for the World Institute, a research and educational entity, can. The Institute can also advocate policies and do some lobbying, but carefully restricts its lobbying in compliance with the law. For an explanation of the restrictions and permissions on lobbying for nonprofit 501(c)(3) charities, check the IRS; or for a good summary, see "Non-Profit Organizations CAN Lobby," July 16, 2013, New Jersey's Center for Non-Profits, http://www.njnonprofits.org/NPsCanLobby.html.

8. Bachus has shared his experience frequently with Bread for the World's board of directors, of which he is a member.

9. David Beckmann, now president of Bread for the World.

10. One exception was a poll taken immediately after the landing. Alexis C. Madrigal, "Moondoggle: The Forgotten Opposition to the Apollo Program," *The Atlantic*, September 12, 2012, http://www.theatlantic.com/technology/archive/2012/09/moondoggle-the-forgotten -opposition-to-the-apollo-program/262254/.

11. The Congressional Budget Office, "A Budgetary Analysis of NASA's New Vision for

Space Exploration," September 2004, estimated the total cost of the Apollo program from 1962 to 1973 to be about $170 billion in 2005 dollars—about $225 billion in 2018 dollars.

CHAPTER 14

1. Letter from *Sojourners*, December 1, 2017.

2. Feeding America reports that 62 percent of the 46,000 local agencies that its food banks serve identify as faith-based, a figure that does not include those motivated by religious faith in the other 38 percent of agencies. *Hunger in America 2014*, executive summary, 4–5.

3. Robert D. Putnam and David E. Campbell, *American Grace* (New York: Simon & Schuster, 2010), 444–58. The authors' survey showed that "volunteering for religious groups and volunteering for secular groups turn out to be positively correlated." More than 90 percent of those who volunteered for a religious group also volunteered for at least one secular group, while 69 percent of those who did not volunteer for a religious group did not volunteer for any secular group either. A similar response appeared regarding financial contributions to religious and secular causes. "Regular churchgoers are more likely to give to secular causes than nonchurchgoers," especially for young people and the needy. Religious people are unusually active in civic life as well. But how religious someone is seems to matter more than which religion he or she belongs to. The contention that religious conservatives are more generous than other Americans is "only half right," the authors say, because "it is their religiosity and not their political ideology that produces the generosity." (By "religiosity" they evidently mean "evidence of their religious commitment," not a superficial display of it.)

4. Putnam and Campbell, *American Grace*, 254–58. Perhaps a sin of omission, the authors suggest, "especially compared to the struggles for social justice that people of faith mounted in comparable periods of American history." A Public Religion Research Institute (PRRI)/ Brookings survey posed this choice: "When Jesus and the prophets urged concern for the poor, they were primarily talking about: our obligation to create a just society [or] charitable acts by individuals." White churchgoers heavily chose "charitable acts" while Hispanic Catholics and black Protestants did the opposite. "Justice v. Charity," *Christian Century*, September 4, 2013, 9. A better question might have allowed also for a both-and response as a third option.

5. Washington Post-Kaiser Family Foundation poll, reported by Julie Zauzmer, "Is Poverty Due to Bad Effort, or to Circumstances?" *The Washington Post*, August 5, 2017, B2. Zauzmer quotes Albert Mohler, president of the Southern Baptist Theological Seminary, as affirming that poverty is a moral issue, but adding that the sin in poverty may be the sins of others, not the poor person. "I think conservative Christians often have a very inadequate understanding of the structural dimension of sin," he said.

6. Putnam and Campbell, *American Grace*, 468–70.

7. David Beckmann's takeaway from *American Grace*, and his conversations with the authors.

8. Matthew 25:24–25.

9. One example is *The Poverty & Justice Bible* (New York: The American Bible Society,

1995, the Contemporary English Version). "Highlighting more than 2000 verses that wake us up to issues of poverty and justice," says the ABS on the back cover.

10. 1 John 4:19. Unless otherwise noted, biblical quotations are taken from the New Revised Standard Version (NRSV).

11. Genesis 1:27.

12. Genesis 4:9-10.

13. Exodus 3-11.

14. Deuteronomy 6:5; Leviticus 19:18; Matthew 22:34-40.

15. Exodus 20:1-17.

16. Leviticus 25:8-28.

17. Leviticus 19:9-10.

18. Deuteronomy 14:28-29.

19. Deuteronomy 15:1-2.

20. Deuteronomy 24:10-22.

21. Deuteronomy 15:7-11.

22. Deuteronomy 15:4.

23. Deuteronomy 17:14-17. I have abbreviated the text.

24. 2 Samuel 11 and 12.

25. 1 Kings 9:15-22; 10:14-29; 12:1-20.

26. 1 Kings 21:1-19.

27. Amos 1:2; 2:6-8; 5:10-15; 8:4-6.

28. Amos 4:1-3.

29. Amos 6:1-7.

30. Amos 5:21-24. I have inserted "hymns" in place of songs. Same meaning.

31. Isaiah 3:13-15.

32. Isaiah 58:6-8.

33. Examples: Psalms 72, 103, and 146.

34. Luke 1:51-53.

35. Luke 4:18-19; Isaiah 61:1-2.

36. Leviticus 25:8-28.

37. Matthew 23:23-24.

38. Luke 5:17-26.

39. Luke 5:27-32; and 7:36-50.

40. Luke 8:1-3.

41. Luke 18:15-17.

42. Mark 7:24-30.

43. Luke 18:9-14.

44. Luke 16:19-25.

45. Luke 10:29-37.

46. Luke 18:18-27.

47. Luke 6:20-26.

48. Luke 12:42-43.

49. Luke 16:19–31.

50. Matthew 25:31–46. My paraphrase of the text.

51. Proverbs 31:9, New Living Translation.

52. Matthew 26 and 27.

53. Romans 1:16.

54. Acts 2:43–47; 5:1–6; 6:1.

55. 2 Corinthians 8 and 9.

56. Romans 13.1–7 and 1 Timothy 2:1–2.

57. Galatians 3:28.

58. Philemon (a two-page letter in the New Testament).

59. Dietrich Bonhoeffer, *The Cost of Discipleship* (New York: Macmillan, 1963), 47.

60. Dietrich Bonhoeffer, *Ethics* (London: SCM Press, 1955), 63.

61. Cited by Eric Metaxas, *Bonhoeffer: Pastor, Martyr, Prophet, Spy* (Nashville: Thomas Nelson, 2010), 280–81.

62. Pope Francis, *The Joy of the Gospel* (*Evangelii Gaudium*), an Apostolic Exhortation (Vatican City: Vatican Library, 2013), section 1.

63. Pope Francis, *The Joy of the Gospel*, sections 53–59.

64. Pope Leo XIII, *Rerum Novarum*, May 15, 1891. This encyclical addressed the revolutionary challenge of Marxism and the deplorable condition of industrial workers. It rejected both extreme socialism and unrestrained capitalism and supported the right of labor to form unions.

65. Garry Wills, *Lincoln at Gettysburg: The Words That Remade America* (New York: Touchstone/Simon & Schuster, 1992), 118. In that race for a seat in the US Senate, Lincoln lost to Stephen Douglas.

66. Romans 13:1–7.

67. Matthew 5:44–45.

68. Philippians 3:20.

69. Matthew 6:10, King James Version.

Index

About the Author

Arthur Simon is founder and president emeritus of Bread for the World, a national citizens' voice urging our nation's decision-makers to help end hunger at home and abroad. He has written a number of books, including *The Politics of World Hunger*, which he coauthored with his brother, Paul Simon, the late US senator from Illinois.